ANCIENT ACCOUNTS OF INDIA AND CHINA

ANCIENT ACCOUNTS
OF
INDIA AND CHINA

BY TWO
MOHAMMEDAN TRAVELLERS.
Who went to those Parts in the 9th Century;
Translated from the ARABIC,

By the late Learned

EUSEBIUS RENAUDOT

With Notes, Illustrations and Inquiries by the same Hand.

GYAN

Published by

Gyan Publishing House
5, Ansari Road
Daryaganj, New Delhi-110002
Phone: 011-47034999, 9811692060
E-mail: books@gyanbooks.com

Distribution Network
gyanbooks.com
India, USA, Canada, UK, Australia, France

ISBN : 978-81-212-3117-6 (PB)
First Published, London, 1733

2nd Impression 2020

Printed at: Gyan Press, Delhi.

Ancient Accounts of India and China
Author: Mohammedan Travellers

ANCIENT ACCOUNTS OF *INDIA* and *CHINA*,

BY TWO

MOHAMMEDAN TRAVELLERS.

Who went to those Parts in the *9th Century*;

Translated from the *ARABIC*,

By the late Learned

EUSEBIUS RENAUDOT.

With *Notes*, *Illustrations* and *Inquiries* by the same Hand.

LONDON:

Printed for *Sam. Harding* at the *Bible* and *Ancher* on the Pavement in St. *Martins-Lane*.

M DCC XXXIII.

TO

HENRY KELSALL, Esq;

THIS

EDITION

IS

Most respectfully Dedicated

and Inscribed by

The English Translator.

THE

PREFACE.

IT ſeemed to me that the Accounts of *India* and *China* I here preſent to the Public, deſerved to be retrieved from the Obſcurity they have hitherto been in; not only becauſe they are written in a very foreign Tongue, but alſo becauſe the Original Manuſcript, which is in the *Comte de Seignelay's* Library, ſeems to be the only one of its kind. Its Age may be ſufficiently aſcertained by the Character it is in; but we have a plain Proof that it was written in the Year of the *Hejra* DLXIX, or the Year of *Chriſt* MCLXXIII: For at the End there are ſome Obſervations, of the ſame Hand, upon the Extent and Circumference of the Walls and Towers of *Damaſcus*, and other Cities in ſubjection to Soltan *Nuroddin*, ſo famous in the Wars Beyond-ſea; and the Writer ſpeaks of him as if then living. Now this Prince dyed in the Year above, and ſo the Manuſcript muſt be about 550 Years old.

The Antiquity of the Manuſcripts which contain theſe two Accounts.

But we may be ſatisfied that our two Authors are more ancient, and that the two

At what Time they were written.

two Dates they give, the one of the Year CCXXXVII of the *Hejra*, which is that of our first Traveller, and the other of the Year of the same CCLIV, when a great Revolution hapned in *China*, are true and just: And these two Dates, correspond with the Years of *Christ* DCCCLI and DCCCLXVII.

They are much older than Marco Polo.

Every body knows that *Marco Polo*, the *Venetian*, was the first that talked to us of *China* with any Knowledge, and that what he writes was formerly much questioned, because of the seemingly incredible Wonders he relates, many of which have been since confirmed for Truths. Now *Marco Polo* returned from his Travels in the Year of *Christ* MCCXCV, whence it follows that our *Arabs* were four hundred Years before him; and as every Thing, we have of the kind, is posterior to him, these Accounts must be far more ancient than what others have penned. Nor will we except any of the *Arabian* and *Persian* Travellers, or Geographers that have written in either Tongue, who have been too partially set forth by some learned Men of our own Times, and very far beyond what they deserve.

The Nubian *Geography beholden to them for many Things.*

The *Geography* commonly called of *Nubia*, and supposed to be the Work of the Sharif *al Edrisi*, which was produced in *Sicily*, and which many Authors call *The Book of Roger*, because it was undertaken at the Command of *Roger* II. King of *Sicily*; is the most ancient we have; and is divided

divided into Climates after the manner of *Ptolomey*, whom the *Arabs* had tranſlated in their Tongue; almoſt all the *Eaſtern Geographies* are methodiſed by the ſame Plan; but it affords you no Poſitions no more than moſt of the reſt, if we except the Geography of *Abulfeda*, to be reſumed hereafter. But this *Nubian Geography* containing the moſt curious Particulars we read in the Authors that have appeared ſince, whether as to natural Hiſtory, or the Cuſtoms and Manners of different Nations, we may ſafely pronounce it to have been pillaged by later Compilers: And very remarkable it is That this *Nubian Geographer*, whoſoever he was, is beholden to our two Authors for moſt of what he relates concerning the Navigation of the *Eaſtern* Ocean, of the *Indies*, and of *China*, which alone may evince them to have been of the higheſt Antiquity among the Writers of their own Nation.

They have ſome Blemiſhes and Defects, but they inform us of ſome very important Things.

But we do not by this mean to extend the Merit of theſe two Accounts beyond due Bounds; we are ready to allow them to contain ſome fabulous Particulars, and many ſo very obſcure that there is no clearing them up; and alſo that their want of Poſitions fruſtrates the Uſe we might otherwiſe have made of the Deſcriptions they give us. But theſe Diſadvantages, which they have in common with all the *Arabian* Geographers, are amply compenſated by a very great number of curi-

curious Things they tell us, and which are ſcarce to be met with elſewhere.

Among others, the old Courſe ſteered for China.

One of their chief Remarkables is the Courſe the *Arabs* and the *Perſians* formerly ſteered from *Baſſora* and *Siraf* to the *Indies* and *China*; and inverſely the Courſe ſteered by the *Chineſe* for *Arabia* and *Perſia*. Many of the Learned who thought with *Martini* That the *Chineſe* ſailed by the direction of the Compaſs as far as *Ceylon*, and there planted a Colony, have perſuaded others That this Voyage was performed by Obſervation. And hence they concluded it almoſt impoſſible but the active and induſtrious *Arabs* muſt have borrowed the uſeful Invention from the *Chineſe*, and have applied it in their long Runs; it appearing by Hiſtory that they ſailed great Lengths, long before the *Portugueſe* diſcovered the *Eaſtern* Parts. Such was the Opinion of the late Mr. *Thevenot*, who knew nothing of our two Authors, and who being very much prepoſſeſſed in favor of the *Chineſe*, concurred with *Martini* That they had had the Uſe of the Compaſs, and that they had ſailed to the Iſland of *Ceylon*, and even much farther; while *Voſſius* inſiſts on the ſame, as a Fact not in the leaſt to be doubted, tho' he does not vouchſafe us the leaſt Proof to countenance his Aſſertion. Our Authors ſo plainly and circumſtantially obſerve to us That the *Indian* and *Chineſe* Ships did not ſtir beyond *Siraf*, that we cannot but ſubmit to them, and eſpecially

as

as they, at the ſame time, acquaint us They dared not go farther, becauſe their Veſſels were unable to ſtand the Aſſaults of the open Sea: But it is not becauſe our two Authors make no mention of the Compaſs That we venture to affirm the *Chineſe* and *Arabians* knew nothing of it; we have other Arguments not to be reſiſted: But tho' we had no other way of proving this Ignorance upon them, the Courſe they ſteered would ſufficiently declare it; they forſaking it as too tedious and dangerous, as ſoon as they came to have the Compaſs.

They contain many remarkable Things which are confirmed by late Travellers.

In theſe Accounts alſo we have many curious Obſervables upon *China*, which agree with *Marco Polo*, and are even confirmed by the moſt ſincere Travellers of later Times: If others there are which claſh with what we elſewhere read, they ought not for that Reaſon alone to be miſtruſted, ſince great Alterations have befallen that Country in the long Courſe of eight hundred Years or upwards. By the Lights *Martini* conveys to us in his *Chineſe Atlas*, we diſcover the Truth of many Things that before appeared fabulous in *Marco Polo*; and the ſame may hereafter be diſcovered of the doubtful Things in our Authors.

Martini is the firſt that told us The great Cities of *China* had often changed their Names; and very poſſible it is that the Names in our two Authors may have obtained in their Time; and tho' they are defective in Poſitions, we preſently know them

them by the Obſervations the *Europeans* have made; for it is in vain to look for them in the *Arabian* Writings; tho' a contrary Opinion has taken ſuch deep Root among us, that it is ſeemingly a Raſhneſs to diſpute the Point. *John Baptiſt Ramuſio*, a Man of great Judgment and very extenſive Learning, having ſeen a ſmall Part of *Abulfeda*'s Geography, and therein obſerved the Names of ſome Places mentioned by *Marco Polo*, conceived a very great Veneration for the Work. *Caſtaldo* made uſe of it alſo for ſeveral Poſitions; and *Schickard* cited ſome parts of it, and promiſed a Tranſlation of the whole. *Greaves* a learned *Engliſhman* actually tranſlated it, and publiſhed two of the Climates. *Thevenot* attempted the Thing after him, but dying, the Copy of his Verſion fell into foreign Hands. All the Learned, and, upon what they have ſaid, all that were Strangers to the Oriental Tongues, have fed up the Public with the exceſſive Commendations they have beſtowed on *Abulfeda*'s Work, tho' often without knowing why or wherefore. *Andrew Muller* who printed *Marco Polo* in *Latin* with tedious Diſſertations, and particularly one upon *Cathay* or *Catai*, regrets a Work *Schickard* had promiſed, concerning *Tartary* and *China*, which he was to have extracted from *Abulfeda*, and was to have been like his *Tarich Regum Perſiæ*.

What we are to judge of the Work Schickard *promiſed.*

The Public may poſſibly think it a great Diſappointment that *Schickard* did not

not print this Work, or translate *Abulfeda*, according to his Word; and it must be most readily believed, after so many learned Orientalists have said it, That the Geography of this Author would completely illustrate *Marco Polo*, and afford us a fair Prospect of *China*, as *Muller* will have it. We happen to live in an Age that has been most minutely and almost triflingly inquisitive into what concerns the Lives and Writings of the Learned: But as it is seldom these Compilers consult any Thing farther than what is contained in Prefaces, and are perfect Strangers both to the Books and Authors mentioned, it may not be amiss to say what is true of *Schickard*, and afterwards of *Abulfeda*.

An Account of Schickard'*s first Work.*

Schickard, who was a Professor in the University of *Tubingen*, got a large Share of Reputation by a Work he intitled *Tarich Regum Persiæ*; which took Birth from the Discovery of a Genealogy written upon a long Scroll, which began with *Adam*, and ended with a *Mohamedan* Prince who had had it done; this *Schickard* took for a very great Curiosity, tho' nothing in the World is less so. He copied the Names, which he often read mistakenly enough, and having collected all that could relate to those Princes; when he comes to the Kings of *Persia*, he does not say a Word of them that he does not borrow from *Teixeira*, a *Portuguese* Author who writes from the *Persian*

Persian Histories with the greatest Fidelity: To this he adds some Citations from the Book intitled *Jukhassin*, which has many Curious Particulars of Oriental History, some Passages from the *Arabian* Geography, but nothing Original. We are sure he had not the least Knowledge of the Authors that wrote this History, which is quite Fabulous, if we except what is said of the latter Kings; and we need only read *Teixeira*, or the Translated Abridgment of the *Persian* Histories called *Leb Towarich*, in the fourth Volume of the late Mr. *Thevenot*'s Collection, by *Gaulmin*; to be convinced of the little value of *Schickard*'s Work, and how unequal he was to the task of writing the History of the *Jenghiz-khanid Tartars*, he ventured to Promise.

He also promised to translate Abulfeda.

Most certain it is also that he in like Manner prromised to Translate *Abulfeda*; but *Greaves*, who, by the Report of those who knew him, was a very worthy Man, not caring to join with *Schickard* in the Undertaking, wrote to him about it. To which he answered, That the Manuscript in the *Vienna* Library, was so obscure that it was absolutely impossible to translate it: He copied it however, and his Copy being afterwards purchased in *Germany*, is now in the King's Library; annexed to it there is part of the Work translated, which requires no great Perusal for us to pronounce it very much an Overmatch for

for *Schickard*. *Greaves* was indeed completely qualified; for besides that he was a perfect Master of the Oriental Tongues, and had travelled in the *Levant*, he was acquainted with the Principal Authors, was profoundly learned, and a consummate Mathematician. He gave us a Specimen of his Work when, in the Year MDCL, he published the Description and Tables of the two Provinces, of *Chowarazm* and *Mawaralnahra* or the *Transoxane*, in *Arabic* and *Latin*. In his Preface he acquaints us he had finished the whole Translation of *Abulfeda*, and he declared as much to some of his learned Friends; but being thrown into Prison by the Parliament, for lending Money to King *Charles* II. his House was ransacked, and his Work lost: This we had from Mr. *Hardy*, a very ingenious Gentleman, who knew him intimately well.

Of Greave's *Translation of* Abulfeda.

The two Climates *Greaves* has given us, are one of the most curious Parts of all *Abulfeda*'s Geography; for it takes notice of Cities unknown to the ancient Geographers, and which we are only told of by the *Mohammedan* History, and our Modern Travels; and what is more, these Parts were subject to the *Seljukid Soltans*, under the third of whom, *Soltan Jelaloddin Malec Shah*, there were very able Geographers, who by his order took very exact Observations, as well towards the *Jelalean* Epoch as the Measure of the Earth. The *Tartar* Princes were actua-

and

ted by the same laudable Spirit of Curiosity; and so *Abulfeda*, who dyed in the Year of *Christ* MCCCXLV, had a great number of pretty exact Tables whereby to settle the true Places of the Cities he mentions. But notwithstanding all this, there are Differences of one, and sometimes two Degrees in the two Climates before us; which is nothing to what there is, of the same kind, throughout the whole Body of the Work, which it may not be amiss to instance by a few Examples.

The Uncertainty of almost all the Positions in Abulfeda.

In order to this we will make Choice of the Country which one would think should have been best known to the *Mohammedans*, and that is *Arabia*: *Abulfeda* speaking of *Medina*, which is sacred among them, because of the Tomb of *Mohammed* which there stands; lays it down in 65 or 67 Degrees of Longitude. *Ailah* a famous City, and formerly very well known, as it was in the Way of the Caravans from *Egypt* to *Mecca*, is according to *Abulfeda* in 53, 54, or 56 Degrees of Longitude. *Tima* in 67 or 68 Degrees. *Tadmor*, the ancient *Palmyra*, in 62 or 66. *Hasantabaz*, the Seat of the ancient Kings of *Yaman* or *Arabia the Happy*, in 65, 67, or 70. *Dafar*, the Seat of the ancient *Homerites*, in 67 or 73. *Najeran* or *Nājran*, a City that often occurs in History, in 67 or 75. *Aden*, still more known, in 65, 67 or 70. Nor is there much more certainty about the Places in other Countries which should have been better known to the Author; nor

nor can any Thing be offered to justify his Ignorance or Negligence as to the Longitude of St. *John d'Acre*, or *Ptolemais*, which he writes to be in either 56, 57, 58, or 70 Degrees. When he gives you but one Number, it is because he found no other in the Books he transcribed, * but it is never the surer for that; he himself does not

* *The chief of these Differences must arise from a difference of Meridians; for Mr.* Renaudot *after all he, in the Body of the Book, says in their behalf as careful Observers and intelligent Mathematicians, must be inconsistent with himself to suppose these Numbers are mere Blunders and Inaccuracies.* Abulfeda *seems to be no more than a Collector, as may be clearly gathered from that Prince's own Preface, and from what Mr.* Renaudot *here acknowledges. That these various Longitudes are perplexing, every Body must allow, it being hard to determin which is to be preferred, as it is impossible to find out the exact Meridian of each; but that they are slips of Ignorance or Negligence cannot well be supposed. Besides, it is well known, That were any Man, like* Abulfeda, *to collect from our own best Geographers, or rather Hydrographers, for what concerns the Sea-Coast in particular, tho' so well known to most of the* European *Navigators, they would be often found to vary a number of Degrees from each other; we need only instance in the Coast of* France, *next to us, and the Coast of* Brasil *in* America, *which now are thought to be rectified, as they doubtless are: But these Variations did not arise from the want of a fixed Meridian, but purely from a mistaken Reckoning or Computation. If some of our best Geographers then have till very lately abounded with Errors of this kind, it is somewhat unreasonable to expect the Orientals to be quite free from them; and as they say,* The Knowledge of a Part, is to be preferred to an Ignorance of the Whole; *so if we can to a Degree or two settle upon the Longitude of most of the noted Cities in the vast extent of* Asia, *which might perhaps be done, it must be somewhat more satisfactory than not to know where to look for them at all.*

not ſuppoſe it, and therein we have where-withal to commend his Sincerity: For it is to be obſerved that of about five hundred and fifty Cities to be found in him, (for Copies vary as to the exact Number) he gives no one Poſition for exact, except that of *Hama* or *Hamath*. After this we may gueſs what Aſſiſtance we are to hope from this ſo applauded Work, towards the Reformation of our *Eaſtern* Geography; as alſo the Account we are to make of Poſitions which vary ſo many Degrees of Longitude from each other, and are not much better agreed as to Latitude.

The Deſcriptions of the Countries more to be valued.

The Deſcription of each Country at the Head of the Tables, is more valuable, and may be of ſome Uſe, particularly for tracing out the Courſe of the great Rivers, the *Nile*, the *Tigris*, the *Euphrates*, *Oxus*, and a few others. The Accounts of the ſeveral Cities in theſe Tables, are very conciſe and exact enough; they do not contain the Fables common in the other *Arabian* and *Perſian* Geographers, not excepting *Yacuti* himſelf, ſo often cited with Commendation, who tho' he divides his Work into Climates, does not oblige us with one Poſition.

We can extract nothing therefrom to illuſtrate the Geography of China.

If what has hitherto been ſaid concerning the little Help we are to expect from *Abulſeda* be true, as doubtleſs it is; it is ſtill more certain That he can ſupply us with no Light as to *China* in particular; to be perfectly ſatisfied of this, we need no other Teſtimony than his own; for thus

thus he delivers himself by way of Preface to the little he says of the chief Cities of this Country: "*China* is, on the West, "bounded by the Desart which divides it "from the *Indies*; on the South, by the "Sea, as also on the East; on the North, "by the Countries of *Gog* and *Magog*, "and others we know nothing at all of. "Geographers, it is true, have the Names "of many Places and Rivers in *China*; "but as we are ignorant of the Pronounciation as well as of the real State of the "Country, they are to us as it were unknown; and the rather as we have no "Body that has been there, of whom "to inform ourselves as we ought; wherefore we will confine ourselves to what "has been written before us." After this he ventures to name some Cities, but so disguised, that it is impossible to guess at them, except *Khansa*, which may be the *Quinsai* of *Marco Polo*, and *Zei un*, which he also mentions. In another Place he speaks of *Cambalic* or *Chanbalig*, and *Catai*, upon the Testimony of *Ebn Said*: These Passages *Muller* has recurred to; and they, it must be said, confirm what the Author himself confesses of the little Knowledge he had of those Parts. With the same Incertitude he declares himself at the beginning of his Universal History.

The Arabians *have related nothing but Fables about it.*

But we must not wonder *Abulfeda* knew so very little of *China*, for the rest that speak of it, tell us nothing but idle Tales and Absurdities, if we except some Passages

ſages in *Yacuti*, *Ebn Wardi*, and the *Perſian Geography*, which ſeem to have been tranſcribed from our Authors, who alone have talked ſeriouſly about *China*. It is aſtoniſhing, indeed, that they are ſo little known, but that they have been known to many is plain, and among the reſt to the Author of the Geography printed at *Rome*, who has taken whole Paſſages from them; this ſuffices to eſtabliſh their Reputation.

Our Authors have ſpoken contemptuouſly of the Chineſe *Learning.*

They may it is poſſible be attacked from another Quarter, and principally becauſe theſe *Arabs* expreſs themſelves ſomewhat irreverently of the *Chineſe* Philoſophy, which has been ſo extolled for about a Century paſt; which deſerving a particular Diſcuſſion ſhall be profeſſedly treated towards the End of this Book, in a Critique upon the *Chineſe* Learning.

Hiſtorical Facts which agree not with our Chineſe *Hiſtory.*

A few hiſtorical Facts alſo in theſe Accounts may be liable to ſome Contradiction; becauſe they agree not with the Hiſtory of *China*, as ſome learned Miſſionaries have extracted it from the Annals of the Country, whoſe Exactneſs they applaud, tho' it be impoſſible to gueſs at it by what they have publiſhed: And if ſome great Men of our own Time have preſumed thereby to reform even the Chronology of Scripture, they did not form their Judgment from any actual Knowledge of the Thing, and *Voſſius* who talks ſo highly of the *Chineſe*, had leſs than any Body; for beſides that he was exceſſively credulous upon this Subject, he could judge

judge but at second hand, being a Stranger to the Tongue, which however was very marvellous with him and more perfect than any other. This Gentleman thought quite otherwise of the *Coptic* Tongue, which he would have to be a barbarous Jargon never heard of till the twelfth Century, tho' there is such a Certainty to the contrary as convicts him of utter Ignorance in *Mohammedan* History, and the History of Christianity in *Egypt*. Fath. *Pezron* approved of what *Vossius* advanced, thereby to vindicate the Chronology of the *Septuagint*; and others have endeavored to reflect an Authority upon the same for particular or private Views not to be regarded when Truth is the Concern.

They have many Things which seem incredible.

In these Accounts also you may meet with some Things hard to believe, like those formerly thought fabulous in *Marco Polo*; and perhaps it were rashness to warrant them all; but it must be granted That the like have often been verified in process of Time; and that for this Reason alone we are to be cautious how we condemn the old Travels, when they in other Respects appear to be true. Such are our two Relations; from the first to the last Word of them there is a Simplicity very uncommon with the Orientals; the other *Arabians* and *Persians* that have written of the *Indies* and *China* particularly, even those so much esteemed by the Learned have avoided nothing more than this attractive Charm, and have collected the most absurd Stories they could set Eyes on. Nor must we wonder they have so many Stories on *China*, which they hardly knew at all, since they have some as ridiculous about *Spain*, which the *Arabs* possessed a long Time, about the City of *Rome*, and about most of the *European* Provinces.

They are cleared up in the Dissertations and Notes without multiplying unnecessary Quotations

In our *Dissertations* and *Notes* we have endeavored to illustrate the most important Passages in our two Authors; but we did not deem it advisable to heap up Quotations from all sorts of Writers, as the Custom too much prevails with the Learned of later Times. *Andrew Muller*, for Example, in his Treatise *De Cataia*, has not omitted one single Passage in the Authors he knew, that could in the least answer his Purpose, tho' most of them were only Transcriptions from Transcribers, who of course could be of no Authority. Yet after this Cloud of Quotations he leaves us in the dark as to the important Part of his Subject, and those who shall know no more of *Cathay* than they have read in *Muller*, will be but very slenderly informed; they will only know the Opinions and Conjectures of several learned Men who have copied one another, and were never thoroughly possessed of their Subject.

Of Benjamin *the* Jew *and his Translators.*

Benjamin the *Jew*, who travelled over a great Part of the *East*, and took Notice of a great many curious and true Particulars,

lars, is no despicable Author, as some would have made him who did not understand him, at the Head of whom we must place those who ventured to translate him, *Arias Montanus*, and after him *Constantine l'Empereur*. They both translated from an Edition printed at *Constantinople*, which being erroneous, and not very fair, might easily puzzle those who did not know whereabouts he was. Accordingly *Arias Montanus*, committed horrid Faults, which the *Dutch* Translator did not afterwards perceive; and both of them by their ill reading of many proper Names of Cities, People, and Provinces, have formed imaginary ones which never were. Hence we every where meet with *Eliman*, which never was, instead of *al Yaman*,* which is *Arabia the Happy*, and many such Faults; *Dougziin*, a People unknown, instead of *Drouziin*, the *Druses*, the Isle of *Nikrokis*; the *Hachisches*, a People who cut Princes with a Saw, and a hundred more of the same Stamp. *Arias Montanus* left his Readers the Task of untying these difficult Knots; but *Constantin l'Empereur* with a more assuming Air, undertakes to illustrate his Authors by Notes, which he has crammed with *Arabian* and *Hebrew* Passages quite wide of his Point; for he had them not from original Authors, or

* *Mr.* Renaudot *writes it* Eliemen, *which does not so much shew the real difference.*

from Geographers and Historians; he did not so much as know one of them except the *Nubian Geographer*, and *Elmacin*, whom he often did not understand. For Instance, he takes up *Benjamin* for talking of the Kalif of *Egypt* who reigned in his Time, because truly he finds another in *Elmacin* of the Family of the *Abassids*; whereas a Man must be quite a Novice to *Mohammedan* History, not to know that, in *Egypt*, the *Fatemites* declared themselves Kalifs, and withdrew Obedience from the *Abassids*, whom they gave out to be Usurpers of the Empire and the Pontificat.

Several great Men have committed vast Faults in Oriental History.

Greater Men by far than *Constantin l'Empereur* have been guilty of as great Absurdities in speaking of what they did not know. So *Joseph Scaliger* attempting the Origin of the Title *Prester John*, commonly applyed to the King of *Ethiopia*, offers one which is neither *Persian*, as he pretends, nor yet *Arabic*. He is in like Manner mistaken in the Etymons of the *Persian* Names, and presuming to exhibit a Series of Kalifs and Soltans of the principal States from the Rise of *Mohammedism*, which *Abraham Zacut*, the *Jew*, had done very exactly, he mangled all the Names, because he saw them in *Hebrew* only, and knew them not originally. *Erpenius*, tho' a good Master of the *Arabic*, is guilty of an infinit number of Faults in his Translation of *Elmacin*, as well in the Text, as in the Geography and proper Names: So that we may justly say we

have

have no body, besides *Golius* and *Greaves*, that we can depend upon for the *Eastern* Geography; to whom indeed we may add *d'Herbelot*, whose *Bibliotheque Orientale* is full of very curious Learning, tho' by the carelessness of the Editors, it is a Work not so perfect as the Author could have made it, intimate as he was with the best *Arabian*, *Turkish* and *Persian* Books.

Of the Description of Arabia the Happy.

There have appeared some new Productions full of *Eastern* Erudition, which it may not be amiss to say a Word to. Of these there is *a Voyage to Arabia the Happy*, wherein are many curious Remarks with regard to the present Times. The Editor quotes *Abulfeda's Arabia*, but he excells that Geographer, who knew but two or three of the principal Cities. What he says of the *Sharifs* of *Mecca*, does not exactly agree with the most certain Records of *Mohammedism*; for not only the Kalifs of the first Race were Masters in that Country; but *Saladin*, a devout *Mohammedan*, if there ever was one, made a Conquest of it by his Brother, and drove out *Abdalnabi*, tho' he pretended to be of the Race of their Prophet.

Chardin's *Travels.*

Sir *John Chardin*, in the last Edition of his *Voyage to Persia*, has favored us with ample Dissertations on the Morality of the ancient *Persians*, as if extracted from their own Authors: And yet most of what he says is borrowed from the *Gulistan* of the Poet *Saadi*, who was, above sixty Years ago, translated into *German* by *Olearius*, and into *Latin* by *Gentius*. The Remainder is no more than Sentences for the most part borrowed from the ancient *Greeks*, and translated into several of the *Eastern* Tongues, and no more peculiar to the *Persians* than to every other Nation in the World. Again, *Mohammedism* glares throughout the whole, and what they would pass upon us for the *Persian* Philosophy and Theology, is taken out of the *Koran*, and belongs to the *Persians* no farther than they have naturalized it of their Language.

Hyde's *Relig. Vet. Pers.*

Dr. *Hyde*, a learned *Englishman*, has undertaken a Work of greater Depth, whereby to explain the Religion of the ancient *Persians*, and which is the more likely to impose on the Reader, as it is full of Quotations from *Persian* and *Arabian* Writers. It also excites the Curiosity by the novelty of the Design, which is to justify the *Worship of Fire* among the old *Persians*, and to prove it to have been a Ceremony of mere Indifference, which intentionally aimed at the true God; for according to him the origin of this *Fire-Worship* was set on foot by the *Israelites*, who, when they were led away Captive, brought it from *Jerusalem*, and retained it to the latter Times, which no body ever knew before *Hyde*. We understood by *Greek* and *Latin* Authors That this *Persian* Superstition and several others were known to them. The ancient Church honoured a great number of Martyrs who suffered Death, in the cruel Persecutions

ſecutions of *Sapor* and *Iſdejerd*, rather than worſhip Fire: Believe not a Word of it ſays *Hyde*, the *Greeks* and the *Latins* knew nothing at all of the *Perſian* Religion, and theſe Martyrs were obſtinate headſtrong People. In ſhort, to prove this Paradox, he has no Authority but a wretched *Perſian* Poet, who wrote about two hundred Years ago: Any Soul alive may be miſled this way, and eſpecially when ignorant of the worth and authenticity of the Authors relied on.

What uſe we are to make of Oriental Learning.

Theſe Digreſſions may ſeem needleſs; but they are far from being ſo, with regard to the Uſe we are to make of *Oriental Literature*; we muſt not extend it farther than is juſt and right, as the common Cuſtom has hitherto been; whereas it ought to be laid down as a ſure and certain Principle That for what concerns ancient Hiſtory and Geography, we can hardly reap any advantage by the *Arabian* and *Perſian* Books, and much leſs by the *Turkiſh*. This alſo has an Eye to the Diſſertations, and Notes inſerted at the End of theſe Accounts; for it had been no difficult Matter to have added a great deal from other *Arabians* and *Perſians*, as well as Modern Travellers; which we thought incumbent on us to avoid, as much as ſome others have thought it not ſo. *Bochart*, for Example, in his *Hierozoicon*, has moſt faithfully amaſſed all the *Greeks* and *Latins* have ſaid about the *Unicorn*; whereto to he adds a great number of Passages from *Arabian* Authors, to which he might have added from Authors he was unacquainted with; but every attentive Reader will at the first Glance observe them to be all Copies from Copies and of each other, and that the Author he particularly follows, whom he calls *Damir*, was nothing less than a Naturalist. It is then amusing the Reader with empty Show, seriously to introduce such Testimonies and not say a Word of Precaution against them, or declare how far or how far not they are to be minded. Every Man that is familiar with the most ridiculous Fables in *Cazwini* and such like Writers, will never imagin we can depend upon what they say, especially about *China*, which they had such confused Notions of; and concerning which they have not a Syllable of Truth that is not taken out of our two Anthors, which again confirms their Antiquity.

Our two Authors have none of the Blamishes common to the other Arabic *Writers.*

They tell us none of the Stories, so common in the *Arabian* Geographers, about the Emperor of *China*, nor insist on the Names *Fagfur* and *Bagbun* they bestow upon him. What they write of the extent of the *Mohammedan* Empire agrees well with the Time they wrote; and the reason given, in the second Account, why *Ebn Wahab* went to *China*, sutes very naturally with the Posture of Affairs about those Times, when the vast Empire of the *Kalifs* began to be rent asunder by the Civil

Civil Wars caused by the Rise of several Independant Princes, which hurryed on its final Ruin. They neither of them have any Fact that betrays a later Time than the Epochs they take notice of, which is a farther Token of their Veracity. For by them it appears That *Persia*, and *Siraf*, from whence the first Traveller departed, were then in Subjection to the Kalifs, which shews that neither the Princes of the House of *Buiya*, or those that destroyed it, had yet made their Appearance in the *East*.

The Indians *were almost all Idolaters in their Time, and there were but few* Mohammedans *in the Country.*

It is seemingly plain also That the *Indies*, which often occur in our two Authors, were still wholly idolatrous, and that the *Mohammedans* had not as yet made any Conquests there, or introduced *Mohammedism* among them, as they afterwards did under the *Gaznavid* Empire of *Sabactakin*, and some other Princes less considerable. Till that Time the *Mohammedans* on the Coast of *Afric*, in the *Indies*, and in *China*, tho' pretty numerous, were there as Merchants only; they traded on the same foot with the *Jews* and *Christians*, and had no manner of Superiority. In the same State they still continue in *China*, and, as is said by Persons very much to be believed, they adhere to their Law with such strictness that they refuse the Degrees taken by the *Literati*, because they think they cannot in Conscience go through the usual Ceremonies.

Most

Most of the Things, our Accounts contain, concerning the Manners and Customs of the *Indians*, are confirmed by Modern Travellers, and the *Portuguese*, as also by the *Arabian* and *Persian* Geographers.

The Description of the Tea-bush, and the Drink the *Chinese* make of its Leaf, is the more remarkable, as many very great Men of our Times, have reported it not to be of such ancient Date; and by what our Authors say of it in general, it is plain they were perfectly informed about it. As much may be said of the Musk Creature they dwell on; and several other Rarities, illustrated in the Notes.

Their Testimony as to the number of Christians in China *is very remarkable.*

We never before heard that Christians had been formerly numerous in *China*; for all that has been written by the *Portuguese*, and others about St. *Thomas*'s Preaching there, can never stand upon the feeble Support of far fetched Conjecture, and bare Probability: The *Chinese* and *Syriac* Inscription indeed, discovered in the Year MDCXXV, assured us the Faith had been taught in *China* in the eight Century at the latest; but no Trace of this Mission was left, and *Kircher* and *Muller* are widely out in their Explanations of this Monument; but here you will have it illustrated in a Dissertation apart, by which it will appear That when our two Authors say, there were numbers of Christians involved in the universal Massacre, at the time a total Revolution befel the Empire, it is not impossible but those who thus perished were descend-

ed

ed of those mentioned on the *Chinese* Stone.

The same Passage gives us to understand what City is meant by the Name of *Cumdan*,* mentioned in the Inscription as being at that Time the Capital of the Empire. Tho' most of the *Arabs* confirm what is said in the Inscription, and have the Name of this City of *Cumdan*, and among the rest the *Nubian Geographer*; yet was this City unknown, his Translators mistaking it for the Name of the River that washed the City, instead of the City itself. Those who undertook to explain the *Syriac* Inscription, afforded us nothing but empty Conjectures; whereas by our two *Mohammedans* we learn two important Facts which cast a great light upon the *Chinese* History; *first* that *Cumdan* was formerly the Capital of the Empire, and *secondly* that the same was *Nankin*, a Thing unknown to the best that have written about *China*.

The Lights they afford us into Geography.

By them also we understand That the City of St. *Thomé* was not so called by the *European* Navigators, as many have thought, seeing it was known by the same Name in the ninth Century. They may be of great Use also for the Coasts of the *Indian* Ocean, if we seriously examin into the little they say, and compare it with

Of the City of St. Thomé.

* *Mr.* Renaudot *writes it* Cumbdan *throughout the whole Preface.*

what

what is in the old *Greek* Geographers, ſeemingly unknown to the *Arabs*, if we except *Ptolomy*'s Tables. By them again, we might clear up many Paſſages in the *Nubian Geography*, which is by no means ſo contemptible a Book as ſome of the Learned would have had it; tho' on the other hand it is not deſerving of the very high Account ſome have made of it. Such as it is, it may ſerve for a Sample of the *Eaſtern* Geographies; for it is void of Poſitions, a Defect it has in common with moſt of the reſt; and indeed they might as well be omitted as given with the Variety, and Incertitude in *Abulfeda*. There is nothing of this kind tolerably exact among the *Perſian* and *Arabian* Geographers, but the Tables of *Ulug Beig*, and *Naſſir Eddin* tranſlated by *Greaves*. The *Nubian Geographer*, tho' his Work has been printed in *Arabic*, and turned into *Latin*, has been of no great Service, becauſe the Tranſlators having nothing but the printed Copy before them, which is very erroneous, could not reſtore their Text by Manuſcripts, which are very ſcarce.

In what manner the proper Names are expreſſed

The proper Names are in the Tranſlation, in the Notes, and in the Diſſertations expreſſed in the moſt ſimple manner poſſible, and according to the Power of our Alphabet, regardful not to depart from Cuſtom, which has fixed the Pronunciation of ſeveral of them. Thus for many Centuries paſt we have been uſed to pronounce the Word which ſignifies a King or Prince

Melik,

Melik, and thus it is written in *Roderic* of *Toledo*, and in other *Spanish*, and *Portuguese* Authors. All the Learned have written and pronounced *Melik Chah*, in ſpeaking or writing of that great *Seljukid* Soltan, who reformed the Calendar, and erected the *Jelalean* Epoch; ſo that a Reader that underſtands no *Arabic*, or is unacquainted with *Eaſtern* Hiſtory, would not know him again by the Name of *Malek Chah*. The ſame it is with the Names of Cities and Provinces, which are variouſly written by *Europeans*, according to their ſeveral Rules of Orthography, which are oftentimes hard to be underſtood. Thus what the *Arabs* call *Aderbijan* [*Adarbejan*] is ſpelt one way by a *German*, and another way by a *Portugueſe*. *Olearius* writes it *Aderbitzian*, *Teixeira* writes it, *Aderbajon*, who alſo cloſes all the *Perſian* Terminations in *N*, with an *M*; becauſe the Natives themſelves pronounce the final *an* almoſt as the *Portugueſe* do their *ao* or *am*. Others of the Learned have imagined we are to adhere to the preſent Rules; and ſo one of the greateſt of them has lately in tranſlating the Hiſtories which mention the Province of *Kowarzem*, ſpelt it *Kariſme*; and will have it that the famous Hiſtorian *Emir Cond*, is to be ſpelt *Emir Cavend*; *Ung-khan* Emperor of the *Moguls*, defeated by *Jenghiz-khan*, *Aveng-khan*, and the ſame of many others. We do not diſpute the preſent Laws of Pronunciation, as to them we muſt hearken to Travellers; but we may venture to ſay The

The *Eastern* Tongues have not been less subject to changes of Pronunciation than the *European*. This is easily understood; for the Geographers of those Parts, aware of the Defect of their Characters or Letters for settling the due and genuin Pronunciation, ascertain it as well as they can, by naming every Vowel in proper Names; and seldom it is they agree with the common way of pronouncing. We pass over the Method taken with the *Eastern* Names by the Translator of *Elmacin* [*Erpenius*]; as for the Translator of the History of *Tamerlan* [*Vattier*] he is quite particular and by himself; for what Soul alive could ever guess that *Gali*, *le Guebase*, *Gabdolle*, are, *Hali* [*Ali*] *Abbas*, *Abdalla*, and so on, which must make all such Translations unintelligible.*

Some Account of the Orthography and Pronounciation of the Eastern Names.

* *This is very justly said, and is a Point which well deserves to be considered at large; but the Reader will not expect us to launch into the Particulars of so wide a Subject, when he perceives that we confine our Views to the narrow Limits of a single Note. Mr.* Renaudot *is perhaps more accurate in his way of spelling the Eastern Names, than any other of his Nation, or perhaps any Foreigner whatsoever; but tho', sensible of the Defect of the* French *Alphabet, he often calls in the* K *and* W *to his assistance, yet he is not always equal and alike in several of his Names; nor has he settled them so, that his Reader shall never be at a loss to know how they are really to be pronounced.*

There

The Diſſertations are rather looſe Eſſays on what might be done towards the Recovery of ſome very obſcure, tho' important, Points, than Tracts in Form. We have endeavored to open the way to thoſe

Of the Diſſertations.

There are two ways of pronouncing the Arabic, *the one peculiar to* Afric, *the other to* Aſia; *which laſt being the Parent of this extenſive Tongue, it ſeems as if we had no room to doubt but the Pronounciation there, is to be preferred to the ſame in* Afric: *But that the* African *Way ſhould, on the other hand, chiefly prevail in* Europe, *is no Wonder, conſidering how long, and how nearly we have had Commerce with the* Moors. *The* Africans *pronounce* el *for* al, *and* Melik *for* Malec *or* Malek, *and ſo on; the* Aſiatics *being more open and full in their Utterance. But it is not only as to Vowels that we are at ſome Uncertainty, but even with regard to Conſonants; whence you have the Ambiguities to be obſerved in ſome parts of this Book, as the Wood called* Hairzan *in one Place, and* Chairzan *in another; the Kingdom of* Gezaz [Jeraz] *or* Haraz; *the Province of* Curiſtan *or* Cuziſtan. *Now theſe ſeveral Ambiguities ariſe from the exact reſemblance of ſome* Arabic *Letters with others which are barely diſtinguiſhed from them by a Point, or two, or three, either above the Letter, or below it; for example, The firſt Letter of* Hairzan *is naked thus* ح, *of* Chairzan *the firſt Letter is with a Point thus* خ; *of* Geraz *the firſt Letter is with a Point thus* ج, *of* Haraz *the firſt Letter, as in* Hairzan, *is naked thus* ح; *in* Curiſtan *the* R *is naked thus* ر, *in* Cuziſtan *the* Z *is with a Point thus* ز: *There is another* R *and* Z, *but the Caſe between them is exactly parallel. It appears then that theſe Variations are produced either by Omiſſion, or Redundancy; if by Omiſſion the Points are wanting: But if by Redundancy, the Points are too much; and that the moſt diligent Tranſcriber may, in the Courſe of a long Copy, be guilty of both, muſt be readily granted.*

The Arabs *are often very careful to prevent any Miſtake in the Pronounciation of proper Names, and eſpecially*

who may hereafter attempt deeper Inquiries, upon the principal Heads that occur.

Two or three Authors, who but copy from each other, suffice to give birth to a Notion which spreads unexamined by those

---

as to Vowels; so that when we neglect them, and, running Riot after our Fancy, deviate from them, nothing can excuse us. Upon this Head many might be severely accused, but we will only instance in Pe'tis de la Croix, Senior, *who, in his History of* Genghiz Khan, *has all along* Capschac *for* Kipjak, Alschasche *for* Alshash, *or the County of* Shash, Carizme *for* Chowarazm, *and infinit others; so that it is with too much Reason Few Gentlemen who have not some previous Notion of Eastern Geography and History, care to read the Books that might instruct them therein. In short, the Evils of this Presumption, or Vanity, or Negligence, or call it what you will, are of the most discouraging Kind, and such as claim a thorough and speedy Reformation.*

Historians, and Geographers should agree upon the most powerful Alphabet they could form out of the several in Europe, *and adhere thereto in their Translations from Eastern Works: Nor ever presume to alter the Names of Persons and Places, or clip them, or stretch them to what they are pleased to call their own Standard, which if they did not, we should always know whereabouts we are, and who is meant. If a little Care were taken, and Men wrote rather to instruct and inform, than to raise themselves a Name, which when their Works come to be strictly examined they must infallibly lose; we should not in a* French *Author, read* Blocquet *for* Blackheath, *or see the thousands of the same Abuses which so abound in their Histories and Geographies. To conclude, If Men were sure That Accuracy and Application would be more required at their Hands, by the Public, than they seem to be; the World would not be pestered with the offensive Lumber of the many Books which stand in such great need of Purification by Fire, or Ablution by Water, no matter which.*

But to digress no farther, we shall only add That we have, as near as we have been able, confined ourselves to the true and genuin Orthography of the Names; and that

who follow them; this throws a Mist over History, and gives an Opportunity to confound Truth with Falshood, and what is Certain with what is mere Conjecture. For Example, Father *Trigaut* misunderstanding some Passages of *Syriac*, declares it very probable That St. *Thomas* preached in *China*. A few Years afterwards, they find the *Chinese* and *Syriac* Inscription, which talks of a Mission from *Judæa* or *Syria*; whereupon it was by some asserted, That the Person, therein mentioned, must have been St. *Thomas*; and at once they prick you down the Track he must have followed, and give you a Map to convince you it was so: But these Systems being confessedly absurd, others

that the Learned Reader is desired to take Notice, That the Ch *in* Chorassan, Chowarazm, Chanbalig *and the like, is to be pronounced like the* Greek χ, *or an* English Kh, *to make it the stronger; and that the* English *Reader may pronounce it as in* Choir, Chimera, Chemistry.

That the U, *wherever it occurs, is to be pronounced nearly like our Dipthong* ou, *or rather our* oo, *as in* Moon, Soon, Boon; *so* Almamun *must be pronounced* Almamoon, Hud, Hood; Asud, Asood; *the same is to be observed generally, wherever the* u *occurs in the Eastern Names, in this Book.*

The i *is to be pronounced as our* ee; *so* Rashid *must be* Rasheed; Walid, Waleed; Yazid, Yazeed.

The a *and the* o *must, in general, be pronounced a little more open than the* English *do, but not quite so broad as the* French.

We had thoughts of using the Circumflex to mark some of these Distinctions, but we apprehended it might perplex the mere English *Reader, as much as it would assist the Scholar.*

 would

would have had this Inscription to be a Forgery, tho' it is certainly a most precious Monument, and of the clearest Authority; as will be proved in one of the Dissertations, which will evince That all hitherto offered upon this Head, and particularly by *Muller*, is Intolerable.

Of the Chinese *Learning.* As for the *Chinese* Learning, we have perhaps exposed our selves to great Contradiction, many of the Learned having a long while been of a quite contrary Opinion, tho' not a Soul of them could be an immediate Judge of what he advanced, ignorant of that dreadful Tongue which requires no less than the Life of Man to be duly attained. The Missionaries, indeed, thought they might safely make the *Chinese* Philosophers instrumental towards the Conversion of the whole Nation, and their view was laudable enough: But others, and especially Libertins have strangely perverted the excessive Things which have been reported of the *Chinese* Antiquities; and have assumed them as a Weapon wherewith to attack the Authority of Scripture, and its Super-structure, the Christian Religion; as also the Universality of the Flood, and to maintain that the World is much older than it is thought to be. The fabulous Accounts which so abound in the *Persian* History, all absurd as they are, have to some seemed worthy of being espoused.

Ignorant People, such as the Author of the *Preadamitic System*, are apt to believe whatever flatters their own Concepticeptions, and especially when such Stories are seriously told by great Men, tho' they, it has since appeared, knew nothing beyond the Titles of the Books they have so vaunted. *Vossius*, who, it must be owned, was deeply read in *Greek* and *Latin* Literature, found wherewithal, in the Ancients, to confirm all he saw, or heard say concerning the *Chinese*. And upon such Authorities have Evil disposed Persons, perverted by a false Metaphysics, given out Opinions which, to them, seemed new; tho' most of the same were familiar to the old Philosophers, and the first Heretics; and tend to no less than the utter Subversion of all Religion. What we are taught by *Jesus Christ*, is too well grounded to want the Concurrence of the *Chinese* Philosophy; and if any believe, it may perfect the Mind, and reform the Manners, tho' they know nothing thereof, but by Paraphrases as obscure as the Text; they are to be advised fairly to inquire into what may be objected to the Antiquity of this proud Nation, to their History and their Philosophy, and compare the Advantages thence to be deduced, with the Abuses that have been made of the Contrary. We hope it will, at least, be granted That we may be well skilled in every Science, great Philosophers, and great Mathematicians, without being beholden to the *Chinese* Books.

THE

The Reader is desired to take Notice, That the Capitals in the Margin of the Two Accounts, are added in this Edition, and refer to the same in the Margin of the Notes, which are in exact Alphabetical Order And that [DD] in the Margin of Page 84 of the *Accounts*, 6 Lines from the bottom, is wanting.

The Reader is also desired to excuse and correct the following most Material Errors of the Press.

In the Two Accounts.

PAG. 2. line 3. from the Bottom, for *Jacquets* read Jackets. p. 9. l. 10. from the bottom, *for* Sugar, Canes, *read* Sugar-canes. p. 18. for *Kaschbin* read *Kashbin*. p. 22. for *Tusng* read *Tusang*. p. 38. *for* the Country of *Kakhan* or *Tibet*, *read* the Country of the *Kakhan* of *Tibet*. p. 47. l. 6. *for* loved *read* love. p. 62. for *Tygris* read *Tigris*. p. 83. l. 8. *for* the King *read* one of the Kings. p. 87. *Gozar* read *Goraz*.

In the Notes and Dissertations.

Page 3. Line 18. *for* possibly *read* possible. p. 7. l. 20. *for* καλαι *read* παλαι. p. 17. l. 22. *for* than *read* then. p. 35. for *Acbem* read *Achem*. p. 46. for *Fanfur* read *Fansur*. p. 47. l. 6. from the Bottom *for* as being a *read* as that a. p. 48. for *Tontang* read *Toutang*. p. 62. l. 12. from the Bottom *for* split Horn *read* cloven Hoof. p. 71. for *Xabicang* read *Xabiang*. p. 72. for *Khan* of *Tibet* read *Kakhan* of *Tibet*. p. 104. l. 8. from the bottom *for* Seet *read* Sect. p. 108. for *Mar-Amba* read *Mar-Ama*. Ibid. for *Selibazaba* read *Selibazaka*. p. 111. for an *Ali read* and *Ali*. p. 115. for *Thadæus* read *Thaddæus*. p. 121. l. 21. *for* Catholics *read* Catholic. p. 122. for *Abasha-Khan* read *Abaka-Khan*. p. 134. for *Eba Shalikan* read *Ebn Kalikan*. p. 135. l. 2. from the Bottom *for* Sping *read* Spring. p. 150. *for* Erythæan *read* Erythræan. p. 175. for cay *Tagazgaz* read call *Tagazgaz*. p. 177. for *Khan* or Emperor read *Kakhan* or Emperor. p. 197. for *Kari* or *Katib* read *Kari* and *Katib*. p. 209. l. 6. *for* express *read* expressed. p. 214. for *Catuian* read *Cataian*. p. 225. for *Epocha Celebrires* read *Epochæ Celebriores*.

ANCIENT ACCOUNTS OF *INDIA* and *CHINA*; BY Two Mohammedan Travellers, Who went to thoſe Parts in the 9th Century.

Tranſlated from the Arabic.

I. ACCOUNT.

[*The Beginning is wanted.*]

* * * * * * * * * * * * *
* * * * * * * * * * * * *

THE third of the Seas we have to mention, is the Sea of *Harkand*. Between this Sea and that of *Delarowi*, are many Iſlands, to the Number, as they ſay, of 1900. They, in ſome ſort, part theſe two Seas from each other,

The Maldives.

[A]

[B]

other, and are govern'd by a Queen. Among these Islands, they find Ambergreese in Lumps of extraordinary bigness; as also in lesser Pieces, in Form of Plants forcibly torn up. This Amber is produced at the Bottom of the Sea, as Plants are upon Earth; and when the Sea is troubled, the Violence of the Wave tears it up from the Bottom, and washes it to the Shore, in form of a Mushroom, or a Truffle.

Coco-nut Trees. Geogr. Nub. p.31. These Islands govern'd by a Woman, are full of that kind of the Palm-tree which bears the Coco-nut; and are one, two, three, or four Leagues distant from each other, all inhabited, and planted with Coco-nut Trees. The Wealth of the Inhabitants consists in Shells [*Cowries,*] and even the Queen's Treasury is full of them. They say there are no Artificers more expert than these Islanders; and that of the Fibres of the Coco-nut they make whole Shirts, all of one Piece, Sleeves, Gussets and all, as also half Vests [or *Jacquets.*] With the same industry, and with the same Tree they build Ships and Houses; and they are skilful in all other sorts of Workmanship. Their Shells they have from the Sea, at times when they rise up to the Surface; at which times the Inhabitants throw Branches of the Coco-nut-tree into the Sea, and the Shells stick to them. They call them *Kabtaje.*

[D] *The Island of* Sarandib *or* Ceylon. Beyond these Islands, in the Sea of *Harkand*, is *Sarandib*, or *Ceylon*, the Chief of all these Islands, which are called *Dobijat.*

It

It is all encompassed by the Sea, and on certain parts of its Coast they fish for Pearl.

Up in the Country there is a Mountain called *Rahun*, to the top of which it is thought *Adam* ascended; and there left the Mark of his Foot in a Rock, on the top of this same Mountain. There is but one Print of a Man's Foot, which is seventy Cubits in Length; and they say that *Adam* at the same time stood with his other Foot in the Sea. About this Mountain are Mines of the Ruby, Opal, and Amethyst. This Island, which is of great extent, has two Kings; and here you may have Wood-Aloes, Gold, precious Stones, and Pearls, which are fished on the Coast; as also a a kind of large Shells, which they use instead of Trumpets, and which they much value.

Adam's *Peek.* *Geogr.*

In this same Sea, towards *Sarandib*, there are other Isles, but not so many in Number, tho' of vast extent and unknown Name. One of these Islands is called *Ramni*, and is under several Princes, being eight or nine hundred Leagues in dimension. Here are Gold Mines, and particularly those called *Fansur*; as also an excellent sort of Camphire. These Islands are not far from some others, the Chief of which is *Alnian*, where is great plenty of Gold. The Inhabitants here have Coco-nut Trees, which supply them with Food; and therewith also they paint their Bodies, and oil themselves. The Custom of the Country is, that no one may marry, till he has slain an Enemy in Battle, and brought off his Head.

[C] *Great Isles of* Ramni.

Alnian.

A remarkable Custom touching Marriage.

If he has killed two, he claims two Wives, and ſo on in proportion; ſo that if he has ſlain fifty, he may marry fifty Wives. This Cuſtom proceeds from the Number of hoſtile Nations which ſurround them; ſo that he, among them, who kills the greateſt Number, is the moſt conſidered.

People that eat Human Fleſh.

Theſe Iſlands of *Ramni* abound with Elephants, Red-wood, and Trees called *Chairzan*; and the Inhabitants eat Human Fleſh. Theſe Iſlands part the Sea of *Harkand* from the Sea of *Shelahet*; and beyond them are others called *Najabalus*, which are pretty well peopled. Both the Men and the Women there go quite naked, except that the Women conceal their Parts with the Leaves of Trees. When Shipping is among theſe Iſlands, the Inhabitants come off in Embarkations, little and big, and bring with them Ambergreeſe, and Coco-nuts, which they truck for Iron: For they want no Cloathing, being free from the extremes either of Heat or of Cold.

Ambergreeſe.

The Sea of Andaman. *Canibals.*

Beyond theſe two Iſlands lies the Sea of *Andaman*; the People on this Coaſt eat Human Fleſh quite raw; their Complexion is black; their Hair frizled; their Countenance and Eyes frightful; their Feet are very large and almoſt a Cubit in length; and they go quite naked. They have no Embarkations; if they had, they would devour all the Paſſengers they could lay Hands on. When Ships have been kept back by contrary Winds, they are often, in theſe Seas, obliged to drop Anchor, on this barbarous Coaſt. for the ſake of Water,

ter, when they have expended their Stock; and upon these Occasions they often lose some of their Men, but most escape.

Beyond this there is a mountainous and inhabited Island, where, as they say, are Mines of Silver; but as it does not ly in the usual Track of Shipping, many have sought for it in vain; tho' remarkable for a very lofty Mountain, which is called *Kashenai*. It happened that a Ship sailing in this Latitude, had Sight of the Mountain, and shaped her Course for it; and being come up with the Land, sent a Boat on shore, with Hands to cut Wood. The Men kindled a Fire, and saw Silver run from it; which gave them to understand there was a Mine of this Metal in that Place; wherefore they shipped as much of the Earth, or Ore, as they saw good. But as they were proceeding on their Voyage, the Sea was ruffled by so furious a Gust of Wind, that, to lighten their Ship, they were under a necessity of throwing all their Ore over board. Since that time the Mountain has been carefully looked for, but it has never since been seen. To conclude, there are many such Islands in the Sea, more in Number than can be said; being partly too dangerous to be approached by Seamen, and partly unknown to them.

[F] *An unknown Island where are Mines of Silver.*

In this Sea there is often beheld a white Cloud, which at once spreads over a Ship, and lets down a long thin Tongue, or Spout, quite to the Surface of the Water,

[G] *A white Cloud, or Water Spout.*

Water, which it disturbs just after the Manner of a Whirl-wind; and if a Vessel happen to be in the way of this Whirlpool, she is immediately swallowed up thereby: But at length this Cloud mounts again, and discharges itself in a prodigeous rain. It is not known whether this Water is sucked up by the Cloud which makes it rise; or in what manner so extraordinuary an effect is brought to pass.

[H] All these Seas are Subject to great Commotions excited by the Winds, which make them boil up like Water over a fire. Then is it that the Surf dashes Ships against the Islands, and breaks them to pieces with unspeakable Violence; and then also is it that Fish, of all sizes, are thrown dead ashore upon the Rocks, like an Arrow from a Bow.

The Wind which commonly blows upon the Sea of *Harkand*, is from another Quarter, it coming from the North-west; but this Sea is also Subject to as violent Agitations as those we have just mentioned. And now is Ambergreese torn up from the Bottom, and particularly where it is very deep; and the deeper it is, the more exquisite is the Amber. It is observed that when this Sea rages in this

[I] violent manner, it sparkles like Fire. In this Sea, moreover, there is a Fish called *Lockham*, which preys upon Men.

[*Here is a Leaf or more wanting in the Manuscript, where the Author began to treat of* China.

* * *

* * * * * which has caused all Goods to lower in their Price. Of the different Causes of this Fall, the frequent Fires which happen at *Cansu* are none of the least. *Cansu* is the Port for all the Ships and Goods of the *Arabs*, who trade in *China*; but Fires are there very frequent, because the Houses are built with nothing but Wood, or else with split Cane [*Bamboo*:] besides, the Merchants and Ships are often lost in going and coming; or they are often plundered; or obliged to make too long a stay in Harbour; or to sell their Goods out of the Country subject to the *Arabs*, and there make up their Cargo. In short, Ships are under a necessity of wasting a considerable time in refitting, not to speak of many other Causes of Delay. Ca nfu.

Soliman the Merchant relates, that at *Cansu*, which is the principal Scale for Merchants, there is a *Mohammedan* appointed Judge over those of his Religion, by the Authority of the Emperor of *China*; and that he is Judge of all the *Mohammedans* who resort to these Parts. Upon Festival Days he performs the public Service with the *Mohammedans*, and pronounces the Sermon or *Kotbat*, which he concludes, in the usual form, with Prayers for the Soltan of the *Moslems*, [or *Muslemen*.] The Merchants of *Irak* who trade hither, are no way dissatisfied with his Conduct, or his Administration in the Post he is invested with; because his Actions, and the Judgments he gives, are just and equitable, and con-

[Q] *A* Mohammedan Kadi *at* Cansu.

conformable to the *Koran* [or *Alcoran*,] and according to the *Mohammedan* Juriſprudence.

[L] *The Courſe to* China. As for the Places whence Ships depart, and thoſe alſo they touch at; many Perſons declare that the Navigation is perform'd in the following order. Moſt of the *Chineſe* Ships take in their Cargo at *Siraf*, where alſo they Ship their Goods which come from *Baſra* or *Baſſora*, *Oman*, and other Parts; and this they do, becauſe in this Sea, (that is, in the Sea of *Perſia* and the *Red Sea*) there are frequent Storms, and ſhole Water in many Places. From *Baſra* to *Siraf* is 120 Leagues, and when Ships have loaded at this laſt Place, they there water alſo; and from thence make Sail for a Place called *Maſcat*, which is in the extremity of the Province of *Oman*, about 200 Leagues from *Siraf*. On the Eaſt Coaſt of this Sea, between *Siraf* and *Maſcat*, is a Place called *Naſif Bani al Safak*, and an Iſland called *Ebn Kahowan*; and in this Sea are Rocks called *Oman*, and a narrow Strait, called *Dordur*, between two Rocks, through which ſmall Veſſels do venture, but the *Chineſe* Ships dare not. There are alſo two Rocks called *Koſſir* and *Howair*, which ſcarce appear above the Water's edge. After we are clear of theſe Rocks, we ſteer for a place called *Shibr Oman*, and at *Maſcat* take in Water, which is drawn out of Wells; and here, alſo, you are ſupplied with Cattle of the Province of *Oman*. From hence Ships take

Geog. Nub. p. 56.

Id. Præf. p. 4. *Lat.*

take their Departure for the *Indies*, and first they touch at *Kaucammali*; and from *Mascat* to this Place, it is a Month's sail, with the Wind aft. This is a Frontier Place, and the chief Arsenal in the Province of the same Name; and here the *Chinese* Ships put in and are in safety. Fresh Water is to be had here, and the *Chinese* pay a thousand Drams for Duties; but others pay only from one *Dinar* to ten *Dinars*.

They are worth about a Gold Crown.

From *Mascat* to *Kaucammali*, it is, as we have said, a Month's Sail; and then, having watered at this last Place, you begin to enter the Sea of *Harkand*; and having sailed through it, you touch at a place call *Lajabalus*, where the Inhabitants understand not the *Arabesque*, or any other Language in use with Merchants. They wear no Cloaths, are white, and unstable on their Feet.

[K]

An Island where no Women are seen.

Palm-wine.

It is said their Women are not to be seen; and that the Men leaving the Island, in Canoes hollowed out of one Piece, go in quest of them, and carry them Coconuts, Sugar, Canes, *Mousa*, and Palm-wine. This Liquor is white, and, if drank fresh, has the Taste of the Coco-nut, and is sweet like Honey; if kept somewhat longer it becomes as strong as Wine; but if it is kept for several Days, it turns to Vinegar. They give it in exchange for Iron; and in like manner they truck the little Amber which is thrown on their Coast, for bits of Iron. The Bargain is driven by by Signs, and Touches of the Hand, because they underſtand not the *Arabeſque*: But they are very ſharp, and are apt to carry off Iron from the Merchants, and leave them nothing in return.

Calabar. From this Place Ships ſteer towards *Calabar*, the Name of a Place and a Kingdom on the Coaſt, to the right Hand beyond *India*. *Bar* ſignifies a *Coaſt* in the Language of the Country, and this depends on the Kingdom of *Zabage*. The Inhabitants are dreſſed in thoſe ſorts of ſtriped Garments, which the *Arabs* call *Fauta*; and they commonly wear but one at a time, which is equally obſerved by Perſons of high Rank, and thoſe of inferior Degree. At this Place they commonly take in Water, which is filled from living Wells, and which they like better than what is drawn out of Ciſterns and Tanks. *Calabar* is about a Months Voyage from a Place called *Kaukam*, which is almoſt upon the Skirts of the Sea of *Harkand*.

[M] Betuma. In ten Days after this, Ships reach a Place called *Betuma*, where they may water if they pleaſe. From thence in ten Days they come up with *Kadrange*, where alſo they may water. It is worth the notice, that in all the Iſlands and Peninſula's of the *Indies*, they find Water when they dig for it.

Senef. In this laſt mentioned Place there is a very lofty Mountain, which is ſcarce Peopled by any but Slaves and fugitive Robbers. From thence in ten Days they arrive

rive at *Senef*. Here is fresh Water, and hence comes the *Aromatic-wood*, we call *Hud al Senefi*: Here is a King; the Inhabitants are black, and wear two striped Garments.

Having watered at this Place, it is a ten Days Passage to *Sandarfulat*, an Island where is fresh Water. Then they steer upon the Sea of *Sanji*, and so to the *Gates* of *China*; for so they call certain Rocks and Sholes in that Sea, between which is a narrow Strait, through which Sips pass. It requires a Month to Sail from *Sandarfulat* to *China*, and it takes up eight whole Days to steer clear of these Rocks. When a Ship has got through these *Gates*, she, with the Tide of Flood, goes into a fresh Water Gulf, and drops Anchor in the chief Port of *China*, which is that of *Canfu*; and here they have fresh Water, both from Springs and Rivers, as they have also in most of the other Cities of *China*. The City is adorned with large Squares, and supplied with all the Necessaries of Defence against an Enemy; and, in most of the other Provinces, there are Cities of Strength, fortified in the same manner.

Sandarfulat.

Canfu.

In this Port it Ebbs and Flows twice in twenty four Hours, but with this Difference; That whereas from *Basra* to the Island called *Bani Kahowan*, it Flows when the Moon is in her mid Course, and Ebbs when she rises and when she sets; from near *Bani Kahowan* quite to the Coast of *China*,

The Tides at Canfu.

China, it is Flood when the Moon rises, and when she is towards her height it is Ebb; and so on, when she sets it is flowing Water, and when she is quite hidden under the Horizon, the Tide falls.

The Island of Muljan. They say that in the Island of *Muljan*, which is between *Sarandib* and *Cala*, on the Eastern Shore of the *Indies*, there are Negroes who go quite naked; and that when they meet with a Stranger, they hang him with his Head downward, and slice

Man-eaters. him into Pieces, which they eat quite raw. These Negroes have no King, and feed upon Fish, *Mousa*, Coco-nuts, and Sugar-canes: They have Ponds and some Lakes.

[N] *Flying Fish.* They report also, that in some parts of this Sea there is a smallish kind of Fish which flies upon the Water, and which they call the *Sea Locust*.

It is moreover said, that in another Part there is a Fish which, leaving the Sea, gets up to the Coco-nut Trees; and having drained them of their Juice, takes to the Sea again.

[O] *A Fish which petrifies.* It is again added, that in this Sea there is another sort of Fish like a Lobster, which petrifies as soon as taken out of its Element; they pulverise it, and it is good for several Diseases of the Eyes.

[P] *A* Vulcano. They say also, that near *Zabage* there is a Mountain called the *Mountain of Fire*, which no one may approach; that, in the day time, it sends up a thick Smoke; and that, in the Night, it throws out Flames. At the Foot of this same Mountain are two

two Springs of fresh Water, the one hot and the other cold.

The Chinese *dress in Silk.* The *Chinese* are dressed in Silk both Winter and Summer; and this kind of dress is common to the Prince, the Soldier, and to every other Person, though of the lowest Degree. In Winter they wear Drawers, of a particular make, which fall down to their Feet. Of these they put on two, three, four, five or more, if they can, one over another; and are very careful to be covered quite down to their Feet, because of the Damps which are very great, and much dreaded by them. In Summer they only wear a single Garment of Silk, or some such Dress, but have no Turbans.

Their common Food is Rice. Their common Food is Rice, which they often eat with a Broth like what the *Arabs* make of Meat, or Fish, which they pour upon their Rice. Their Kings eat Wheaten Bread, and all sorts of Animals, not excepting Swine, and some others.

Fruits of China. They have several sort of Fruits; Apples, ~~Lemons~~, Quinces, *Moulas*, Sugar-canes, Citruls, Figs, Grapes, Cucumbers of two sorts, Trees which bear Meal, Walnuts, Almonds, Filberds, Pistachios, Plums, Apricocks, Services, and Coco-nuts; but they have no store of Palms; they have only a few about some private Houses.

Drink made of Rice. Their drink is a kind of Wine made of Rice; they have no other Wine in the Country, nor is there any brought to them; they know not what it is, nor do they

they drink of it. They have Vinegar alſo, and a kind of Comfit like what the *Arabs* call *Natef*, and ſome others.

They are not very nice in point of cleanlineſs, and waſh not with Water when they eaſe Nature, but only wipe themſelves with Paper. They eat alſo of dead Animals, and practice in many other things like the *Magians*; and, in truth, the Religion of the one and the other is much the ſame. The *Chineſe* Women appear uncover'd, and adorn their Heads with ſmall Ivory and other Combs, of which they ſhall wear ſometimes a Score together. The Men are covered with Caps of a particular make.

The Ornament of the Chineſe *Women.*

The Law they obſerve with regard to Thieves, is to put them to Death as ſoon as caught.

Some Particulars relating to the Indies *and to the Kings of the ſame Countries.*

[R] *Four great Kings.*

Both the *Indians* and *Chineſe* agree, that there are four great or principal Kings in the World; they allow the King of the *Arabs* to be the firſt, and to be, without diſpute, the moſt Powerful of Kings, the moſt wealthy, and the moſt excellent every way; becauſe he is the Prince and Head of a great Religion, and becauſe no other ſurpaſſes him in Greatneſs, or Power.

The Emperor of *China* reckons himſelf next after the King of the *Arabs*, and after him the King of the *Greeks*; and laſtly, the *Balhara*, King of *Moharmi al Adan*,

The Balhara.

Adan, or of *Those who have their Ears bored*. This *Balhara* is the most illustrious Prince in all the *Indies*; and all the other Kings there, tho' each is Master and independant in his Kingdom, acknowledge in him this Prerogative and Pre-eminence. When he sends Ambassadors to them, they receive them with extraordinary honours, because of the respect they bear him. This King makes magnificent Presents after the manner of the *Arabs*; and has Horses and Elephants in very great Number, and great Treasures in Money. He has of those Pieces of Silver called *Thartarian* Drams, which weigh half a Dram more than the *Arabesque* Dram. They are coined with the Die of the Prince, and bear the Year of his Reign from the last of the Reign of his Predecessor. They compute not their Years from the Æra of *Mohammed* as do the *Arabs*, but only by the Years of their Kings. Most of these Princes have lived a long time, and many of them have reigned above Fifty Years; and those of the Country believe that the length of their Lives, and of their Reigns, is granted them in recompence for their Kindness to the *Arabs*. In truth, there are no Princes more heartily affectionate to the *Arabs*; and their Subjects profess the same Friendship for us.

The Balhara, *a Name common to all these Kings.*

Balhara is an Apellative common to all these Kings, as was *Cosroes*, and some others, and is not a proper Name. The Country which owes Obedience to this Prince, begins

gins on the Coaſt of the Province called *Kamkam*, and reaches by Land to the confines of *China*. He is ſurrounded by the Dominions of many Kings, who are at War with him, and yet he never marches againſt them. One of theſe Kings is the King of *Haraz*, who has very numerous Forces, and is ſtronger in Horſe than all the other Princes of the *Indies*; but is an Enemy to the *Arabs*, tho' he at the ſame time confeſſes their King to be the greateſt of Kings; nor is there a Prince in the *Indies* who has a greater Averſion to *Mohammediſm*. His Dominions are upon a Promontory, where are much riches, many Camels, and other Cattle. The Inhabitants here Traffic with Silver they waſh for; and they ſay there are Mines of the ſame on the Continent. There is no talk of Robbers in this Country, no more than in the reſt of the *Indies*.

The Kingdom of Tafek.

On one ſide of this Kingdom lies that of *Tafek*, which is not of very great extent; this King has the fineſt White Women in all the *Indies*; but he is ſubject to the Kings about him, his Army being but ſmall. He has a great Affection for the *Arabs*, as well as the *Balhara*.

Rahmi.

Theſe Kingdoms border upon the Lands of a King called *Rahmi*, who is at War with the King of *Haraz*, and with the *Balhara* alſo. This Prince is not much conſidered either for his Birth, or the Antiquity of his Kingdom; but his Forces are

are more numerous than thoſe of the *Balhara*, and even than thoſe of the Kings of *Haraz*, and *Tafek*. They ſay that when he takes the Field, he appears at the Head of fifty thouſand Elephants; and that he commonly marches in the Winter Seaſon, becauſe the Elephants not being able to bear with thirſt, he can move at no other Time. They ſay alſo that in his Army there are commonly from ten to fifteen thouſand Tents. In this ſame Country they make Cotton Garments, in ſo extraordinary a manner, that no where elſe are the like to be ſeen. Theſe Garments are for the moſt part round, and wove to that degree of fineneſs, that they may be drawn through a Ring of a middling Size.

Shells are current in this Country, and ſerve for ſmall Money, notwithſtanding that they have Gold and Silver, Wood-Aloes, and Sable-Skins of which they make the Furniture of Saddles and Houſings. In this ſame Country is the famous *Karkandan* or *Unicorn*, who has but one Horn upon his Forehead, and thereon a round Spot with the Repreſentation of a Man. The whole Horn is black, except the Spot in the middle, which is white. The Unicorn is much ſmaller than the Elephant; from the Neck downwards he pretty much reſembles the Bufflar; for Strength he is extraordinary, therein ſurpaſſing all other Creatures; his Hoof is not cloven; and from his Foot to his Shoulder he is all of a Piece. The Elephant flies from the Unicorn, whoſe low-

The Unicorn.

C ing

ing is like that of an Ox, with ſomething of the Cry of a Camel. His Fleſh is not forbidden, and we have eaten of it. There are great Numbers of this Creature in the Fens of this Kingdom, as alſo in all the other Provinces of the *Indies*; but the Horns of theſe are the moſt eſteemed, and upon them are generally ſeen the Figures of Men, Peacocks, Fiſhes, and other Reſemblances. The *Chineſe* adorn their Girdles with theſe ſorts of Figures; ſo that ſome of theſe Girdles are worth two or three thouſand pieces of Gold in *China*, and ſometimes more, the Price augmenting with the Beauty of the Figure. All the things, we have here enumerated, are to be purchaſed in the Kingdom of *Rahmi* for Shells, which are the current Money.

Kaſchbin. After this Kingdom there is another which is an inland State, diſtant from the Coaſt, and call'd *Kaſchbin*. The Inhabitants are white, and bore their Ears: They have Camels, and their Country is a Deſart, and full of Mountains.

Hitrange. Farther on, upon the Coaſt, there is a ſmall Kingdom called *Hitrange*, which is very poor; but it has a Bay, where the Sea throws up great Lumps of *Ambergreeſe*. They have alſo Elephants Teeth and Pepper; but the Inhabitants eat it green, becauſe of the ſmallneſs of the Quantity they gather.

Mujet. Beyond theſe Kingdoms, here mentioned, there are others of number unknown, and among the reſt that of *Mujet*. The Inhabitants

habitants are white, and dreſs after the *Chineſe* Mode: Their Country is full of Mountains with white Tops and of very great Extent. Here are great Quantities of Musk, eſteemed the moſt exquiſite in the World. They have War with all the neighbouring Kingdoms. The Kingdom of *Mabed* is beyond that of *Mujet*; therein are many Cities, and the Inhabitants have a great Reſemblance of the *Chineſe*, even more than thoſe of *Mujet*; for they have Officers or Eunuchs like thoſe who govern the Cities among the *Chineſe*. The Country of *Mabed* is conterminous with *China*, and is at peace with the Emperor of *China*, but is not ſubject to him. Mabed.

The *Mabed* ſend every Year Ambaſſadors and Preſents to the Emperor of *China*, who on his part ſends Ambaſſadors and Preſents to them. Their Country is of great Extent; and when the Ambaſſadors of the *Mabed* enter *China*, they are carefully watched, and never once allow'd to ſurvey the Country, for fear they ſhould form Deſigns of conquering it, which would be no difficult Task for them; becauſe of their great Numbers, and becauſe they are parted from *China*, only by Mountains, or by Rocks. *The* Mabed *ſend Ambaſſadors to* China.

They ſay, that in the Kingdom of *China* there are above two hundred Cities which have Juriſdiction over ſeveral others, and have each a Prince or Governor, and an Eunuch or Lieutenant. *Canfu* is one of theſe Cities, being the Port for all Shipping, and preſiding over twenty Towns. *The Number of Cities in* China.

A Town is dignify'd with the Title of City, when it is allowed some of those great *Chinese* Trumpets which are fashion'd after this manner: They are three or four Cubits in length, and are as much about as can be grasped with both Hands; but they grow narrower towards the End, which is fitted to the Mouth of a Man: On the Outside, they are coloured with *Chinese* Ink, and may be heard a Mile off. Each City has four Gates, at each of which are five of these Trumpets, which the *Chinese* sound at certain Hours of the Day and of the Night. Moreover, in each City are ten Drums, which they beat at the same time; and this they do as a public Token of their Obedience to the Emperor, as also to signify the Hour of the Day and of the Night; to which end they have also Dials and Clocks with Weights.

Trumpets.

Drums.

Copper Money.

They coin a great deal of Copper Money like what the *Arabs* know by the Name of *Falūs*. They have Treasures like other Kings; but no others have this sort of small Money, which, and no other, is current all over the Country: For tho' they have Gold, Silver, Pearls, Silk, and rich Stuffs in great abundance, they consider them only as Moveables and Merchandize, and the Copper Pieces are the only current Coin. From foreign Parts they have Ivory, Frankincense, Copper in Pigs, Tortoise Shell, and the Unicorns Horns which we have mention'd, and with which they adorn their Girdles. Of their own Stock,

Stock, they have Numbers of Beasts of Burthen; Horses, Asses, and Dromedaries; but they have no *Arabian* Horses. They have an excellent kind of Earth, wherewith thy make a Ware of equal Fineness with Glass, and equally transparent. *Porcelaine*

When Merchants enter *China* by Sea, the *Chinese* seize on their Cargo, and convey it to Warehouses; and so put a stop to their Business for six Months, and till the last Merchantman be arrived. Then they take three in ten, or thirty *per Cent.* of each Commodity, and return the rest to the Merchant. If the Emperor wants any particular thing, his Officers have a right to take it preferably to any other Persons whatsoever; and paying for it to the utmost Penny it is valued at, they dispatch this Business immediately, and without the least Injustice. They commonly take Camphire, which they pay for after the rate of fifty *Fakuges per Man*, and the *Fakuge* is worth a thousand *Falus* or Pieces of Copper. When it happens that the Emperor does not take Camphire, it sells for half as much again. *Vid. M. P. l. 2. c. 79.* *Merchants how us'd in* China.

The *Chinese* bury not their dead till the Day twelvemonth of their Decease. Till the Expiration of this Term, they keep them in Coffins; for having previously dried them with quick Lime, that they may keep, they place them in some part of their Houses. The Bodies of their Kings are embalmed with Aloes and Camphire. They mourn for three whole Years, all which time they weep their dead, and whoso- *The Burials of the* Chinese.

ever ſhould not do ſo, would be chaſtiſed with the Bamboo, a Puniſhment both Men and Women are liable to, at the ſame time that they are reproached, *What then thou art not concerned at the Death of thy Parent* [or *Relation*]? They bury their dead in deep Pits, much like thoſe in uſe with the *Arabs*, till which is done, they conſtantly ſet Victuals before the Corpſe; and as it is in the Evening that they thus adminiſter meat and drink to their dead, if the next Morning they find nothing left, they imagine that they have both eaten and drank, and ſay, *The deceaſed hath eaten.* They ceaſe not from bewailing their dead, nor from ſetting Meat and Drink before them as long as they are kept in the Houſe; inſomuch that their Expences upon theſe Occaſions, and in thus paying the laſt Duties to their departed Relations, are ſo exorbitant, as often to ruin them, and conſume their Wealth and Eſtates. Formerly they, with the dead Bodies of their Kings or others of the Royal Blood, buried very rich Apparel and thoſe ſorts of Girdles which we have obſerv'd to coſt ſo much; but this Cuſtom is now no more; becauſe it has happened that the Bodies of ſome have been dug up by Thieves, for the ſake of what was buried with them.

The Chineſe *learn to read and write.*

The *Chineſe* both poor and rich, great and ſmall, learn to read and to write. The Titles of their Kings or Governors are varied to the Dignity and Rank of the Cities under them; thoſe of the ſmaller Cities are called *Tuſng*, and this Word ſignifies

nifies the Governor of a Town. Thoſe of the greater Cities, as *Canfu* for Example, are ſtiled *Difu*; and the Eunuch or Lieutenant is titled *Tukam*. Theſe Eunuchs are ſelected from the Inhabitants of the Cities. There is alſo a ſupreme Judge, and him they call *Lakſhi-ma-makvan*; other Names they have for other Officers which we know not how properly to expreſs.

No one is raiſed to the Dignity of a Prince or Governor of a City, till he has attained his fortieth Year, *For then*, ſay they, *he hath Experience*. When one of theſe Princes or petty Kings, keeps his Court in a City, he is ſeated upon a Tribunal, and receives the Petitions or Complaints of the People. Behind his Tribunal, is an Officer called *Licu*, who keeps ſtanding, and, according to the Order he receives from the Prince, commits his Anſwer to Writing; for they never anſwer by Word of Mouth to any Buſineſs whatſoever, nor will they give any Anſwer at all to any thing that is not written. Before the Parties preſent their Petitions to the Prince, they get them examined by an Officer, who, if he diſcovers any Fault, ſends them back again. For no Man may draw up theſe Writings which are to be preſented to the Prince, except a Clerk verſed in Buſineſs, and at the Bottom of each Writing they put, *Written by ſuch a one, the Son of ſuch a one*; and if, in this Caſe, there happen any Blunder or Miſtake, the Clerk is bamboo'd. The Prince never

Governors of Cities.

ſeats himſelf on his Tribunal, till he has eaten and drank, for fear he ſhould be miſtaken in ſomething; and each of theſe Princes or Governors has his Subſiſtance from the publick Treaſury of the City he commands.

The Emperor of China.

The Emperor of *China*, who is above all theſe Princes or petty Kings, never appears in public but once in ten Months; ſaying, That if he ſhewed himſelf oftner to the People, they would loſe the Veneration they have for him. For he holds it as a Maxim, That Principalities cannot ſubſiſt but by force, and that the People know not what Juſtice is; and that thus Conſtraint and Violence muſt be uſed to maintain, among them, the Majeſty of Empire.

Taxes.

They have no Impoſt upon their Lands, but are ſubject only to a Poll Tax, which is levied upon Men only, and that, according to their Condition and Capacity. When any *Arabs*, or other Strangers are in this Country, the *Chineſe* tax them in proportion to their Subſtance. When any Dearth makes Neceſſaries very dear, then does the King open his Storehouſes, and ſell all Sorts of Proviſions much cheaper than they are to be had at Market; and hence no Dearth is of any long Continuance among the *Chineſe*.

The public Treaſury.

The Sums that are gathered from the Capitation Tax, are laid up in the public Treaſury; and, I believe, that, from this Tax, fifty thouſand *Dinars* are every Day paid into the Treaſury of *Canfu* alone,

alone, although this City be none of the largest in *China*.

The Emperor also reserves to himself the Revenues which arise from the Salt Mines, and from a certain Herb which they drink with hot Water, and of which great Quantities are sold in all the Cities, to the amount of great Sums. They call it *Sah*, and it is a Shrub more bushy than the Pomegranate-tree, and of a more taking Smell, but it has a kind of Bitterness with it. Their way is to boil Water, which they pour upon this Leaf, and this Drink cures all sorts of Diseases. Whatever Sums are lodged in the Treasury arise from the Poll Tax, and the Duties upon Salt and upon this Leaf. *The Emperor's Revenues.*

In each City there is a small Bell hung to the Wall above the Prince's or Governor's head; and this Bell may be rung by a String which reaches about three Miles, and crosses the high Way, to the end that People may get at it. When the String is pulled, the Bell strikes over the Governor's Head, and strait he commands, that the Person, who thus demands Justice, be brought before him; and accordingly the Complainant sets forth his Case in Person, and the Wrongs he suffers. And the same Practice is in use throughout all the other Provinces. *A small Bell.*

If a Man would travel from one Place to another, he must take two Passes with him; the one from the Governor, the other from the Eunuch or Lieutenant. The Governor's *Passes for Travellers.*

nor's Paſs permits him to ſet out on his Journey, and takes notice of the Name of the Traveller, and of thoſe alſo of his Company, the Age and Family of the one and the other: For every body in *China*, whether a Native, or an *Arab*, or any other Foreigner, is obliged to declare all he knows of himſelf, nor can he poſſibly be excuſed the ſo doing. The Eunuch's or Lieutenant's Paſs ſpecifies the Quantities of Money or Goods which the Traveller and thoſe with him, take along with them. And this is done for the Information of the Frontier places, where theſe two Paſſes are examined; for whenever a Traveller arrives at any of them, it is regiſtered, *That ſuch a one, the Son of ſuch a one, of ſuch a Family, paſſed through this Place on ſuch a Day, in ſuch a Month, in ſuch a Year, and in ſuch Company.* And by this means they prevent any one from carrying off the Money or Effects of other Perſons, or their being loſt: So that if any thing has been carried off unjuſtly, or the Traveller dies on the Road, they immediately know what is become of the Things, and they are either reſtored to the Claimant, or to the Heirs.

Adminiſtration of Juſtice. The *Chineſe* adminiſter Juſtice with great Strictneſs in all their Tribunals. When any Perſon enters his Action againſt another, he ſets down his Claim in writing, and the Defendant writes down his Defence, which he ſigns, and holds between his Fingers. Theſe two writings are delivered

livered in together, and being examined, Sentence is pronounced in writing, and the Parties have each his Paper returned to him; but first they give back to the Defendant his writing of Defence, that he may acknowledge it. When one Party denies what the other affirms, he is ordered to return his Writing; and if the Defendant thinks he may do it safely, and accordingly delivers in his Paper again, they also call for that of the Plaintif, and then they say to him who denies what the other seems to have reason to maintain, *Exhibit a Writing whereby to make it appear that your Antagonist has no right to demand of you what is in debate; but if it clearly betrays the Truth of what you deny, you shall undergo twenty Strokes of the* Bamboo *upon the Backside, and pay a Fine of twenty* Fakuges, which make about two hundred *Dinars*. Now this Punishment is such as the Criminal could not survive: It is so grievous that no Person in all *China*, may, of his own Authority, inflict it upon another, upon pain of Death, and Confiscation of goods And so no Body is ever so hardy as to expose himself to so certain a Danger; wherefore Justice is well administred, and very exactly distributed to every one. They require no Witness, nor put the Parties upon Oath.

Their Methods with Bankrupts.

When any Man becomes a Bankrupt, and has wasted the Substance of his Creditors, they throw him into a Prison in the Governor's Palace, and he is immediately put upon his Declaration. After he has been a Month in Prison, he is re-

leased

leased by the Governor's Order, and Proclamation is made, *That such a one, the Son of such a one, has consumed the Substance of such a one; and that if he has any Effects in the Hands of any Person, Lands, Reversions, or Wealth in any other Shape whatsoever, it must be made known within the Term of a Month.* In the mean time the Bankrupt is bamboo'd on the Backside, if Discovery is made of any Effects of his, and at the same time is upbraided with having been a Month in Prison, eating and drinking, tho' he had wherewithal to satisfy his Creditors. He is chastised in the same manner, whether he makes Declaration of his Effects or not. They reproach him that his Business is to get the Substance of private Persons into his Hands, and embezzle it; and that he ought not so to defraud those he had dealings with, by stripping them of their Property. But after all, if they cannot discover him to have been guilty of any Fraud, and if it is proved to the Prince that the Man has nothing in the World, the Creditors are called in, and receive a part of their Debt out of the Treasury of the *Bagbun*, (this is the ordinary Title of the Emperor of *China*, and signifies *The Son of Heaven*; but we commonly pronounce it after a different manner, and call him, *Magbun.*) Then it is publickly forbidden to buy of, or sell any thing to this Man upon pain of Death, and so he cannot defraud any of his Creditors by concealing their Money. If discovery be made that he has any Sums in the

the Hands of another, and if the Person he intrusts makes no Declaration, he is bamboo'd to death, and nothing is said to the Proprietor or Bankrupt. The Sums that they discover are divided among the Creditors, and the Debtor or Bankrupt must never more concern himself with Trade.

A Stone on which is the Price of Medicines.

The *Chinese* have a Stone ten Cubits high, erected in the public Squares, and on this Stone are graved the Names of all sorts of Medicines, with the exact rates of each; and when the poor stand in need of any Relief from Physic, they go to the Treasury, where they receive the Price each Medicine is rated at.

Poll Tax.

There is no Land Tax in *China*; they only levy so much *per* Head, according to the Wealth and Possessions of the Subject. When a Male Child is born, his Name is immediately entered into the King's Books, and when this Child has attained his eighteenth Year, he begins to pay for his Head; but they demand it not of the Man who has seen his eightieth Year; on the contrary he receives a Gratification, by way of Pension, from the public Treasury; and in doing this, the *Chinese* say, That they give him this Gratification in his old days, in acknowledgment for what they receiv'd of him when he was young.

Schools.

There are Schools in every Town for teaching the Poor and their Children to write and read, and the Masters are paid at the public Charge. The Women wear nothing

nothing on their Heads but their Hair, whereas the Men are covered.

In *China* there is a Hamlet called *Tayu*, which is a Caſtle advantagiouſly ſeated on a Hill, and all the Strong-holds in *China* are called by the ſame Name.

The *Chineſe* are for the moſt part handſom, of comely Stature, fair, and by no means addicted to Exceſſes of Wine; their Hair is blacker than the Hair of any other Nation in the World; and the *Chineſe* Women curl theirs.

[S] *Proof by red hot Iron.*

In the *Indies*, when one Man accuſes another of a Crime puniſhable with Death, it is cuſtomary to ask the Accuſed if he is willing to go thro' the Tryal by Fire; and if he anſwers in the affirmative, they heat a Piece of Iron till it is red hot: This done, they tell him to ſtretch forth his Hand, and upon it they put ſeven Leaves of a Tree they have in the *Indies*, and upon theſe Leaves they put the red hot Iron; and in this Condition he walks backwards and forwards for ſome time, and then throws off the Iron. Immediately after this, they put his Hand into a leathern Bag, which they ſeal with the Prince's Signet; and if at the End of three Days he appears and declares that he has ſuffered no Hurt, they order him to take out his Hand, when, if no Sign of Fire is ſeen, they declare him innocent, and delivered from the Puniſhment which threatned him; and his Accuſer his condemned to pay a *Man* of Gold as a Fine to the Prince. Some-

Sometimes they boil Water in a Caldron till it is ſo hot that no one may approach it; then they throw an Iron Ring into it, and command the Perſon accuſed to thruſt his Hand down, and bring up the Ring. I ſaw one who did this, and receiv'd no manner of Hurt. The Accuſer is in this Caſe alſo to pay a *Man* of Gold. *Scalding Water.*

When a King dies in the Iſland of *Sarandib*, they lay his Body on a Car, in ſuch a manner that his Head hangs backwards till it almoſt touches the Ground, and his Hair is upon the Earth; and this Car is followed by a Woman with a Broom in her Hand, therewith to ſweep Duſt on the Face of the deceaſed, while ſhe cries out with a loud Voice; *O Men! behold your King who was yeſterday your Maſter; but now the Empire he exerciſed over you is vaniſhed and gone. He is reduced to the State you behold, having left the World; and the Arbiter of Death hath withdrawn his Soul. Reckon therefore no more upon the uncertain Hopes of Life.* This Cry, and ſome others like it, they continue for three Days, after which the dead Body of the King is embalmed with Sandal Wood, Camphire, and Saffron, and is then burnt, and the Aſhes are ſcatter'd abroad to the Wind. It is a univerſal Cuſtom all over the *Indies*, to burn the Bodies of the dead. The Iſland of *Sarandib* is the laſt of the Iſlands of the *Indies*. When they burn a King it is uſual for his Wives to jump into the Fire, and [T] *The Funeral Rites of the King of* Sarandib. [AA]

to

to burn with him; but this they are not constrained to do if they are not willing.

Indian *Penitents.*

In the *Indies* there are Men who profess to live in the Woods and Mountains, and to despise what other Men most value. These abstain from every thing but such wild Herbs and Fruits as spring forth in the Woods, and put an Iron Buckle upon their natural Parts, that they may not be able to have any Commerce with Women. Some of them are quite naked, or have only a Leopard's Skin thrown over them, and in this Plight keep standing with their Faces turned to the Sun. I formerly saw one in the Posture I have described, and returning to the *Indies* about sixteen Years afterwards, I found him in the very same Attitude, and was astonished he had not lost his Eyesight by the Heat of the Sun.

The Succession of Families in one and the same Business.

In all these Kingdoms the sovereign Power resides in the Royal Family, and never departs from it; and those of this Family succeed each other. In like manner there are Families of Learned Men, of Physicians, and of all the Artificers concerned in Architecture, and none of these ever mix with a Family of a Profession different from their own.

Balhara.

The several States of the *Indies* are not subject to one and the same King, but each Province has its own King; nevertheless the *Balhara* is, in the *Indies*, as King of Kings.

[U]

The Chinese *not given to Wine.*

The *Chinese* are fond of Gaming and all manner of Diversions: On the contrary, the

the *Indians* condemn them, and have no Pleaſure in them. They drink no Wine, nor admit Vinegar, becauſe it is made of Wine; and yet they abſtain not therefrom as a religious Duty, but for another Reaſon: They ſay that if a King is given to Wine, he ought not to be deemed a King; for, add they, as there are frequent Wars with the neighbouring States, how ſhould a Drunkard manage the Affairs of his Kingdom?

Wars with their Neighbours.

The Wars they wage with the neighbouring Princes, are not uſually undertaken with a view to poſſeſs themſelves of the adjoining Dominions; and I never heard of any, but the People bordering upon the Pepper Country, that have ſeized on the Poſſeſſions of their Neighbours after a Victory. When a Prince makes himſelf Maſter of ſome Kingdom, he confers the Government thereof upon ſome Perſon of the Royal Family of the conquered Country, and thus he keeps it in Subjection to himſelf, apprehending the Natives would never agree to be otherwiſe governed.

The Puniſhment of bad Governors.

When any one of the Princes or Governors of Cities, within the Dominions of the Emperor of *China*, is guilty of a Crime, he is put to death, and eaten; and in general it may be ſaid, that the *Chineſe* eat all thoſe that are put to death.

Marriages.

When the *Indians* and *Chineſe* are about to marry, both Parties come to an Agreement, then Preſents are made, and at laſt the Marriage is celebrated with the

Sound of many ſorts of Inſtruments and Drums. The Preſents they ſend conſiſt of Money, and in this every one does what he can afford.

The Puniſhment of a Rape. If any Man in the *Indies* runs away with a Woman, and abuſes her Body, they kill both him and the Woman, unleſs it be proved that ſhe was forced, then the Man only is puniſhed with death; but if the Woman conſented to the evil Deed, they are puniſhed with death, both the one and the other. Theft is always death, as well in the *Indies* as in *China*, whether the

Of Theft. Theft be conſiderable or inconſiderable; and particularly in the *Indies*, where if a Thief has ſtolen but the value of a ſmall Peice of Money, or a thing of greater worth, they take a long, ſtrong, and ſharp Stake, which they apply to his Fundament, and thruſt it through, till it comes out at his Neck.

The Debauchery of the Chineſe. The *Chineſe* are addicted to the hateful Vice, and the filthy Practice of it they number among the indifferent things they perform in honour of their Idols.

Buildings. The *Chineſe* Buildings are of Wood; whereas the *Indians* build with Stone, Plaſter, Brick and Mortar. After the ſame manner they build in many parts of *China*.

Polygamy. The *Chineſe* and *Indians* are not ſatisfied with one Wife; but both the one and the other marry as many as they pleaſe.

Rice their chief Food. Rice is the moſt common Food of the *Indians*, who eat no Wheat; whereas the

Chineſe

Chinese eat of Rice and Wheat indifferently. Circumcision is practised neither by the *Indians* nor the *Chinese*.

The *Chinese* worship Idols, pray to them, and fall down before them; and they have Books which explain the Articles of their Religion. *Idolatry.*

The *Indians* suffer their Beards to grow; and I have seen one of them with a Beard three Cubits long. They wear no Whiskers; but the *Chinese*, for the most part, have no Beard, and shave all smooth. The *Indians*, upon the death of a Relation, shave both Head and Face. *Beards.*

When any Man in the *Indies* is cast into Prison, they allow him neither Victuals nor Drink for seven Days together; and this, with them, answers the end of other Tortures to extort from the Criminal a Confession of the Truth. *Vide Barbos. p. 305. d.*

The *Chinese* have Judges, besides the Governors, who decide in Causes between Subject and Subject, and the same they have in the *Indies*. *Judges in private Causes.*

Both in *China* and in the *Indies* there are Leopards and Wolves; but no Lions in the one Country or the other. Highway Robbers are punished with death. *No Lion.*

Both the *Chinese* and the *Indians* imagine the Idols they worship speak to them, and give them Answers. *Superstition.*

Neither the one nor the other kill their Meat by cutting the Throat, as do the *Mohammedans*, but by beating them on the Mouth till they die. *Vide Mar. Pol. l. 2. Manner of killing Meat.*

Cleanliness Trig. 1. *p.* 71. They wash not with Well-Water. The *Chinese* wipe themselves with Paper; whereas the *Indians* wash every Day before they eat.

The *Indians* touch not their Wives while their Custom is upon them, but turn them out of their Houses and avoid them. The *Chinese*, on the contrary, have commerce with them during that time; and turn them not out of their Houses.

The *Indians* wash, not only the Mouth, but the whole Body also, before they eat, which the *Chinese* observe not.

Extent of China. The Country of the *Indies* is more in Extent than that of *China*, and exceeds it by the one half. The number of Kingdoms is greater in the *Indies* than in *China*, but *China* is the most populous of the two. It is not usual to see Palm-Trees either in the *Indies* or in *China*; but they have all other sorts of Trees, and Fruits which we have not. The *Indians* have no Grapes, and the *Chinese* have not many; but both abound in numbers of other Fruits, tho' the Pomegranate thrives more plentifully in *India* than in *China*.

The Chinese *ignorant of the Sciences.* The *Chinese* have no Sciences, and their Religion and most of their Laws are derived from the *Indians*; nay, they are of Opinion, that the *Indians* taught them the Worship of Idols, and consider them as a very religious Nation. Both the one and [Y] the other believe the *Metempsychosis*; but they differ in many Points touching the Precepts of their Religion.

Physic

Physic and Philosophy are cultivated among the *Indians*, and the *Chinese* have some Skill in Medicine; but it almost wholly consists in the Art of applying hot Irons, or Cauteries. They have also some smattering of Astronomy; but therein the *Indians* surpass the *Chinese*. Thevenot v. 3. p. 170.

I know not that there is any one of either Nation that has embraced *Mohammedism* or speaks *Arabic*. *Few have embraced* Mohammedism.

The *Indians* have but few Horses, and there are more in *China*; but the *Chinese* have no Elephants, and cannot endure to have them in their Country, for they abhor them. *Horses and Elephants.*

The *Indian* Dominions furnish a great number of Soldiers, who are not paid by the King, but when they are rendezvoused for War, take the Field entirely at their own Expence, and are no charge to the King; whereas the *Chinese* allow their Forces much the same the *Arabs* allow theirs. *Soldiers.*

China is a pleasant and a fruitful Country. Most of the *Indian* Provinces have no Cities; whereas in *China* they are many in number, great in Extent, and well fortified. *Beauty of the Country.*

The Climate of *China* is more wholesom, and the Country itself is less fenny; the Air there is also much better; and scarce is their a One eyed, or a Blind Person to be seen, or any one subject to the like Afflictions; and the same Advantage is enjoyed by several Provinces of the *In-* *The Climate.*

dies. The Rivers of these two Countries are large and surpass our greatest Rivers.

Rains. Much Rain falls in both these Countries. In the *Indies* are many Desart Tracts; but *China* is inhabited and peopled throughout its whole Extent.

The Persons of the Chinese. The *Chinese* are more handsom than the *Indians*, and come nearer to the *Arabs*, not only in Countenance, but in their Dress, in their way of Riding, in their Manners, and in their processional Ceremonies. They wear long Garments, and Girdles in form of Belts, or Baldrics.

The *Indians* wear two short Vests; and the Men as well as the Women wear golden Bracelets, adorned with precious Stones.

Targazgaz. Beyond the Continent of *China*, there is a Country called *Tagazgaz*, from the Name of a Nation of the *Turks*, who there inhabit; and also the Country of *Kakhan* or *Tibet*, which is conterminous with the Country of the *Turks*.

Isles of Sila. Seaward are the Islands of *Sila*, inhabited by white People, who send Presents to the Emperor of *China*, and who are persuaded that if they did not send him Presents, the Rain of Heaven would not be showered down upon their Country. None of our People have been there to inform us concerning them. They have white Falcons.

THE

THE SECOND ACCOUNT: OR, THE DISCOURSE OF *Abu Zeid al Hasan* of *Siraf*.

Concerning the Voyage to the Indies *and* China.

The Author's Preface.

I HAVE carefully examined the Book I have been ordered to peruse, that I might confirm what the Author relates, when he agrees with what I have heard, concerning the Things of the Sea, the Kingdoms on the Coasts, and the State of the Countries; and that I might also add, upon this Head, what I have elsewhere gathered concerning them, and is not to be found in this Book.

I find it was written in the Year of the *Hejra* CCXXXVII, and that the Accounts the Author gives touching the Things of the Sea were, in his Time, very true and agreeable to what I have underſtood from Merchants who depart from *Irak*, to ſail upon thoſe Seas. I find alſo that all the Author writes is agreeable to Truth, excepting ſome Paſſages.

Of J. C. DCCCLI.

Meat ſet before the Dead.

Speaking of the Cuſtom of ſetting Meat before the Dead, which he attributes to the *Chineſe*, he ſays, When they have ſerved up the Meat over Night, and find nothing the next Morning, they cry *the Deceaſed hath eaten.* This ſame Thing we had been told and believed it, till we met with a Man of undoubted Credit, whom he asked concerning this Cuſtom; and he anſwered that the Fact was not ſo, and that this Notion was groundleſs, as well as what is vulgarly ſaid of the idolatrous Nations, that they imagin their Idols ſpeak to them.

Alterations in China.

He told us alſo that ſince thoſe Days the Affairs of *China* had put on quite another Face; and ſince much is related, to ſhew the Reaſon why the Voyages to *China* are interrupted, and how the Country has been ruined, many Cuſtoms aboliſhed, and the Empire divided, I will here declare what I know of the Cauſes of this Revolution.

The great Troubles which have embroiled the Affairs of this Empire, which have put a Stop to the Juſtice and Righteouſneſs

teousness there formerly practised, and which have, in fine, interrupted the ordinary Navigation from *Siraf* to *China*, sprang from this Source.

A great Revolution in China.

An Officer, who was considerable for his Employ, though not of the Royal Family, revolted some Time ago. This Man's Name was *Baichu*, and he began with Hostilities in the Country, marching his Arms into many Places to the great Loss of the Inhabitants, till winning a Party over to him by his Liberalities, he got together a Multitude of Vagabonds and abandoned People, whom he formed into a considerable Body of Troops. His Hands thus strengthened, and himself in a Condition to undertake any Thing, he betrayed his Design of subduing the Empire to himself, and strait marched to *Cansu*, one of the most noted Cities in *China*, and, at that Time, the Port for all the *Arabian* Merchants. This City stands upon a great River, some Days distant from the Entrance, so that the Water there is fresh: But the Citizens shutting their Gates against him, he resolved to besiege the Place, and the Siege lasted a great while. This was transacted in the Year of the *Hejra* CCLXIV, and of *Christ* DCCCLXXVII. At last he became Master of the City, and put all the Inhabitants to the Sword. There are Persons fully acquainted with the Affairs of *China*, who assure us, that besides the *Chinese*, who were massacred upon this Occasion,

Occaſion, there periſhed one Hundred and twenty Thouſand *Mohammedans*, *Jews*, *Chriſtians*, and *Parſees*, who were there on Account of Traffic. The Number of the Profeſſors of theſe four Religions, who thus periſhed, is exactly known; becauſe the *Chineſe* are extremely nice in the Accounts they keep of them. He alſo cut down the Mulberry Trees, and almoſt all the Trees of other Kinds; but we ſpeak of the Mulberry in particular, becauſe the *Chineſe* carefully cultivate it for the ſake of its Leaf, wherewith they ſubſiſt and propagate their Silk-worms. This Devaſtation is the Cauſe why Silk has failed, and that the Trade which us'd to be driven with it, in the Countries under the *Arabs*, is quite ſtagnated.

Many Cities taken by the Rebel.

Having ſacked and deſtroyed *Canfu*, he poſſeſſed himſelf of many other Cities, which he attacked one after another, the Emperor of *China* not having it in his Power to ſtop his Progreſs. He advanced then to the capital City called *Cumdan*; and the Emperor left this his royal Seat, making a confuſed Retreat to the City of *Hamdu*, on the Frontiers towards the Province of *Tibet*. Mean while the Rebel, puffed up by his great Succeſſes, and perceiving himſelf Maſter of the Country, fell upon the other Cities, which he demoliſhed, having firſt ſlain moſt of the Inhabitants, with a View in this general Butchery to involve all the Branches of the Royal Blood, that no one might

might ſurvive to diſpute the Empire with him. We had the News of theſe Revolutions and of the total Ruin of *China*, which ſtill continues.

The King of Tagazgaz *aſſiſts the Emperor of* China.

Thus were Affairs, and the Rebel ſtood uncontroled by any Diſadvantage that might take away from his Power and Authority. At laſt the Emperor of *China* wrote to the King of *Tagazgaz*, in *Turkeſtan*, which whom, beſides the nearneſs of his Dominions, he was in ſome degree allyed by Marriage; and at the ſame Time ſent an Embaſſy to him to implore his Deliverance from this Rebel. Upon this the King of *Tagazgaz* diſpatched his Son, at the Head of a very numerous Army, to fight the Rebel; and after many Battles, and almoſt continual Skirmiſhes, he utterly defeated him. It was never known what became of the Rebel. Some believe he fell in Battle, while others think he ended his Days another way.

The Emperor returns to Cumdan.

The Emperor of *China* returned then to *Cumdan*; and altho' he was extremely weakned, and almoſt diſpirited becauſe of the Embezzlement of his Treaſures, and the Loſs of his Captains and beſt Troops, and becauſe of all the late Calamities; he nevertheleſs made himſelf Maſter of all the Provinces which had been conquered from him. However he laid no Hands on the Goods of his Subjects, but ſatisfied himſelf with what remained in his Coffers, and the Fragments

ments of the Public Money. His Condition indispensibly obliged him to take up with what his Subjects would give him, and to require nothing from them but Obedience to his Mandates, forbearing to squeeze Money from them, because the Kings or Governors had made away with it.

The Division of China *into many Principalities.*

And thus *China* became almost like the Empire of *Alexander*, after the Defeat and Death of *Darius*, when he divided the Provinces, he took from the *Persian*, between several Princes, who erected themselves into so many Kings. For now each of these *Chinese* Princes joined with some other to wage War upon a third, without consulting the Emperor; and when the strongest had subdued the weakest, and become Master of his Province, all was wasted, and unmercifully plundered, and the Subjects of the vanquished Prince were unnaturally devoured; a Cruelty allowed by the Laws of their Religion, which even permit human Flesh to be exposed to Sale in the public Markets.

Disorders consequent to the Civil Wars.

From these Combustions there arose many unjust Dealings with the Merchants who traded thither, which having gathered the Force of a Precedent, there was no Grievance, no Treatment so bad but they exercised upon the foreign *Arabs*, and the Masters of Ships. They extorted from the Merchants what was uncustomary, they seized upon their Effects, and

and behaved towards them in a Method of Procedure quite contrary to the ancient Usages. And for these Things has God punished them by withdrawing his Blessings from upon them in every Respect, and particularly by causing the Navigation to be forsaken, and the Merchants to return in Crouds to *Siraf* and *Oman*, pursuant to the infallible Orders of the Almighty Master, whose Name be blessed.

The Punishment of Adultery, Homicide, and Theft.

The Author, in his Book, notes some Customs and Laws of the *Chinese*, but mentions not the Punishment inflicted on married Persons, when convicted of Adultery. This Crime, as well as Homicide, and Theft is punished with Death, and they execute the Criminal in this Manner: They bind both the Hands together, and then force them backwards over the Head till they rest upon the Neck; they then fasten the right Foot to the right Hand, and the left Foot to the left Hand; so that both Hands and Feet are strongly bound behind the Back, and thus bundled up it is impossible for the Criminal to stir, nor wants he any Body to hold him. This Torture disjoints the Neck, makes the Vertebræ start from their Connections, and dislocates the Thighs; in short, the Party is in so miserable a Condition, that were he to continue therein but for a few Hours, there would be no need of any Thing else to make an End of him. But when they have bound him, as we have said, they strike him with a

Staff

Staff [*Bamboo*] which they always uſe upon the like Occaſions, and which alone were ſufficient to kill the Criminal. With this they give him a certain Number of Blows, a Number they never exceed, and then leave off, when he is at the very laſt Gaſp of Life, and forſake the Body to People who eat it.

Public Women.

There are Women in *China* who refuſe to marry, and chuſe rather a diſſolute Life, and perpetual Debauchery. The Cuſtom is, for theſe Women to preſent themſelves in full Audience before the commanding Officer of the Garriſon in the City, and declare their Averſion to Marriage, and their Deſire to be numbered with the public Women. They then deſire to be regiſtred in the uſual Form, among theſe Proſtitutes, and the Form is ſuch: They write down the Name of the Woman, her Family, the Number of her Jewels, the ſeveral *Items* of her Attire, and the Place of her Abode; thus is ſhe admitted a public Woman. After this they put about her Neck a String, at which hangs a Copper Ring, with the King's Signet; and deliver to her a Writing, which certifies that ſhe is received into the Liſt of common Proſtitutes, and intitles her to a yearly Stipend of ſo many *Falus* to be paid her out of the public Treaſury, and threatens with Death the Perſon who ſhould take her to Wife. They every Year give public Notice of what is to be obſerved with regard to

theſe

these Women; and turn off those who are too barren of Charms. In the Evening these Women walk abroad in Dresses of different Colours, without any Veil, and prostitute themselves to all new comers that loved Debauchery; but the *Chinese* themselves send for them to their Houses, whence they depart not till the next Morning. Praised be God, who hath rescued us from the like Infamy!

Copper Money.

The *Chinese* coin no Money besides the little Pieces of Copper, like those we call *Falus*, nor will they allow Gold or Silver to be wrought into Specie, like the *Dinars* and *Drams* that are current with us. For, say they, if a Thief goes, with an evil Intent, into the House of an *Arab*, where is Gold and Silver Coin, he may carry off ten thousand Pieces of Gold, and almost as many Pieces of Silver, and not be much burdened therewith, and so be the ruin of the Man who should suffer this Loss; whereas if a Thief has the same Design upon the House of a *Chinese* Artificer, he cannot ,at most, take away above ten thousand *Falus* or Pieces of Copper, which do not make ten *Miticals* or *Dinars* of Gold. These Pieces of Copper are allayed with something of a different kind, and are of the Size of a *Dram*, or Piece of Siver called *Bagli*; and in the middle they have a pretty large Hole to string them by. A thousand of them are worth a *Mitical* of Gold, or a *Dinar*; and they string them by thousands, with a Knot between every hundred. All their

their Payments in general are made with this Money, whether they buy or sell Lands, Furniture, Merchandize, or any thing else. There are some of these Pieces at *Siraf*, with *Chinese* Characters upon them.

Chinese. *Buildings.* There is no particular Remark to be made upon the frequent Fires which happen in *China*, and the *Chinese* manner of Building. The City of *Cansu* is built in the manner he describes, that is, of Wood; with Canes interwoven just like our Works of split Cane. They do the whole over with a particular consistence they make of Hemp-Seed, which becomes as white as Milk, and when the Walls are covered therewith, they have a wonderful Gloss.

Varnish.

Inside of their Houses. They have no Stairs in their Houses, nor do they build with different Stories; but put every thing they have into Chests which run upon Wheels, and which, in cases of Fire, they can easily draw from place to place, without any hindrance from Stairs, and so save their things presently.

Eunuchs in Office. As for the inferior Officers in their Cities, they commonly have the Direction of the Customs, and the Keys of the Treasury. Some of these have been taken on the Frontiers, and castrated; others of them have been cut by their own Fathers, who have sent them as a Present to the Emperor. These Officers are at the head of the principal Affairs of State, of the Emperors private Affairs, and of his Treasures; and those, particularly, who are sent to *Cansu*, are selected from this Body.

It

It is customary for them, as well as the Kings or Governors of all the Cities, to appear abroad, from time to time, in solemn Procession. At these times they are preceded by Men who carry great Pieces of Wood, like those the Christians, of the *Levant*, use instead of Bells. The Noise they make is heard afar off, and as soon as it is heard, no Man stands in the way of the Eunuch, or Prince. If a Man is at his Door, he goes into his House, and keeps his Door shut, till the Prince, or Eunuch of the City is gone by. So no Soul is to be seen in the way; and this is injoined that they may be held in the greater Veneration, to strike a Dread, that the People may not see them often, and that they may not grow so familiar as to speak to them. *Their solemn Appearance in the Cities.*

The Eunuch or Lieutenant, and the principal Officers wear very magnificent Silk Dresses, of so fine a kind, that none thereof is brought into the Country Subject to the *Arabs*, the *Chinese* keep it up at so high a rate. One of the chief Merchants, whose words cannot be called in question, relates that he waited on an Eunuch, whom the Emperor had sent to *Cansu*, in order to purchase some things he wanted from among the goods that are carried thither from the Country of the *Arabs*: And that upon his Breast he perceived a short Vest, which was under another silk Vest, and which seemed to be even between two other Vests of the same kind; *Their Dress.*

that the Eunuch obſerving him to look ſtedfaſtly upon his Breaſt, ſaid, *I ſee you keep your Eyes ſixed upon my Stomach; what may be the meaning of it?* The Merchant anſwered; *I am ſurpriſed at the Beauty of that little Veſt, which appears under your other Garments.* The Eunuch laughed and held out his Shirt Sleeve to him, *Count,* ſays he, *how many Veſts I have above it.* He did ſo, and counted five, one upon another, and the Waſtecoat or ſhort Veſt was underneath. Theſe Garments are wove with raw Silk which has never been waſhed nor ſulled; and what is worn by the Princes or Governors is ſtill more rich, and more exquiſitely wrought.

The Chineſe *expert Artiſts.*

The *Chineſe* ſurpaſs all Nations in every kind of Art, and particularly in Painting; and, with their Hands, they perform ſuch perfect Works as others can but faintly imitate. When an Artificer has finiſhed a fine Piece, he carries it to the Prince's Palace to demand the Reward, he thinks he deſerves for the beauty of his Performance; and the Cuſtom is for the Prince to order him to leave his Work at the Palace Gate, where it muſt ſtand a whole Year. If during that time no Perſon finds a Fault in it, the Artificer is rewarded, and admitted into the body of Artiſts; but if the leaſt Fault he found, it is rejected, and the Workman is ſent away empty. It happened once, that one of their Painters drew an Ear of Corn, with a Bird perched on it, upon a piece of Silk; and his Performance

was

was so exceeding fine, that all who beheld it were astonished thereat. This Piece stood exposed to public View, till, one Day, a crooked Fellow, passing by the Palace, found Fault with the Picture, and was immediately conducted to the Prince or Governor of the City, who at the same time sent for the Painter. Then he asked this crooked Fellow what Fault he had to find with this piece of Paint; to which he answered, *Every body knows that a Bird never settles upon an Ear of Corn but it bends under him; and here this Painter has represented his Ear bolt upright, though he has perched a Bird upon it; and this is the Fault I have to find.* This was pronounced a very just Observation, and the Prince bestowed no Reward upon the Artist. They pretend by this, and other means, to stimulate their Workmen to the Attainment of Perfection, by thus engaging them to be extremely nice and circumspect in what they undertake, and to apply their whole Mind to what is to go out of their Hands.

The Story of an Arab *who went to* China.

There was formerly a Man of the Tribe of *Koreish*, whose Name was *Ebn Wahab*, descended of *Hebar* the Son of *Al Asud*, and he dwelt at *Basra*. This Man left *Basra*, when that City was sacked, and came to *Siraf*, where he saw a Ship ready to make sail for *China*. The mind took him to go on board of this Ship, and in her he went to *China*, where in the Sequel he had the Curiosity to travel to the Emperor's Court; and leaving *Cansu* he reached *Cumdan* after a Journey of two Months. He ſtaid a long Time at the Emperor's Court, and preſented ſeveral Petitions, wherein he ſignified that he was of the Family of the Prophet of the *Arabs*. Having waited a conſiderable while, the Emperor at laſt ordered him to be lodged in a Houſe, appointed for him, and to be ſupplied with every thing he ſhould want. This done, the Emperor wrote to the Governor of *Canſu*, commanding him carefully to inform himſelf, among the Merchants, concerning the Relation this Man pretended to bear to the Prophet of the *Arabs*: And the Governor, by his Anſwers, confirming the Truth of what he had ſaid, touching his Extraction, the Emperor gave him Audience, and made him rich Preſents, wherewith he returned to *Irak*.

His Diſcourſe with the Emperor concerning the Arabs.

This Man, when we ſaw him, was well advanced in Years, but had his Senſes perfectly about him; and told us that, when he had his Audience, the Emperor asked him many Queſtions about the *Arabs*, and particularly how they had deſtroyed the Kingdom of the *Perſians*. *Ebn Wahab* made anſwer, that they did it by the Aſſiſtance of God, and becauſe the *Perſians* were involved in Idolatry, adoring the Stars, the Sun, and Moon, inſtead of worſhipping the true God. To this the Emperor replied, that the *Arabs* had conquered the moſt illuſtrious Kingdom of the whole Earth, the beſt cultivated,

vated, the most opulent, the most pregnant of fine Wits, and of the most extensive Fame. Then said he, *What Account do the People in your Parts make of the other Kings of the Earth?* To which the *Arab* replied, that he knew them not. Then said the Emperor to the Interpreter, *Tell him we esteem but five Kings; that he whose Kingdom is of widest Extent is the same who is Master of* Irak, *for he is in the midst of the World, and surrounded by the Territories of other Kings; and we find he is called the King of Kings.* After him we reckon our Emperor, here present, and we find that he is stiled the *King of Mankind*; for no other King is invested with a more absolute Power and Authority over his Subjects, nor is there a People, under the Sun, more dutiful and submissive to their Sovereign than the People of this Country; we therefore, in this respect, are the *Kings of Men*. After us is the King of the *Turks*, whose Kingdom borders upon us, and him we call the *King of Lions*. Next, the *King of Elephants*, the same is the King of the *Indies*, whom we also call the *King of Wisdom*; because he derives his Origin from the *Indians*. And, last of all, the King of *Greece*, whom we stile the *King of Men*; for, upon the face of the whole Earth, there are no Men of better Manners, nor of comlier Presence than his Subjects: These, added he, are the most illustrious of all Kings, nor are the others to compare with them.

The Emperor's Questions concerning the Arabs and others.

Then, ſaid *Ebn Wahab*, he ordered the Interpreter to ask me, *If I knew my Maſter and my Lord, meaning the Prophet, and if I had ſeen him?* I made anſwer, *How ſhould I have ſeen him, who is with God?* He replyed, *That is not what I mean, I ask you what Sort of a Man he was in his Perſon.* I replyed, that he was very handſom. Then he called for a great Box, and, opening it, he took out another contained therein, which he ſet before him, and ſaid to the Interpreter, *Shew him his Maſter and his Lord*; and I ſaw in the Box the Images of the Prophets, whereat I moved my Lips, praying to my ſelf in honour of their Memory. The Emperor did not imagin I ſhould know them again, and ſaid to the Interpreter, *Ask him why he moves his Lips?* I anſwered, I was praying in Memory of the Prophets. *How do you know them?* Said the Emperor. I replied, that I knew them by the Repreſentation of their Hiſtories: *There*, ſaid I, *is* Noah *in the Ark, who was ſaved with thoſe that were with him, when God ſent down the Waters of the Flood; and he afterwards peopled the whole Earth with thoſe that were with him at the ſame time*; and I made the uſual Salute to *Noah* and his Company. Then the Emperor laughed and ſaid; *Thou art not miſtaken in the Name of* Noah, *and thou haſt named him right; but as for the univerſal Deluge it is what we know not. It is true, indeed, that a Flood covered a part of the Earth; but it reached not* our

Noah.

The Flood.

our Country, nor even the Indies. I made my Anſwer to this, and endeavoured to remove his Objections the beſt I could, and then ſaid again to him, *There is* Moſes *with his Rod and the Children of Iſrael.* He agreed with me as to the ſmall Extent of their Country, and the Manner how the ancient Inhabitants, there, were deſtroyed by *Moſes.* I then ſaid to him, *He there, is Jeſus upon an Aſs, and here are his Apoſtles with him. He,* ſaid the Emperor, *was not long upon Earth, ſeeing that all he did was tranſacted within the Space of ſomewhat better than thirty Months.* After this *Ebn Wahab* ſaw the Hiſtories of the other Prophets, repreſented in the ſame Manner we have briefly declared, and he fancied that what was written in great Characters under each Figure, might be the Names of the Prophets, the Countries whence they were, and the Objects of their Prophecies. Moſes Jeſus Chriſt.

Then, ſaid the ſame *Ebn Wahab, I ſaw the Image of* Mohammed *riding upon a Camel, and his Companions about him on their Camels, with Shooes of the* Arabeſque *Mode on their Feet, and leathern Girdles about their Loins. At this I wept, and the Emperor commanded the Interpreter to ask me why I wept? I anſwered, There is our Prophet, and our Lord, who is alſo my Couſin.* He ſaid I was right, and added that he and his People had ſubdued the fineſt of all Kingdoms; but that he had not the Satisfaction of enjoying his Conqueſts, tho' his Succeſſors had. Mohammed.

Indian Prophets. I afterwards saw a great Number of other Prophets, some of them stretching forth their right Hand, and with their three Fingers bent down between the Thumb and the Fore-finger, just like those who lift up the Hand to make oath. Others were standing and pointed to the Heavens with their Finger, and others were in different Postures. The Interpreter took them to be the Figures of their Prophets and those of the *Indians*.

Questions concerning the Kalifs. The Emperor then asked me many Questions concerning the *Kalifs*, their Mode of Dress, and concerning many Precepts and Injunctions of the *Mohammedan* Religion, and I answered him the best I could.

The Age of the World. After this he said, *What is your Opinion concerning the Age of the World?* I made answer, that Opinions varied upon that head; that some were for six Thousand Years; that others would not allow so many; and that others reckoned it at a still higher Rate; but that it was, at least, as old as I had said. At this, the Emperor and his first Minister, who was near him, broke out into a Laughter, and the Emperor made many Objections to what I had advanced. At last said he, *What does your Prophet teach upon this Subject? Does he say as you do?* My Memory failed me, and I assured him that he did. Hereupon I observed I had displeased him, and his Displeasure appeared upon his Countenance.

Then

Then he ordered the Interpreter to ſpeak to me in the following ſtrain: *Take heed of what you ſay; for Kings never ſpeak but to be informed of the Truth of what they would know. What did you mean by giving the Emperor to underſtand that there are, among you, various Opinions concerning the Age of the World? If ſo it be, you are alſo divided upon the Things your Prophet has ſaid, at the ſame time that no Diverſity of Opinion is to be admitted on what the Prophets have pronounced, all which muſt be revered as ſure and infallible. Take heed, then, how you talk after ſuch a Rate any more.* To this he ſubjoined many other Things which, through Length of Time, have eſcaped my Remembrance.

Sequel of the Converſation with the Emperor.

At laſt he asked me, *How is it that thou haſt forſaken thy King, to whom thou art nearer, not only by the Place of thy abode, but by Blood alſo, than thou art to us?* In return to which, I informed him of the Revolutions which had hapned at *Baſſora*, and how I came to *Siraf* where I ſaw a Ship ready to ſpread Sail for *China*; and that having heard of the Glory of his Empire, and its great abundance of Neceſſaries; Curioſity excited me to a Deſire of coming into his Country, that I might behold it with mine own Eyes. That I ſhould ſoon depart for my Country, and the Kingdom of my Couſin, and that I would make a faithful report of what I had ſeen of the Magnificence of the Empire of *China*, and of the vaſt extent of the Provinces

vinces it contains; and that I would make a grateful Declaration of the kind Usage, and the Benefactions I there met with; which seemed to please him very much. He then made me rich Presents, and ordered that I should be conducted to *Cansu* upon Post Horses. He wrote also to the Governor of the City, commanding him to treat me with much Honour, and to furnish me with the like Recommendations to the other Governors of the Provinces, that they might entertain me till the Time of my Departure. Thus was I treated every where, being plentifully supplied with all the Necessaries of Life, and honoured with many Presents till the Time of my Departure from *China*.

Cumdan. We asked *Ebn Wahab* many Questions concerning the City of *Cumdan*, where the Emperor keeps his Court. He told us that the City was very large, and extremely populous; that it was divided into two great Parts, by a very long and very broad Street; that the Emperor, his chief Ministers, the Soldiery, the supreme Judge, the Eunuchs, and all belonging to the imperial Household, lived in that Part of the City which is on the right hand Eastward; that the People had no manner of Communication with them; and that they were not admitted into Places watered by Canals, from different Rivers, whose Borders were planted with Trees, and adorned with magnificent Dwellings. The Part on the left hand Westward, is inhabited

habited by the People and the Merchants, where are alſo great Squares, and Markets for all the Neceſſaries of Life. At break of Day you ſee the Officers of the King's Houſehold, with the inferior Servants, the Purveyors, and the Domeſtics of the Grandees of the Court, who come, ſome on foot others on Horſeback, into that Diviſion of the City, where are the public Markets, and the Habitations of the Merchants; where they buy whatever they want, and return not again to the ſame Place till the next Morning.

This ſame Traveller related that this City has a very pleaſant Situation, in the midſt of a moſt fertile Soil, watered by ſeveral Rivers. Scarce any Thing is wanted, except Palm-Trees, which grow not there.

Communication between the Ocean and the Mediterranean.

In our Times, Diſcovery has been made of a Thing quite new, and unknown to thoſe who lived before us. No Body imagined that the Sea which extends from the *Indies* to *China*, had any Communication with the Sea of *Syria*, nor could any one take it into his Head, Now behold what has come to paſs in our Days, according to what we have heard. In the Sea of *Rum*, or the Mediterranean, they found the Wreck of an *Arabian* Ship which had been ſhattered by Tempeſt; for all her Men periſhing, and ſhe being daſhed to Pieces by the Wave, the Remains of her were driven by Wind and Weather into the Sea of *Chozars*, and from thence to the Canal of the Mediterranean Sea, and at laſt were

thrown

thrown on the Shore of *Syria*. This evinces that the Sea ſurrounds all the Country of *China*, and of *Cila*, [or *Sila*,] the uttermoſt Parts of *Turkeſtan*, and the Country of the *Chozars*, and that then it enters at the Strait till it waſhes the Shore of *Syria*. The Proof of this is deduced from the Built of the Ship we are ſpeaking of; for none but the Ships of *Siraf* are ſo put together, that the Planks are not nailed [or *bolted*], but joined together in an extraordinary Manner as if they were ſewn; whereas
[E] the Planking of all the Ships of the Mediterranean Sea, and of the Coaſt of *Syria*, is nailed and not joined together the other way.

We have alſo heard ſay, that Ambergreeſe has been found in the Sea of *Syria*, which ſeems hard to believe, and was unknown to former Times. If this be as is ſaid, it is impoſſible that Amber ſhould have been thrown up in the Sea of *Syria*, but by the Sea of *Aden* and of *Kolzum*, which has Communication with the Seas where Amber is found. And, becauſe God hath put a Seperation between theſe Seas, if this Story be true, it muſt neceſſarily have been that this Amber was driven firſt from the *Indian* Sea into the others, and that, from the one to the other, it at laſt came into the Sea of *Syria*.

Of the Province of Zapage.

Province of Zapage.

We will now begin to ſpeak of the Province of *Zapage*, which is oppoſite to *China*, and a Month's Sail diſtant therefrom by by Sea, or leſs, if the Wind be fair. The King of this Country is called *Mehrage*, and they ſay it is nine hundred Leagues in Circumference, and that this King is Maſter of many Iſlands which ly round about; thus this Kingdom is above a thouſand Leagues in Extent. Among theſe Iſlands there is one called *Serbeza*, which is ſaid to be four hundred Leagues in Circuit, and that alſo of *Rahmi* which is eight hundred Leagues in Compaſs, and produces Red-wood, Camphire, and many other Commodities. In this ſame Kingdom is the Iſland of *Cala*, which is in the Mid-paſſage between *China* and the Country of the *Arabs*. This Iſland, they ſay, is fourſcore Leagues in Circumference; and hither they bring all Sorts of Merchandiſe, Wood Aloes of ſeveral Sorts, Camphire, Sandal-wood, Ivory, the Lead called *Cabahi*, Ebony, Red-wood, every Kind of Spice, and many other Things too tedious to enumerate. At preſent the Commerce is moſt uſually carried on from *Oman* to this Iſland, and from this Iſland to *Oman*. The *Mehrage* is ſovereign over all theſe Iſlands, and that which he makes his Abode, is extremely fertile, and ſo very populous that the Towns almoſt croud one upon the other. A Perſon of great Probity relates, that when the Cocks here crow at their accuſtomed Hours, juſt as with us, at rooſt upon Trees, they anſwer each other a hundred Leagues around and more, becauſe of the Proximity of the

Villages

Villages which almoſt touch each other; and he adds that no Part of it is uninhabited, nor any of its Land uncultivated. Thoſe who travel in this Country may ſtop at every Step, and find Shelter from the Beams of the Noon-day Sun, and if they are tired they may repoſe themſelves every Day at Noon, go which way they will.

Particulars of the Country of Zapage.

Now what follows, which we have from the Teſtimony of ſeveral Perſons, is the moſt remarkable Particular we have heard concerning the Iſland of *Zapage*. There was formerly a King, who was called *Mehrage*. His Palace is ſtill to be ſeen on a River as broad as the *Tygris* at *Bagdad* or at *Baſſora*. The Sea intercepts the Courſe of its Waters, and ſends them back again with the Tide of Flood; and during the Tide of Ebb, it ſtreams out freſh Water a good way into the Sea. This River is let into a ſmall Pond cloſe to the King's Palace, and every Morning the Officer who has Charge of his Houſehold, brings an Ingot of Gold wrought in a particular Manner, which is unknown, and throws it into the Pond in the Preſence of the King. The Tide riſing with the Flood covers it with many others, its fellows, and quite conceals it from Sight; but low Water diſcovers them, and they appear plain by the Beams of the Sun. The King comes to view them at the ſame Time that he repairs to an Apartment of State

which

which looks upon this Pond. This Custom is very ſcrupulouſly obſerved, and thus they every Day throw an Ingot of Gold into this Pond, as long as the King lives, nor touch the ſame upon any Account. When the King dyes, his Succeſſor cauſes them all to be taken out, and not one of them is ever miſſed: They count them, and melt them down, and this done, the Sums provening from this great Quantity of Gold, are diſtributed to thoſe of the Royal Houſehold, to the Men, to the Women, and to the Children, to the ſuperior and to the inferior Officers, each receiving a Part, in Proportion to the Rank he bears, and according to the Order eſtabliſhed, among them, for this Diſtribution; and the Surplus is given away to the Poor, and to the infirm. Then they reckon up the Number of Ingots, and what they weigh, and ſay; Such a one reigned ſo many Years, for he left ſo many Ingots of Gold in the Pond of the Kings, and they were diſtributed, after his Death, to the People of his Kingdom. It is a Glory, with them, to have reigned a long while, and to have thus multiplied the Number of theſe Ingots, to be given away at their Death.

A Story of the King of Komar *and the* Mehrage.

Their ancient Hiſtory relates, that one of the Kings of *Komar* would have waged War with him of this Iſland. This Country of *Komar* is the ſame from whence they bring the Wood Aloes called *Hud al Komari*; nor is there a Kingdom proportionably

ably more populous than that of *Komar*. The Inhabitants are all very courageous, and Debauchery with Women, and the Use of Wine are forbidden among them, nor have they any Wine in their Country. This Kingdom was at Peace with that of *Zapage*, where reigned the *Mehrage*. They are divided from each other by a Passage of ten, or twenty Days sail, with a very easy Gale. They say that in former Days there was a young and turbulent King in this Island of *Komar*. This King was one Day in his Palace, which looks upon a River much like the *Euphrates* at the Entrance, and but a Day Distant from the Sea. His prime Minister was with him, and, in the Discourse they had together, mention was made of the Kingdom of the *Mehrage* and its Glory, how well it was peopled and cultivated, and the Croud of Islands which owed Obedience thereunto. Then said the King of *Komar* to his Minister, *I am taken with a Desire, which I most earnestly could wish to see accomplished*. The Minister, who was a wise and a prudent Man, and no Stranger to the Levity of his Master, addressed him; *My Lord, what is your Desire? I could wish*, replied the King, *to see before me, in a Dish, the Head of the* Mehrage *King of* Zapage. The Minister, well aware it was Jealousy that inspired him with this Irregularity, made Answer, *My Lord, I could wish you would not disturb your Mind with such Thoughts, since nothing ever happened between those People and us, to furnish us with Matter of Complaint; seeing they never offended*

offended us either by Word or deed, and never did us the least Injury. Moreover, they are in an Island divided from us, and have no Manner of Communication with our Country; nor do they betray any Thoughts of making a Conquest of this Kingdom. No one therefore ought to hearken to such Discourse, or make one Word of Answer upon this Head. The King was enraged at this Return, and replyed not thereto; but without any Regard had to the sage Advice of his first Minister, he opened the same Thing to the principal Officers of State, and to all those of his Court that were present.

The Enterprise of the Mehrage *against the King of* Komar.

This Matter being rumored about by several Persons, became of public Notoriety, and at length reached the Ears of the *Mehrage.* He, who then reigned, was a wise and an active Prince, of consummate Experience, and as yet in the Flower of his Days. He called for his first Minister, and having acquainted him with what he had heard, said to him; *It is by no means proper to declare the Behavior of this giddy Prince, or to betray how little we esteem him, because of his Youth and little Experience. Nor is it proper to divulge what he has said against me; for such Speeches, cannot but be prejudicial to the Dignity of a King, make him contemptible, and take away from his Reputation.* Having thus injoined his Minister to conceal what had passed between them, he, at the same Time, commanded him to prepare a thousand Ships of middling Burthen, and to equip them with all Things necessary, Arms and Ammunition, and to man them with as many of his best Forces as they could carry; then he gave out That he would take a Voyage among the neighbouring Islands, under his Dominion, to divert himself. He wrote to all the tributary Princes of these same Islands to acquaint them That he designed them a Visit, to recreate himself in their Islands: And this being the public Talk, each of these Kings prepared for the Reception of the *Mehrage*. Mean while, when every Thing was in readiness as he had ordered, he went on board his Ships, and with a powerful Army sailed over to the Kingdom of *Komar*. The King and those belonging to his Court were effeminate Creatures, who, all the Day long, did nothing but consult their Faces and rub their Teeth, eternally with Mirrors and Tooth-picks in their Hands, or carried after them by Slaves. So the King of *Komar* discovered nothing of the *Mehrage*'s purpose, till he appeared in the Mouth of the River, which was crowned by the Palace of the King of *Komar*, and till he had landed his Troops, who immediately invested him with great vigor, and took him. The King was taken in his Palace, and all that belonged to him fled without fighting.

Then the *Mehrage* instantly caused Proclamation to be made, That he granted entire Security of Life and Effects to all the Inhabitants of the Country; and seating himself on the Throne of the King of *Komar*, now a Captive, he ordered him to be brought

brought into his Preſence, together with his firſt Miniſter. Then ſaid he to the King of *Komar: Who was it filled your Head with a Project unequal to your Strength, and abſolutely impoſſible for you to compaſs? What would you have done if you had gained your End?* This Prince, who had nothing to ſay for himſelf, made no Anſwer. Then continued the *Mehrage, If you had enjoyed the Pleaſure you wiſhed, of ſeeing my Head in a Diſh before you, you would have ſpoiled my Kingdom, and made your ſelf Maſter thereof, after you had committed all Sorts of Violence: I will not ſo behave with regard to you; but yet I will execute upon you, what you wiſhed concerning me, and then will I return into my Kingdom, without touching any Thing in your Dominions, and without carrying away ought ſoever of great Value or ſmall, deſirous only that you may be recorded an Example for the Inſtruction of thoſe who ſhall come after you; that no one may exceed the Bounds of his Power, that each may be contented with his own, and that thoſe you have diſturbed may be reſtored to perfect Security.* This ſaid, he ordered them to ſmite off his Head; and then turning to the Miniſter, he ſaid; *You have done all a good Miniſter could do, I know you offered good Advice to your Maſter, and that he hearkened not unto you. Conſult who may beſt ſucceed this* Fool, *for the good of the Kingdom, and ſet him upon the Throne:* Then ſtrait the *Mehrage* departed for his own Territories, and neither did he, or any of his, lay Hands on the leaſt Thing in the Kingdom of *Komar*.

 When

When he arrived in his own Kingdom, he ſat down upon his Throne, and, being in the Place which looked upon the Pond before-mentioned, he cauſed the Head of the King of *Komar* to be put into a Baſon, and ſet before him; and calling in the Chiefs of his Kingdom, he acquainted them with all he had done, and with the Reaſons which had induced him to the Expedition we have related; And they approved the Deed with Acclamations and Prayers for his Proſperity. Then he ordered the Head of the King of *Komar*, to be waſhed, and embalmed, and put into a Coffer; and ſent it back to the King *Komar* who had been appointed in the Room of him he had put to Death, at the ſame time writing a Letter to this new Prince, couched in the following Terms; *What inclined us to do what we did to your Predeceſſor, and your Lord, was his known Malevolence towards us, and that we might ſet an Example to his Equals. We have been ſo happy as to treat him as he would have treated us: But we think it convenient to ſend his Head back to you, having had no Deſign of detaining it, or of arrogating any Glory to our ſelves from the Advantage we obtained over him.* The News of this Action being conveyed to the Kings of the *Indies* and of *China*, it added to the Reſpect they before had for the *Mehrage*: And from that Time it has been a Cuſtom with the Kings of *Komar*, every Morning they riſe, to turn towards the Country of *Zapage*, and to proſtrate themſelves on the Ground, and to make

make the most profonnd Inclinations, in Honour of the *Mebrage*.

[Y] *The* Indians *hold the Metempsychosis.*

All the Kings of the *Indies* and of *China* believe the Metempsychosis or Transmigration of Souls, and make it an Article of their Religion. A Person of Credit relates, That one of these Princes being newly recovered of the Small-Pox, and beholding himself in a Glass, was deeply troubled to see how sadly his Face was disfigured; and that turning himself towards one of the Sons of his Brother, he said to him, Sure it never hapned to any Man as to me, to remain in his Body after such a Change; but this Body is only a Vessel puffed out with Wind, and when the Soul leaves it, she migrates into another; go get upon the Throne, for I am about to separate my Body from my Soul, until I return in another Body. At the same Time he called for a sharp and keen *Cangiar*, with which he commanded his Nephew to cut off his Head, which the other did, and he was afterwards burnt.

The Author begins again to speak of China *and several Affairs relating to that Country.*

The Story of an Arabian *Merchant.*

The *Chinese* were wonderfully regular in their Government, before the last Revolutions entirely destroyed and reduced it to the State it is in at present. There was a certain Merchant, a Native of *Chorassan*, who coming into *Irak*, did there deal to a considerable Amount, and having bought up a Quantity of Goods went to

China. This Man was extremely Selfish and of invincible Avarice. It hapned that the Emperor of *China* had sent one of his Eunuchs to *Cansu*, the City for all the *Arabian* Traders, there to purchase what he wanted, and was to be had on board of the Ships that were arrived. This Eunuch was one of those who shared the most considerably in his Master's good Opinion and Confidence, and was Keeper of his Treasure and of all his most precious Things. A Dispute arose between this Eunuch and this Merchant, about some Pieces of Ivory and other Goods, and it ran so high, that the Merchant refused to deal with him: But this Affair making a great Noise, the Eunuch pushed it so far, that he forced from him the Choice of his Goods, regardless of whatever the other could say to him.

The little Bell. The Merchant withdrawing himself, went privately to *Cumdan*, where the Emperor resides, and which is two Months distant from *Cansu*; and being arrived he went to the String of the Bell mentioned in the first Book. The Custom was, That whoever pulled it should be sent a ten Days Distance from thence, as a Kind of Banishment; it was ordained also, that he should be committed to Prison, there to remain for two whole Months, which expired, the King or Governor of the Province released him, and said, *You have involved your self in an Affair which may turn to your utter Ruin, and to the Loss of your Life, if you speak not the real Truth; forasmuch as the Emperor hath appointed*

appointed Ministers and Governors to distribute Justice to you and to your Fellows, nor is there any one of them that would not right you. If, when you appear before the Emperor, your Wrongs are not such as may intitle you to have recourse to him, it will, most certainly, cost you your Life; to the end that every Man who would presume to do as you have done, may be deterred from the same. Withdraw therefore immediately, and be gone about your Business. Now if the Party endeavoured to fly he was chastised with fifty Strokes of the *Bamboo*, and was then sent back to the Country whence he came; but if he persisted in his Demand of Redress, he was admitted to an Audience of the Emperor.

The *Chorassanian* strenuously persisted in his Demand of Justice, and of leave to be admitted to the Emperor, which was at length granted him. The Interpreter asking him his Business, he related what had befallen him with the Emperor's Officer, and how he had forced from him a Part of his Effects. This Thing was soon divulged, and noised about at *Cansu*. In the mean time the Emperor commanded the Merchant to be cast into Prison, and that Care should be there taken he wanted for neither Victuals nor Drink. At the same time he ordered his prime Minister to write to the Governor of *Cansu*, charging him to inform himself concerning the Complaints of this Merchant, and to examine into the Grounds thereof. At the same Time also three principal Officers received the same Order. These Officers are called *of the*

Right, of the Left, and of the Midst, and, according to their Rank, have the Command of the Emperor's Forces, under the prime Minster; he trusts them with the Guard of his Person, and when he takes the Field for some military Enterprise, or on any other Account, each of them, according to his Rank, marches near him. These three Officers wrote, each apart, what they had, upon the strictest Enquiry, discovered of the Matter; and assured the Emperor that the Merchant's Complaint was just and true. These first Informations were followed and confirmed by many more, sent to the Emperor from divers Parts, and the Eunuch was cited to appear. No sooner did he arrive than the Emperor seized on all his Effects, and deprived him of his Office as Treasurer, and then said to him; *Death ought to be thy Doom for giving this Man, who is come from* Chorassan, *on the Frontiers of my Kingdom, cause of Complaint against me. He hath been in the Country of the* Arabs, *whence he came into the Kingdoms of the* Indies, *and at last to my City, seeking his Advantage by Trade; and thou wouldst have had him return, cross these Kingdoms, and have said to all the People in his way, I have been abused in* China, *where they have stript me of my Substance. I grant thee thy Life, in Consideration of thy former Services in the Rank thou holdest in my House; but I will conferr on thee a Command among the Dead, forasmuch as thou hast not been able to acquit thy self of thy Duty in that thou holdest over the Living.*

And

ſtrait he ordered him to be ſent to the Tombs of the Kings, to guard them, and there to remain for Life.

One of the Things moſt worthy to be admired in *China*, before the late Commotions, was the good Order they obſerved in the Adminiſtration of Juſtice, and the Majeſty of their Tribunals. To fill them they made Choice of ſuch Men as were perfectly verſed in their Laws, and ſuch, conſequently, as were never at a Stand when they were to paſs a Judgment; Men of Sincerity, zealous in the Cauſe of Juſtice upon every Occaſion, nor to be byaſſed by what the Great could offer to embroil a Diſpute; ſo that Juſtice was always adminiſtred to him who had Right on his ſide. In a Word, they made Choice of upright Men, of Men who equally abſtained from the ſlender Subſtance of the Poor, and from the Preſents of thoſe who would have bribed them therewith.

The Order obſerved in the Chineſe *Tribunals.*

When they deſigned to promote any Man to the Office of principal Judge, they previouſly ſent him to all the chief Cities of the Empire, in each of which he ſtaid a Month or two. In the mean time it was his buſineſs, moſt minutely, to inquire into the Affairs of the People, into all that paſſed in the City, and into the various Cuſtoms. He informed himſelf of all ſuch as deſerved to be believed upon their Word of Teſtimony, and this Knowledge was of uſe to him in the Sequel, as Occaſion required. After he had gone through all

The Promotion of a ſupreme Judge.

all the Cities, in the Manner abovesaid, and made a Stay of some Time in the most considerable of them, he repaired to the imperial Court, where he was invested with the Dignity of supreme Judge. To him then the Emperor referred the Nomination of all the other Judges, and by him were they appointed, after he had acquainted the Emperor with those, who, in his whole Dominions, were most worthy of exercising Jurisdiction, each in his own City, or in others; for he knew those who were commendable for their Understanding, and so no one was raised, who possessed not the same Endowments, or who bore not Testimony according to Truth, when he was interrogated.

The Emperor allows none of his Judges to write to him upon any Affair, when he is informed of the contrary, and even deprives them of their Office. The supreme Judge causes Proclamation, every Day, to be made before his Gate, and in his Name they cry out, If any Man hath been wronged by the King or Governor, who is not to be seen of the People, or by any one of his Relations or Officers, or by any one of the Body of the People; I will do him ample Justice, as soon as the Offender is put into my Hands, and that I have Charge of him: This Proclamation is thrice repeated. It is an ancient Custom with them, never to degrade a King or Governor of a City, but by virtue of Letters issued out by the Council or Divan of Kings; and this is commonly executed for some flagrant Malversation, or when

when Judgment is suspended or delayed. But when the Governor avoids these two Things, it is seldom he is disturbed with Letters of Revocation, which are never drawn up but on a lawful Account. The Posts of Judicature are conferred on none but Persons of Probity and Lovers of Justice; and so is good order maintained in the Kingdom.

Of Chorassan.

This Province is almost conterminous with *China*. From *China* to the *Sogd* it is about a two Months Journey, through impracticable Desarts, and through a Country all over covered with Sand, where no Water is to be found. It is not watered by any Rivers, nor is there any Habitation in the Purlieus of this Province; and for this Reason it is that the *Chorassanians* can make no Irruptions into *China*. That Part of this Empire which lies farthest westward, is the Province of *Madu*, which borders upon *Tibet*, so that on this side the two Nations are at perpetual War with each other. Among those of our time who have travelled into *China*, we were acquainted with one who told us he had seen a Man that had a Vessel with Musk in it, on his Back, and had travelled on Foot from *Samarcand* to *Cansu*, the Port for all Merchants from *Siraf*. He had, by Land, traversed all the Cities of *China*, one after another, which he might easily do, because the Provinces of *China* and *Tibet*, where the

Madu.

Musk of Tibet.

the Musk-creature is met with, are contiguous and not divided by any Separation. The *Chinese* carry off as many of these Creatures as they can lay Hands on, and those of *Tibet*, on their Part, do the same. But the Musk of *Tibet* is far preferable to that of *China* for two Reasons: *First* in *Tibet* this Creature feeds on aromatic Pastures, while in *China* he has nothing to subsist him but what is common. *Secondly* the *Tibetians* preserve their Bladders or Cods of Musk in the pure natural State, while the *Chinese* adulterate all that come into their Hands. They dip them also into the Sea, or else expose them to the Dew, and having kept them some time, they take off the outward Membrane, and then close them up; and this Musk passes in the Country of the *Arabs* for Musk of *Tibet*, because of its Excellence.

The most exquisite of all the Sorts of Musk, is what the Roe-Bucks, that yield it, leave behind them when they rub themselves against the Rocks in the Mountains; for the Humor, whence it is generated, falling down towards the Navel of the Creature, it there gathers into a Quantity of turbid Blood, just after the Manner of Biles, and such like Tumors. When this Swelling is ripe, the Creature, who is sensible of a painful Itching, seeks out for Stones and rubs himself against the same, till he opens his Sore, and the Contents run out. Now as soon as this Matter falls from the Creature, it coagulates, the Wound closes, and

and the ſame Kind of Humor gathers to a Head again as before.

In *Tibet*, there are Men who go in queſt of this Musk, and are very ready at knowing it; and having found it, they carefully collect it, and put it up in Bladders; and it is carried to their Kings. This Musk is moſt exquiſite when it has, as we may ſay, ripened in the Bladder of the Creature which bears it: It ſurpaſſes all others in goodneſs, juſt as Fruit is better when it is gathered ripe from the Tree, than when it is pulled green.

Another Sort of Musk.

There is ſtill another way of getting Musk. They inſnare the Creature in Toils, and ſhoot him with Arrows: But it often happens that the Hunters cut the Tumors of the Creature before the Musk is elaborated; and in this Caſe it has, at firſt, an ill Scent that prevails till the Matter is thickened, which ſometimes does not happen in a great while, but as ſoon as it coagulates it turns to Musk.

The Musk-Creature.

The Musk-Creature is like our Roe-Buck, his Skin and Colour the ſame, with ſlender Legs, a ſplit Horn, ſtrait, but ſomewhat bending withal. On each ſide, he has two ſmall white Teeth, which are ſtrait, and riſe above his Muzzle, each half a Finger, or ſomewhat leſs, in length, and in turn not unlike the Teeth of the Elephant; and this is the diſtinguiſhing Mark between theſe Creatures and other Roe-Bucks.

The Emperor of China*'s Letters conveyed by Poſt Horſes*

The Emperors of *China* write to the Kings or Governors of Cities, to the Eunuchs

nuchs or Lieutenants, and their Letters are conveyed by Post-Horses with a cut Tail, disposed almost like the Posts among the *Arabs*, in the Order every Body knows.

Several Chinese *Customs.* Besides what we have here related concerning the *Chinese* Customs, it is usual for the Princes, and even the People, to make Water standing. Persons of Dignity, as the Kings and the principal Officers, have gilded Canes, a Cubit long, which are bored through; and these they use when they make Water, standing upright all the time, and the Tube carries the Water a good Distance from them. They are of Opinion that Pains in the Kidneys, the Strangury and Stone, are caused by making Water in a sitting Posture; and that the Reins cannot free themselves of those Humors but by standing to evacuate, and that thus this Posture contributes to the Preservation of Health.

They suffer their Hair to grow, for the Men will not round the Head of a Child, when he comes into the World, as do the *Arabs*: For they say it causes a considerable Alteration in the Brain, and that common Sense is notably impaired thereby. They suffer the Head then to be all covered with Hair, which they carefully comb.

Their Marriages. As for their Marriages, they observe the Degrees of Consanguinity after this Manner. They are divided, among themselves, into Families and Tribes, like the *Arabs*, and some other Nations; and they know each other by the Difference of their Descents. No one marries in his own Tribe, just as the

the Children of *Thummim* among the *Arabs*, take not to Wife a Daughter of the Race of *Thummim*, and a Man of one Family espouses not a Woman of the same; but, for Example, a Man of the Family of *Robayat* marries into that of *Modzar*, and, inversely, a *Modzar* conjoins with a *Robayat*. They are of Opinion that such Allyances add to the Nobility of the Children.

Some Particulars concerning the Indies.

In the Kingdom of the *Balhara*, and in all the other Kingdoms of the *Indies*, there are Persons who burn themselves. This Custom proceeds from their Notion of a Metempsychosis or Transmigration, which they firmly believe as a Truth never to be called in Question among them. [AA] Indians *that burn themselves.*

There are Kings who upon their Accession observe the following Ceremony. They dress a great Quantity of Rice, and pour it out upon Leaves of the *Mousa*, in Sight of the King. Then three or four Hundred Persons come of their own accord, without the least Constraint on the part of the King, and present themselves before him. After he has eaten some of this Rice, he gives a little of it to each of them, as fast as they come up to him, one after another, and they eat it in his Presence. By eating of this Rice they all engage to burn themselves on the Day the King dyes, or is slain, and they punctually fulfil their Promise, throwing themselves into the [Z]

Fire

Fire till the very last, so that not one Soul of them is left behind.

[AA] *Their Manner of burning themselves.* When a Man is determined to burn himself, he first goes to the King's Palace to ask leave so to do; and having obtained it, he goes round the public Squares of the City, and makes his way to the Place where the Pile is heaped up with Store of dry Wood; while round about it stand many Persons who feed the Fire, so that it is very violent and blazes prodigiously. At last the Person comes preceded by a Number of Musical Instruments, and surrounds the Place in the midst of his Friends and Relations. During which, some put upon his Head a Garland of Straw or dry Herbs, which they fill with burning Coals, whereon they pour Sandarac, which catches Fire as strongly as Naphtha. Nevertheless he continues the Procession, although the Crown of his Head be all on Fire, and the Stench of his burnt Flesh be smelt, not so much as changing Countenance, in the least Degree, or betraying the least Sense of Pain. At last he comes to the Pile, throws himself into it, and is soon reduced to Ashes.

A certain Person says he saw one of these *Indians* burn himself; and avers that when he came near to the Pile, he drew out a *Cangiar*, and with it ript down from his Breast to the Rim of his Belly; and that this done, he with his left Hand pulled out a Flap of his Liver, and with the *Cangiar* cut off a Piece of it, which he gave to one of his Brothers, talking all the Time, and

and diſplaying an invincible Contempt of Death, and a wonderful Patience under his Torments, till at laſt he leaped into the Fire, to go to Hell.

Indians *who have particular Opinions.*

The Perſon who told this, added that, in the Mountains of this ſame Country, there are *Indians* who, in Opinions and Manners, differ but little from thoſe we call *Kaniſians* and *Jelidians*, and who are addicted to all Manner of Superſtition and Vice. There is a great Emulation between theſe Mountaineers and the People on the Coaſt; the latter continually going up to the Mountains to dare the Inhabitants there to do as they do; and the Mountaineers, on their part, as frequently coming down to the Coaſt with Defiances of the ſame Nature.

A very remarkable Story.

Among others, There once came down a Man on this Errand, and having gathered a Number of the Inhabitants of the Coaſt about him, who came as well out of Curioſity to ſee the Sight as with Intent to imitate him; He told them to do what he was about to perform, or, if they deſpaired of doing it, acknowledge themſelves overcome. He ſat himſelf down then in a Place planted with Canes, and directed them to bend one of them down to the Ground. Theſe Canes are like our Sugar-Canes, bend like them, and have a very large Stem: When they are laid hold on at Top, they obey and ſtoop to the Ground; but as ſoon as they are let go, they violently fly up to their firſt Rectitude. One of the largeſt of theſe he cauſed to be bowed down to his Height, and fastened his Hair strongly thereto; when taking in hand his *Cangiar* which sparkled like Fire, so keen it was, he said to those about him, *I am going to cut off my Head with this Cangiar,—as soon as it is severed from my Body, let go the Cane, and when it flies up with my Head I will laugh, and so you shall hear me do.* The People of the Coast had not Courage enough to imitate him. The Person who related these Things to us, did it without Emotion or Wonder, and in our Times these Facts are very generally known; for this part of the *Indies* is in the Neighbourhood of the Country of the *Arabs*, and we hear from thence every Day.

Aged Indians *request to be thrown into the Fire.*

Farthermore, it is a customary Thing for Men and Women, of the *Indian* Blood, to desire those of their Family to throw them into the Fire, or drown them, when they are grown old, or perceive themselves to sink under the Weight of their Years; firmly believing they are to return in other Bodies. They burn their Dead.

The bold Actions of Indian *Robbers.*

It has oftentimes hapned in the Isle of *Sarandib*, where there is a Mine of precious Stones in a Mountain, the Pearl-Fishery, and other rare and extraordinary Things, That an *Indian* would come into the *Buzar* or Market-place, with his *Kri*, as they call a Kind of *Cangiar* they wear, made after a particular Manner, and seize on the most wealthy Merchant there present, and holding his *Kri* to his Throat, lead him, by the Vest, out of the City, in the midst of a Throng of of People, while not a Soul of them dared to attempt his Reſcue: For if any Attempt of the Kind was made, the *Indian* was ſure to kill the Merchant, and make away with himſelf. When he had got him out of the City, he obliged him to redeem himſelf with a great Sum of Money. This Outrage continued till the Kings ordained, That every *Indian*, who preſumed upon the like, ſhould be ſeized; but offering to execute this Order, the *Indian* killed the Merchant firſt, and then himſelf. The ſame Misfortune befel many other Merchants, and after this Manner did a Number, both of *Arabs* and *Indians*, periſh; wherefore the Merchants ſought after other Means to ſecure themſelves, and the *Indians* were no longer apprehended.

Mines of precious Stones in the Iſle of Sarandib.

In the Mountain of *Sarandib* they find precious Stones of various Colours, Red, Green, and Yellow, moſt of which are, at certain times, forced out of Caverns and other Receſſes by Waters and Torrents. In theſe Places the King has his Officers to keep an Eye over thoſe who pick them up. Many times alſo they are dug out of Mines, juſt like Metals, and they ſometimes find precious Stones in the Ore, which muſt be broken to get at them.

Laws of Sarandib.

The King of this Iſland has Laws which are the Groundwork of the Religion and Government of the Country. Here are Doctors, and Aſſemblies of learned Men like thoſe of the *Hadithis* among the *Arabs*. The *Indians* repair to theſe Aſſemblies and

[BB] Theſe are the Repoſitaries of

the Mohammedan Tradition. write down what they hear of the Lives of their Prophets, and the various Expositions of their Laws. Here is a very great Idol of the finest Gold; but concerning the Weight thereof Navigators are not agreed. Here also are Temples where great Sums of Money are expended.

Jews *and other Sects.* In this same Island there is a very great Multitude of *Jews*, as well as of many other Sects, even *Tanwis* or *Manichees*, the King permitting the free Exercise of every Religion. At the End of this Island are Valleys of great Length and Breadth, which extend quite to the Sea. Here Travellers stay two Months, and more in that called *Gab Sarandib*, allured by the Beauty of the Country, bedecked with Trees and Verdure, Water and Meads, and blessed with a wholesom Air. This Valley opens upon the Sea called *Harkand*, and is transcendantly pleasant. You there buy a Sheep for half a Dram, and for the same you purchase as much of their Drink as may suffice many Persons. This Drink is made of Palm-Honey boiled, and prepared with the *Tari* [*Taddi*] or Juice which runs from the Tree.

The Pastimes of the Inhabitants. Gaming is the most usual Occupation of the Inhabitants here. They play at Draughts, and their other principal Pastime is fighting of Cocks, which are very large in this Country, and better provided with Spurs than Cocks commonly are; and besides this the *Indians* arm them with Blades of Iron in the Fashion of *Cangiars*. Upon these Combats they bet Gold, Silver, Lands, Farms,

Farms, and many other Things which are won by the Maſter of the Cock that beats. They play alſo at Draughts, and venture great Sums upon the Chance of this Game, but with ſuch Fury, That thoſe who have not wherewithal, Debauchees and deſperate People, often play away the Ends of their Fingers. While they are at play, they have a Fire by them, and thereon a Pot of Walnut, or *Seſame* Oil; they have no Oil of Olives; and they place a little, but very ſharp, Hatchet between them. When one of them has won a Game, the other lays his Hand upon a Stone, and the Winner cuts off the End of the Loſer's Finger with the Hatchet; and the Patient dips his injured Part into the boiling Oil, to cauteriſe the Wound. And yet they cannot ſhake off this evil Habit of Gaming; on the contrary, they ſometimes perſiſt in it ſo obſtinately and ſo long, that, before they part, they have all their Fingers thus mutilated. Some of them will take a Wick, and ſoaking it in Oil, apply it to ſome Member, ſet Fire to it, and let it burn ſo that the Scent of the burnt Fleſh is ſmelt by thoſe who play with them, while the Parties themſelves betray not the leaſt Senſe of Pain.

Exceſſive Debauchery.

Debauchery runs high in this Country, as well among the Women as among the Men; for they are laid under no Reſtraint. It runs ſo high, that ſometimes a foreign Merchant, juſt arrived from Sea, ſhall ſend for the Daughter of a King of the Country, and ſhe ſhall come to him to the Fiſhing grounds, with her Father's Consent and Privity. Wherefore the *Mohammedan* Doctors of *Siraf* strictly warn young People not to go that way.

Rains in the Indies.

In the *Indies* there are heavy Rains, which the People of the Country call *Jasara*. They last three whole Months, during Summer, incessantly Night and Day, and scarce does the Winter stop them. The *Indians*, to the best of their Abilities, prepare themselves against these Rains, some Time before they fall; and no sooner do they come on than they shut themselves up in their Houses, made of Wood and Cane interwoven, and thatched with Leaves. They stir not out during all this Time, and no Soul is seen abroad, no not even the Artificers, who now do their Work at Home; and during this Season they are subject to several Sorts of Ulcers in the Sole of the Foot, caused by the Damps.

These Rains fecundate the Land.

These Rains are the Life of the *Indians*; were they to fail, they would be reduced to the deepest Want. For their Fields, sown with Rice, are watered only by Rains, and are fecundated thereby; if great Store of Water ly upon the Rice Grounds they need no other help, or to be watered by Art. But when the Rains are plentifully showered down, the Rice thrives abundantly, and even becomes much better in Kind. It never Rains in the Winter.

[BB] Bramins, Indian Devotees.

The *Indians* have Devotees and Doctors known by the Name of *Bramins*. They have Poets also who compose Verses, stuffed with Flattery, in Praise of their Kings; Astrologers

Astrologers they have, Philosophers, Soothsayers, and Men who observe the Flight of Birds, and others who pretend to the Calculation of Nativities, particularly at *Kanuge*, a great City in the Kingdom of *Gozar*.

In the *Indies*, there are certain Men called *Bicar*, who go all their Life-time naked, and suffer their Hair to grow till it hides their hinder Parts, and the rest of their Body. They suffer also their Nails to grow, so that they become pointed and sharp as Swords, nor do they ever cut them, but leave them to break and fall off as it happens; and this they observe as a religious Duty. Each of them has a String about his Neck, whereto hangs an earthen Porringer; and when they are pressed by Hunger, they stop at the Door of some *Indian* House, and those within immediately and joyfully bring out Rice to them, believing there is great Merit in so doing; while they eat out of the Porringer and withdraw, never returning to make the same Request, if not by Necessity urged thereto. *Indian Penitents.*

The *Indians* have many Laws and religigious Precepts, by which they imagin they please God: Of such as these it is written in the *Koran, The Wicked have a mighty Pride.* One part of their Devotion consists in building of *Kans* or Inns, upon the Highways, for the Accommodation of Travellers; where also they set up Dealers, of whom the Passengers may purchase what they may happen to want. They there also settle public Women, such as are in the *Indies*, who expose *Religious Precepts.* [CC] themselves to Travellers; all which the *Indians* number among their meritorious Deeds.

[EE] *Public Women.* In the *Indies* they have public Women called *Women of the Idol*, the Origin of whose Institution is such: When a Woman has laid herself under a Vow, that she may have Children; if it happens that she brings forth a handsom Daughter, she carries the Child to the *Bod*, so they call the Idol they worship, and there leave her. When this Girl has attained a proper Age, she takes an Apartment in this public Place, and spreads a Curtain before her Door, and waits the Arrival of Strangers, as well *Indians* as Men of other Sects, to whom this Debauchery is made lawful. She prostitutes herself at a certain rate, and delivers her Gains into the Hands of the Idol's Priest, to be by him disposed of, for the use and Support of the Temple. We praise the Almighty and Glorious God, who hath chosen us to be free from the Sins which defile the Men involved in Infidelity.

[FF] *The Idol of* Multan. Not very far from *Almansur* there is a famous Idol called *Multan*, whither they resort in Pilgrimage from the remotest parts, even from distances of several Months. Some of the Pilgrims bring with them the odoriferous Wood *Hud al Camruni*, so called from the City of *Camrun*, where they have an excellent Wood Aloes, which they offer to this Idol; delivering it to the Priest of the Temple that he may burn it before his God. Some of this Wood is worth two hundred

hundred *Dinars* the *Man*, and is commonly marked with a Seal, to distinguish it from another kind of the same Wood, of less Value. It is usual for Merchants to buy it of these idolatrous Priests.

Particular Devotion.

There are, among the *Indians*, certain Men who make Profession of Piety, and whose Devotion consists in seeking after unknown Islands, or such as are newly discovered, there to plant Coco-nut Trees, and to sink Wells of Water for the Use of Ships that sail to those Parts.

Whole Ships built, &c. with the Coco-nut Tree.

There are People, at *Oman*, who cross over to the Islands that produce the Coco-nut, carrying with them Carpenter's and all such like Tools; and having felled as much Wood as they want, they let it dry, then strip off the Leaves, and with the Bark of the Tree they spin a Yarn, wherewith they sew the Planks together, and so build a Ship. Of the same Wood they cut and round away a Mast; of the Leaves they weave their Sails, and the Bark they work into Cordage. Having thus compleated their Vessel, they load her with Coco-nuts, which they bring and sell at *Oman*. Thus is it that, from this Tree alone, so many Articles are convertible to use, as suffice not only to build and rig out a Vessel, but to load her when she is compleated, and in a Trim to sail.

The Country of the Zinges *or* Negroes.

The Country of the *Zinges* or *Negroes* is of vast Extent. They there commonly sow Millet, which is the chief Food of the Negroes. Sugar-canes also they have, and other

other sorts of Trees; but their Sugar is very black. These People have a Number of Kings, who are eternally at war with each other. About their Kings they have certain Men called *Moharamin*, because each of them bores his Nose, and there wears a Ring. They have Chains also fastned about their Necks; and when they are at war, and going to fight, they each take one end of his Neigbour's Chain, and pass it thro' the Ring that hangs under his Nose; two Men hold this Chain, and so prevent the rest from advancing towards the Enemy till Deputies have been, from Side to Side, to negotiate a Peace, which if it is concluded, they take their Chains about their Necks again, and retire without fighting: But when they once begin to unsheath the Sword, no Soul of them quits his Post till he is slain.

They have great Respect for the Arabs.

In their Hearts they have all a profound Veneration for the *Arabs*, and when they chance to see any one of them, they fall down before him, and cry, This Man comes from the Kingdom where flourishes the Date-bearing Palm, for they are very fond of Dates.

Dervises, Preachers.

Among these People there are Preachers, who harangue them in their own Tongue, nor may the *Caiebs* or Orators of any other Nation whatsoever be compared with them. Some of these profess a religious Life, and are covered with the Skin of a Leopard or Ape. One of these Men, with a Staff in his Hand, shall present himself before them, and

and, having gathered a Multitude of People about him, preach all the Day long to them; he ſpeaks of God, and recites the Actions of their Countrymen who are gone before them. From this Country they bring the Leopards Skins called *Zingiet*, ſpotted with red and black, very great and very broad. [GG]

In this ſame Sea is the Iſland of *Socotra*, whence the *Socotrin* Aloes. This Iſle lies near the Land of the *Zinges*, and near alſo to the Country of the *Arabs*, and moſt of its Inhabitants are Chriſtians, which is thus accounted for: When *Alexander* ſubdued the Kingdom of the *Perſians*, his Preceptor, *Ariſtotle*, to whom he had by Letters communicated his Conqueſts, wrote back to him to deſire That by all means he would ſeek after the Iſland of *Socotra*, which afforded Aloes, an excellent Drug, and without which they could not make up the famous Medicament called *Hiera*. That the beſt way would be to remove the Inhabitants thence, and, inſtead of them, plant a Colony of *Greeks*, that they might ſend Aloes into *Syria*, *Greece*, and *Egypt*. Accordingly, *Alexander* gave the neceſſary Orders to diſpoſſeſs the Inhabitants, and to ſettle a Colony of *Greeks* in their ſtead. Then he commanded the Kings of the Nations, who divided his Empire, after he had ſlain the great *Darius*, to execute the Orders he had iſſued out for the Preſervation of theſe *Greeks*. They remained then as a Guard upon this Iſland, till God ſent *Jeſus Chriſt* into the World; when the *Greeks* of this ſame Iſle, being

The Iſland of Socotra. V. Geogr. Nubi. p. 24.

This is the Eaſtern Notion.

being informed concerning his Advent, embraced the Christian Faith, as the other *Greeks* had done before them; and in the Profession of this Faith have they persevered to this Day, as well as all the Inhabitants of the other Isles.

The Seas of those Parts. In the first Book, no mention is made of the Sea which stretches away to the right, as Ships depart from *Oman* and the Coast of *Arabia*, to launch into the great Sea: But the Author describes only the Sea on the left hand, in which are comprehended the Seas of *India* and *China*, which he seems to have particularly had in his Eye. In this Sea, which is, as it were, on the right of the *Indies*, as you leave *Oman*, is the Country of *Sihar* [*Shihr*] where Frankincense grows, and other Countries possessed by the Nations of *Ad*, *Hamyar*, *Jorham*, and *Thabateba*. The People of this Country have the *Sonna* in *Arabic*, of very ancient Date, but, in many things, different from what is in the Hands of the *Arabs*, and containing many Traditions to us unknown. They have no Villages, and they lead a hard and a very miserable Life.

These are Tribes of *Arabs*.

[HH]

The Country they inhabit extends almost as far as *Aden* and *Judda* upon the Coast of *Yaman* or *Arabia the Happy*. From *Judda* it stretches up into the Continent as far as the Coast of *Syria*, and ends at *Kolzum*. The Sea is, in this part, divided by a Slip of Land, which God hath fixed as a Line of Separation between these two Seas, as it is written in the *Koran*. From *Kol-*

zum

zum the Sea stretches along the Coast of the *Barbarians* to the West Coast, which is opposite to *Yaman*, and then along the Coast of *Ethiopia*, from whence you have the Leopard Skins of *Barbary*, which are the best of all, and most skilfully dressed; and lastly, along the Coast of *Zeilah*, whence you have Amber and Tortoise-shell.

The Navigation of the Siraf *Traders.*

When the *Siraf* Ships arrive in this Sea, which is to the right of the Sea of *India*, they put into *Judda*, where they remain; for their Cargo is thence transported to *Kahira* [*Cairo*] by Ships of *Kolzum*, who are acquainted with the Navigation of the Red Sea, which those of *Siraf* dare not attempt, because of the extreme Danger, and because this Sea is full of Rocks at the Water's Edge; because also upon the whole Coast there are no Kings, or scarce any inhabited Place; and, in fine, because Ships are every Night obliged to put into some Place of Safety, for Fear of striking upon the Rocks; they sail in the Day time only, and all the Night ride fast at Anchor. This Sea, moreover, is subject to very thick Fogs, and to violent Gales of Wind, and so has nothing to recommend it, either within or without. It is not like the Sea of *India*, or of *China*, whose Bottom is rich with Pearls and Ambergreese; whose Mountains of the Coast are stored with Gold and precious Stones; whose Gulfs breed Creatures that yield Ivory; and among the Plants of whose Shores are Ebony, Red-wood, the Wood of *Hairzan*, Aloes, Camphire, Nutmegs, Cloves, Sandal

V. Lud. Barth. p. 155.

dal Wood, and all the other Spices and Aromatics; where Parrots and Peacocks are Birds of the Foreſt; and Muſk and Civet are collected upon the Lands. In ſhort, ſo productive are theſe Shores of eſtimable things, that it is impoſſible to reckon them up.

Ambergreeſe. Ambergreeſe, which is thrown upon the Coaſt of this ſame Sea, is waſhed to Shore by the Swell: It begins to be found on the *Indian* Sea, but whence it comes is unknown. We only know that the beſt of it is thrown upon the *Barbarian* Coaſt, or upon the Confines of the Land of Negroes, towards *Sihar*, and Places thereabouts. It is of a bluiſh white, in round Lumps. The Inhabitants of this Country have Camels trained up to the Buſineſs, which they mount by Moonſhine, and ride along ſhore. Theſe Camels are broke to this, and as ſoon as they perceive a piece of Amber, they bend their Knees, and their Rider picks it up.

Another ſort of Amber. There is another ſort which ſwims in great Lumps upon the Surface of the Sea, almoſt like the Body of an Ox, or a little leſs, and weigh a great deal. When a certain Fiſh of the Whale-kind, called *Tal*, ſees theſe floating Lumps, he ſwallows the ſame, and is killed thereby. Then they ſee the Whale floating upon the Surface, and inſtantly the Men who are accuſtomed to this ſort of Fiſhery, and know when theſe Whales have ſwallowed Amber, go out to him in their Boats; and darting him with Iron Harpoons, they tow him to ſhore, where

where they ſplit him down the Back, and take out the Amber: What they find about the Belly of the Creature is commonly ſpoiled with the Wet, and contracts an unpleaſant Scent. You may buy the Bones of this Fiſh, at the Druggiſts of *Bagdad* and *Baſſora*. The Amber which has not been infected by Ordure, in the Belly of the Whale, is perfectly good. It is a uſual thing to make Stools of the *Vertebræ* of the Back-bone of this Whale called *Tal*.

They ſay, that in a Village, ten Leagues from *Siraf*, called *Tain*, there are old Houſes neatly enough built, the Lintels of whoſe Doors are of the Rib of this Whale. I have heard a Perſon ſay, That formerly one of them was thrown upon the Coaſt, not very far from *Siraf*; and that going to view him he ſaw People getting upon the Back of this Creature with Ladders; and that the Fiſhermen expoſed him to the Sun, ſliced away his Fleſh, and having digged a Pit, gathered up the Greaſe which was melted by the Sun; and that having drained off all the Oil, they ſold it to the Maſters of Ships. This Oil, mixed up with another kind of Stuff, in uſe with Seamen, ſerves for calking of Ships, to ſecure the Seams of the Planking, and to ſtop up Leaks. This Whale Oil is negotiated for great Sums of Money.

Buildings of Whale Ribs.

Whale Oil.

Of Pearls.

Before we ſpeak of Pearls, and the manner of their Formation, Let us praiſe God, who

who hath created them by his Providence, who hath produced all Creatures upon Earth, and who even from them produces others, and many and various Things which Men know not, wherefore do we aſcribe unto him all Majeſty, and bleſs his mighty and glorious Name.

The Formation of Pearls.

Pearls begin to be formed of a Subſtance, at firſt, ſomewhat like the Plant called *Anjedana*, being of Size the ſame, in Colour and Figure pretty alike, ſmall, thin, and tender, juſt like the Leaves of this Plant. At firſt it ſwims feebly on the Surface, and ſticks to the Sides of Ships, under Water; where, in time, it hardens, grows, and gets covered with a Shell. When theſe Oyſters become heavy, they fall down to the Bottom of the Sea, where they ſubſiſt after a manner to us unknown. They appear no other than a piece of red Fleſh, like the Tongue towards the Root, without Bones, Sinews, or Veins.

Different Opinions upon this Head.

But there are various Opinions touching the Production of Pearls; and ſome ſay, When it rains the Oyſters riſe up to the Surface, and that, gaping, the Drops of Water they catch turn to Pearls. Others ſay they are generated in the Oyſters themſelves, which is moſt likely, and is confirmed by Experience. For moſt that are found in Oyſters, are fixed and move not: When they are looſe the Merchants call them *Seed Pearl*. God alone knoweth how this Matter is. Now this is the moſt wonderful thing we have heard concerning the Subſiſtance of Oyſters.

A

The Story of a Pearl.

A certain *Arab* came formerly to *Bassord*, and brought with him a Pearl worth a great Sum of Money: He shew'd it to a Druggist of his Acquaintance, and, ignorant of the Value thereof, asked him what he thought of it. The Merchant telling him it was a Pearl, the *Arab* asked him what it might be worth; and he valued it at a hundred Pieces of Silver. The *Arab*, all astonished at his Words, asked if any Person would be willing to give him what he had said; whereupon the Merchant counted out a hundred Drams to him; and with this Money did the *Arab* purchase Corn to carry back into his own Country. The Merchant, on the other hand, brought the Pearl to *Bagdad*, and sold it at a very high rate, which inabled him to deal very considerably thereafter. Now this same Merchant declared, that he had examined the *Arab* touching the Origin of Pearls, and that he delivered himself to the following Effect.

Recital touching the Origin of Pearls.

I was going along, said he, by *Saman*, in the District of *Bahrein*, not very far distant from the Sea; and upon the Sand I saw a dead Fox, with something, at his Muzzle, that held him fast. I drew near, and saw a white, lucid Shell, in which I found the Pearl I took. Hence he gathered, that the Oyster was upon the Shore, driven thither by Tempest, which very often happens. The Fox passing by, and leering at the Meat of the Oyster, whose Shell stood open, did jump thereon, and thrust in his

Muzzle to ſeize the Fiſh, who, cloſing, locked him faſt, as has been ſaid. For it is a Property of theirs, never to let go their hold of any thing, except forcibly opened by an Iron at the Edges. This is the Oyſter that breeds Pearls, which it as carefully keeps as a Mother her Child. When therefore it was ſenſible of the Fox, it withdrew, as to avoid an Enemy; and the Fox feeling himſelf ſqueezed, did beat the Ground on each hand, till he was ſtifled, and ſo dyed. The *Arab* found the Pearl, and God would have it that he ſhould apply himſelf to the Merchant, a very happy thing for him.

Kings of the Indies *wear Ear-rings.*

The Kings of the *Indies* wear Ear-rings of precious Stones ſet in Gold. They wear alſo Collars of great Price, adorned with precious Stones of divers Colours, but eſpecially green and red; yet Pearls are what they moſt eſteem, and their Value ſurpaſſes that of all other Jewels; they at preſent hoard them up in their Treaſures, with their moſt precious things. The Grandees of their Court, the great Officers and Captains, wear the like Jewels in their Collars. They dreſs in a half Veſt, and carry a Paraſol of Peacocks Feathers to ſhade them from the Sun; and are ſurrounded by thoſe of their Train.

Indians *who refuſe to eat with each other.*

There are certain *Indians*, who never eat two out of the ſame Diſh, or upon the ſame Table, and would deem it a very great Sin if they ſhould. When they come to *Siraf*, and are invited by the conſiderable Merchants, were they a hundred in in Number, more or leſs, they muſt each have a ſeparate Diſh, without the leaſt Communication with the reſt.

Plates and Diſhes made of the Coco-nut Leaf.

Their Kings, and Perſons of high Quality, have freſh Tables made for them every Day, together with little Diſhes and Plates, wove of the Coco-nut Leaf; in which they eat what is prepared for their Subſiſtance: And their Meal over, they throw the Table, the Diſhes and Plates, into the Water, together with the Fragments they have left. Thus at every Meal they have a new Service.

To the *Indies* they formerly carried the *Dinars*, called *Sindiat*, or Gold Pieces of the *Sind*, and the *Dinar* there paſſed for three of ours, and even more.

Thither alſo are carried Emeralds from *Egypt*, which are ſet for Rings.

REMARKS, OR NOTES

UPON THE

CHIEF PASSAGES
Of the Two Foregoing Accounts.

Of the Sea of Harkand.

THE Author, doubtless, intends the *Maldives*, which, according to the Eastern Geographers, divide the Sea of *Delarowi*, or the Sea of the great Gulf of *India*, as far as *Ras Kemori*, or Cape *Comerin*, from that of *Harkand*. The *Arabs* and the other Orientals have Names for the Seas, which bear no Affinity with those of the other Languages. These Seas, without comprehending the Ocean which they call *Bah-Mahit*, are, the Sea of *China*, the Sea of *India*, the Sea of *Persia*, the Sea of *Kolzum*, or the *Red Sea*, so call'd from a Town which is thought to be the *Clysma* of the Ancients; the Sea of *Rum*, or of *Greece*, which is the *Mediteranean*; the Sea call'd *Al-Chozar*, or the *Caspian*, and the Sea of *Bont*, or the *Pontus Euxinus*. But these are not all the Names they give them; for the Sea of *India* is very often called the *Green Sea*; that of *Persia*, the Sea of *Bassora*; and other Names they have for particular Parts of these Seas. In like manner the Sea of *Harkand*, the Sea of *Delarowi*, the Sea of *Zinge*, or that on the Coast of *Barbary*, and the *Dark Sea* which was almost unknown to the *Arabs*, it stretching away beyond the Island of *Madagascar* or St. *Lawrence*, have different Names [A]

from

from the different Coasts they wash, and which they also call the *Salt Sea*.

Geograph. Arabic. Clim. 1. *p.* 8. The Sea of *Shelabet* our Author mentions to be divided by the Islands of *Ramni*, that is, by a Part of the Continent of the *Indies*, must be somewhere in that extent of Sea from Cape *Rasalgat* to *Malabar*: But as this extent seems to be very great, one would be apt to think this Sea extends but from *Shelabet*, which, according to *Abulfeda*, is a Town of the *Manibar*, which is a Part of the *Peninsula* of *India* within the *Ganges*, stretching from *Gizerat* or *Guzarat*, to *Coulam* or *Coulan*.

[B] *In these Seas are about* 1900 *Islands.*

The *Arabs* had but a very imperfect Knowledge of these Islands, and hence our Authors reckon them but at 1900; but our exact Navigators and Travellers, and particularly *Pyrard*, have it that the Inhabitants talk of above twelve thousand, and that the King of the *Maldives* assumes the Stile of *King of the twelve thousand Islands*. The *Nubian* Geographer calls them, with our Authors, *Robaiat* or *Robibat*, although the Name *Maldive* be more agreeable to the *Malabaric* Tongue, in which *Dive* is an Island; whence we have *Sarandib* or *Sarandive*, *Angedive*, and many others. *Garcias de Orta*, a learned *Portuguese* Physician, says, they must be written *Naledive*, or the *Four Islands*, or rather as *Barros*, the *Thousand Islands*; if after all it would not be better to say they borrow their Name from *Maly*, *Maley*, or *Male*, the chief of them, where the King resides. The Ancients knew next to nothing of these Islands; and we cannot tell when the *Arabs* landed among them to propagate *Mohammedism*, which they professed when first discovered by the *Portuguese*. *Barros* relates that the *Portuguese* of his time had run about three hundred Leagues along these Islands, from those of *Mamal*, a Moor of *Cananor* who was Master of the Northermost, about forty Leagues from the Coast of *Malabar*, and in the Latitude of 12 Degrees and 30 Minutes; and that the Southermost they knew

Dec. 3. *l.* 3. *c.* 7.

were

were thoſe of *Candu*, and *Adu* in the ſeventh Degree of the Antartic Hemiſphere: But that in the Sea Charts of the Moors, theſe Iſlands lay in a Cluſter along the Coaſt of *India*, from the Flats or Shelves of *Padua*, to the Parallel of Mount *Deli*; and then ran away Eaſtward till they almoſt touched *Java-head*, and the Coaſt of *Sunda*. The *Portugueſe* and *Dutch* Charts, which place theſe Iſlands of *Adu* and *Candu* a little more Northerly, take no Notice of the others which ſhould have been found out after ſo many Voyages, to and again, in theſe Seas: But the Mooriſh Charts are ſo very inaccurate, that it is very poſſibly they ſtretch out this String of Iſlands much farther than it really goes; for by the later Voyages it is certain that theſe Iſlands, of a Cluſter of which, according to *Pyrard*, each Province or Group is formed, each of which they call an *Atollon*, reach not farther than 5 Degrees South. The *Arabian* Geographer had certainly ſeen what our Author writes of theſe Iſlands, which he deſcribes accurately enough, except when he relates that the Capital is call'd *Anabona*; whereas in the original Text, which is corrupted in the *Roman* Edition, it is ſaid that the King of the Iſles *Robihat*, the ſame with the *Maldives*, reſides in the Iſland called *Maly*, or *Male*, which this Geographer writes of the King of the Iſland or *Peninſula* of *Comar*, which forms the Point and Part of the Eaſtern Coaſt of *India*. *Clim.* 1. *p.* 8.

He alſo calls theſe Iſlands *Robihat*; whereas our Author ſays, that all the Iſlands were comprehended under this Name, not excepting *Ceylon* or *Sarandib*; and whereas the Original from whence this Tranſlation is borrowed, reads *Dobijat*. In the *Indian* Tongue *Dive* is an Iſland or Iſle, but the *Arabs* write it *Dib*, as appears by their *Sarandib*, or *Sielendiba*, as it is written in the Fragment of *Coſmas Indopleuſtes*.

Our Author ſays, theſe Iſlands were governed by a Queen; and the *Nubian* Geographer reports that they have a King, but that his Wife has all the Power in her own Hands, that ſhe is uncontrolable by the King, and orders all matters of State and Property to her own good liking. The Hiſtory of theſe Iſlands is too much in the dark for us to examine *Voyages de Thevenot.* *Ubi ſupra.*

 mine

mine into the Origin of this Custom, which was abolished before the *Portuguese* first came hither. Perhaps the *Arabs*, who settled here, introduced, with *Mohammedism*, many of their Customs, and among the rest that of excluding Women from all public Employs; or it may have happen'd that when the *Arabs* discovered these Islands, some Woman ruled as Regent during her Son's Minority, such being the known Custom over all the *Molucca* Islands; which also prevailed among even the *Moguls*, whose Empire, during the Minority of *Gayuk Khan*,

Leb.Tarik. was governed by *Turakia Katun* his Mother. And thus the first Discoverers giving it out, that the Islands were under a Queen, easily persuaded others that it was the usual Form of the Government; and as Voyages hither did not happen often, they remained a long time under this Mistake. And so it was with the King of *Morocco*, who in the Year 1685, speaking of the *English*, said, they were not to compare with other Nations, because they obey'd a Woman; for this Prince who valued himself upon his Parts, had in some of his Histories read many things concerning Queen *Elizabeth*, in whose Reign the first Treaties of Commerce, with the Kingdom of *Morocco*, were managed by *Edmund Hogan*, her Majesty's Ambassador to *Muley Abdal-Malec* King of *Morocco*, in the Year MDLXXVII.

Hackluyt 1 Edit. p. 156.

What is said of the Ambergrease, which so abounds in these Islands, is confirm'd by *Garcias de Orta*, *Pyrard*, *Barbosa*, and many other Travellers.

The Shells are still current among the *Maldivese*, and in many Parts of the *Indies*, they pass for small Money; and not only in the *Indies*, but on the Coast of *Guinea*, and in the Kingdoms of *Benin* and *Congo*, were they are used in Traffic. *Barros* thus expresses himself thereon. *They have a kind of Shells about the Size of a Snail, but they are of another Shape, hard, white, and lucid; and some of them are so well illuminated, and stained of divers Colours, that being set in Gold for Buttons, they look like enamel. Ships ballast with these Shells for* Bengal *and* Siam, *where they are used at Market for change like our small Copper Pieces.* The same Author takes Notice of the Way

Way they take these Shells, and therein agrees with our Author; and *Pyrard* confirms what he says of the Treasures of these Shells the Princes of the Country have. P. 73. 1. *Barb. loc. citat.*

In the same Sea towards the Island of Sarandib *are many Isles.* [C]

It were to be wished our Author had expressed himself a little clearer in this Passage and many others, which relate to the Position and Place of the Coasts and Islands of the *Indian* Sea; which cannot easily be gathered from so imperfect a Description. He says, that in the Sea beyond the *Maldives*, there is a great Number of Islands, or Peninsula's, the *Arabs* having no Word to express these last: Wherefore they call *Spain*, *Jezirat-al-Andalus*, *The Island of* Andalusia, because it is washed by the Sea on three Sides. They therefore called Islands or Peninsula's that vast extent of Coast from Cape *Comorin* to *China*, where, it seems, we must place those Nations, who are but partly known to us, and under very different Names. In those Countries we find all that our Authors and the *Nubian* Geograper, their Copist, attribute to these great Islands, but which cannot hold good of the Islands of *Sumatra*, *Java*, and *Borneo*, which possibly are some of those described in the Sequel.

The Isles our Authors call *Ramni*, are otherwise called *Rani*, or *Rana*, and at this day give Title to a *Raja* or idolatrous Prince of the *Indies*, who derives his origin from King *Porus*. In the *Arabian* Geography this Island is called *Rami* as in the *Oriental Library* of Mr. *d'Herbelot*.

The Islands of *Najabalus*, or *Lajabalus*, (for the Name is spelt both ways) are, it is probable, the small Isles of *Nicobar*, where Ships still generally touch when bound to some Parts of the *Indies*.

Our Authors observe, that in these Islands there was a barbarous Race of Man-eaters; and this *Teixeira* confirms, adding thereto a still more barbarous Custom of eating their Relations when *Geo. Arab. supra.*

 they

P. 188. they are grown old. He places these Barbarians between the Isles of *Nicobar* and *Tanacarim* or *Tanasarim*: And this Custom remains to this Day, if we may believe *Navarette*; *It is certain they eat alive those* Europeans *they can catch*.

L. 1. c. 18. *Marco Polo* tells us, that the Inhabitants of the Island he calls *Angaman*, devoured all those they could lay Hands on. *Teixeira* says also of the *Javans*, that about an hundred Years before he wrote, that is, about two hundred Year ago, they ate Human Flesh, a Custom they unnaturally adhered to, till such time as they imbraced *Mohammedism*. The *Peguans* were guilty of the same, and sold Human Flesh publickly. Most of the *Cafres* on the Coast of *Barbary* are Anthropophagites also, and particularly those call'd *Zimbas*. These in the Year 1589 made an Incursion into the interior *Afric*, to the Number of 80000, and devoured all the Persons that fell into their Hands; and thus desolated a Tract of above three hundred Leagues. The *Mumbos* and most of the other *Cafres* of *Afric* are Devourers also of the same kind; and the *Portuguese* of *Mosambique*, and the Neighbouring Parts, agree that they ate the Bodies of such as were executed. *M. Polo*, besides other Parts of the *Indies* and *China*, where he observes the People to be Anthropophagites, says, that in the Kingdom of *Felech*, which is one of the eight of the lesser of *Java*, the Inhabitants ate Human Flesh as well as those of the Kingdom of *Samara*, those of *Dragojan*, and those of the greater *Java*, according to *Barthema*, who sold their ancient Relations to Men, who bought them to eat.

Joa. dos Santos Hist. de Ethiopia, Or. l. 2. p. 69.
L. 3. c. 11. c. 13. 14.
L. 3. c. 29.

The same *M. Polo*, speaking of the Astrologers, or Magicians of the great Khan of the *Tartars*, says, that when a Man was condemned to Death, they took him, dress'd him, and ate his Flesh.

P. 314. c. 319. *Barbosa* writes almost the same of *Siam* and the *Celebes*, and adds, that when a Criminal was to be sentenc'd to Death, they begg'd him of the King to eat. *Nicolo di Conti* observes also of the Inhabitants of the Isle of *Andramania*, or that of *Andaman*, and those of *Sumatra*, that they would eat Human Flesh;

P. 339. c.

Flesh; and according to *Pigafetta*, there were certain hairy People in the *Molucca's*, who having killed a Man, ate his Heart with Lemon Juice. *P. 364. l.*

Of the Island of Ceylon. [D]

The Orientals know the Island of *Ceylon* by no other Name than *Sarandib*, which has some affinity with the Σιελεδίβα of *Cosmas*, the Author of the *Christian Topography*. *Dive*, in the *Indian* Tongue, is an Island, and the *Arabs*, who have no V Consonant, do, after the manner of the *Greeks*, end their last Syllable with a B. Thus all the *Indian* Names ending in *Dive*, give you to understand that the Place meant, is either an Island or a Peninsula; for most of the Orientals have but one Word for the one and the other. From *Ceylon* the *Arabs* have formed *Saran*; for the two Liquids L and R are often converted into each other. *Arrian* writes, that Westward there lies an Island called παλαισιμούνδου, and by the Ancients *Taprobana*, where you must correct his Text, νῆσος λεγομένη καλαὶ ταπροβάνη· παρὰ δὲ τοῖς ἀρχαίοις αὐτῆς Σιμούνδου; which wants it, by a Mistake of the Transcribers, who have of the λ and α in ΣΙΛΑΝΔΟΥ formed a μ. *Voya de Thevenot. T. 1. Vide Bardos. p. 312. e. f.*

The same *Cosmas* gives it for the *Taprobana* of the Ancients. He says, it is about nine hundred Miles in Circumference, and that it was governed by two Kings, one of whom was Master of the Mines of *Yacinth*, or *Iacinth*, a general Name under which are comprehended several sorts of coloured Stones, which the *Arabs* call *Yacut* or *Iacut*; that some *Persian* Christians were there settled, and had a Priest, a Deacon, and all the Church Liturgy; that the Kings and most of the Inhabitants were Strangers; that Commodities were brought hither from all Parts, and even from *China*, this Island being as it were in the Heart of all the *Indies*; that it is five Days distant from the Continent of the *Indies*; and that its chief Scale was call'd *Marallo*; in fine, that there were found the κοχλίους, or Pearl Oysters, as our Author confirms.

What the *Arabs* relate of the Print of a Foot upon the top of a Mountain, which they say is *Adam's Step*; is to be found in most of the *Arabian* Authors, who are very fond of such Stories; and is confirmed by the Tradition of the Country, handed down to our present Times. *Robert Knox*, an *Englishman*, who lived twenty Years in this Island, and who publish'd an ample Account of it in the Year 1681, expresses himself to this effect. "Southward of *Conde-Uda* there is a Mountain, "supposed to be the highest in the Island, and "called *Hamalell* in the Language of the *Chingulas*, but the *Portuguese*, and the other *Europeans* "call it *Adam's Peek*. This Mountain is in the "Form of a Sugar-loaf, very steep, and upon the "top of it is a flat Stone, on which is seen the "Impression of a Man's Foot, but larger than the "Life, being about two Foot in length. The People of this Island reckon it a meritorious Work, "to visit this Trace or Impression, and fall "down before it; and generally towards the beginning of their New Year, which is in the "Month of *March*, the Men, Women and Children resort to this great and lofty Mountain, there "to perform their Devotions."

Lud. Barthem. l. 3. 4.

It is the common Opinion, that the *Chinese* peopled part of this Island, and that the Name of *Chingulas* or *Chingalas*, is derived from a *Chinese* Colony, settled on the Point *de Gale*, and descended from certain *Chinese* driven hither by stress of Weather.

Mart. Hist. 236. *Teixeira, l.* 1. *p* 184. *Vid. Marc. Pol. l.* 3. *c.* 19 & 23.

This, Father *Martini* confirms, saying, *Cingala* is *Sinarum Syrtes*, so called because here perished a Fleet an Emperor of *China* had fitted out to conquer this Island; and that *Ceylon*, or *Sinlan*, signifies *Chinese*. In another place he takes Notice that the *Chingulas* are much braver than the other Natives of the Country: But as *Navarette* very pertinently animadverts, This Proof makes quite against what it is intended to demonstrate, since it does not seem likely that they should inherit from the *Chinese* a Courage they never possessed.

Some

Some Authors have pretended that *Ceylon* is not the *Taprobana* of the Ancients, but that *Sumatra* is the Place. These are *Andrew Corsali*, *Maximilian* of *Transylvania*, *Barthama*, *Gaspar Barreyros*, *Pigafeta*, and some others. P. 180. P. 348. P. 184. P. 256. P. 372.

Ships built in the Indies. [E]

This same sort of Ships is exactly described by *Marco Polo*, under the Name of Ships of *Ormuz*; for at that time all the Commerce of *Siraf*, which was afterwards transacted at the Isle of *Kis*, was remov'd to *Ormuz*. "The Ships of *Ormuz* are very "bad and dangerous, and Merchants often run a very "great Risque in them. For they cannot fasten "their Planks with Bolts, because the Wood is as "hard and as brittle as Earthen-ware; so that when "they attempt to drive so much as a Nail into it, "the Nail starts back and breaks. Wherefore "they bore the ends of their Planks as gently as "possible with an Augre, and then drive in Tree-"nails, and so make them fast. Then they bind "them or rather sew them together with a strong "Thread of Coco-nut, which Nut is large, and "all over cover'd with strong Fibres like Horse "Hair. They then launch them, and when every "other part of them is decayed, these Threads are "clean and unhurt; and of the same they make "Cordage and Cables, which preserve a long time "in the Water. They use no pitch to save their "Ships from rotting, but use, instead of it, a Fish "Oyl. * L. 1. c. 16. p. 2.

* *Le navi d'Ormuz sono pessime & pericolose, on de li mercanti spessa volte in quelle pericolano: & la causa e questa, par che non si ficano con chiodi per esser il legno col quale si fabricano duro, & di materia fragile a modo di vaso di terra, & subito che si ficca il chiodo, si ribatte in se medesimo, & quasi si rompe. Ma le tavolo si foranno con trivello di ferro piu leggiermente che possono nell' estremita, & doppo vi si mettono alcune*

chiavi

Almost all the Modern Writers who have treated of the *Maldives* and the Coco-nut, agree with our Ancient Traveller in the manner of building these *Indian* Embarkations; and add, as a remarkable Circumstance, That this Tree alone not only affords Materials wherewithal to build a Ship, but to load her also when she is finished. The great Planks of the Trunk serve for her Hull and Masts; with the Filaments or Fibres of the Nut they spin the Cordage and the Sails; and they calk her with the coarser Stuff, and the Oil extracted from the Tree. They load her with Nuts both green and dry, and of the Liquor they draw from them, which is very pleasant and sweet at first, but turns into a Vinegar if kept, they make a kind of Cream, Comfits, Butter, and an excellent Oil for Wounds.

[F] *An unknown Isle where are Mines of Silver.*

Amidst such a Number of Islands as are scatter'd up and down the *Indian* Sea, quite up to the Coast of *China*, it is a hard matter to single out which of them our Author means. It seems that even in his Days, the Course to be steered for this Island was lost, and that Chance only directed Ships thither. There are Silver Mines in most of these Islands, as Travellers say.

[G] *A white Cloud, or Water-spout.*

This white Cloud, which has such extraordinary Effects, is very exactly described in the Second Volume

---

chiavi di legno, con le quali si serrano: doppo le legano, o vero cuciono con un filo grosso, che si cava di sopra il scorzo della noci d'India, le quali sono grandi: & sopra vi sono fili, como sete di cavallo, li quali posti in aqua com e putrefatta la sostanza rimangono mondi, & se ne fanno corde, con le quali legano le navi, & durano longamente in aqua: alle qual navi non si pone pesce per dissea della putrefattione ma s'ungono con olio fatto di grasso de pesci, & calcasi la stoppa.

of

of Mr. *Thevenot* the Younger. It is commonly call'd a Water-spout; and the *Arabian* Geographer speaks of it in almost the same terms. This sort of Whirlpool is not only seen all over the *Indian* Sea, but in the Sea of *Persia* also. *James Lancaster* observed one of them in the Straits of *Malacca*, on the way of *Achem*, attended with the same disturbance and rising of the Water described by our Authors. *Purchas Vol.* I. *p.* 159.

Tufan, Tuffoon, or Whirl-wind.

[H]

Our Authors observe that the Coast of *China* is subject to violent Storms, and particularly to those Squalls or Frets of Wind called, in their Language, *Tufan*, from a *Greek* Word τυφῶν, which signifies almost the same thing. The *Portuguese* and *Spaniards* derive from the *Arabs* their Word *Tufaon*, or *Tufon*, which, on the Coast of *China*, comes on from the Eastern Board, and begins in the Month of *August*. *Navarette* is in the wrong when he looks for the Etymology of this Word in the *Chinese* Language, in which, says he, *Tung fung* is an Easterly Wind. *P.* 423. The *Indians* of *Manila* call it *Bagio*, and it is to the full as violent as the Hurricans among the *American* Islands. These *Typhons* are much to be dreaded, especially in the Passage from the *Indies* to *China*, as we may perceive by many Examples to be found in the Writings of the most famous Navigators of these last Ages. But although this Word is originally *Greek*, and signifies rather a Storm attended with Thunder than a *Tufan* or Hurrican, during which the Wind shall shift to every Point of the Compass; yet the *Arabs* derive it from a Word of theirs which signifies *to turn*, believing it a Native of their Tongue, just as *Navarette* took it for an Offspring of the *Chinese*. *Varenius* says, the *Arabs* called it *Olifant*; he means *Al-Tufan*; but tho' he is out as to this, he describes it very exactly in his *Universal Geography*. *L.* 1. *p.* 283. *Edit.* II.

It appears like Sparks of Fire.

[I]

This was observed by Father *Martini* on the Coast of *China*: And *John Davis*, an *Englishman*, took Notice

Purchas. Vol. 1. p. 132. tice of the ſame Phænomenon in the Year 1604, being in 7 Degrees of Southern Latitude, not far from the Iſle of *Fernand de Noronha*; he ſays, the Glare was ſo ſtrong he could eaſily ſee to read by it.

[K] *An Iſland without Women.*

This, very probably, is the Iſland mentioned by *Marco Polo*: " Beyond *Cheſmacoran*, about five hundred " Miles in the main Sea, ſomewhat Southerly, there " are two Iſlands, the one *Maſculine*, and the other " *Feminine*, about thirty Miles wide of each other. In " the one the Men live without the Women, and this " is called the *Maſculine Iſland*; and in the other, " which is called the *Feminine Iſland*, the Women " live without the Men. The Inhabitants of theſe " Iſles are one People, however, and are baptized " Chriſtians. The Men croſs over to the Female " Iſland, and ſtay there three Months together, (*viz.*) " *March*, *April*, *May*, each in his Houſe with his " Wife; and then return to the Male Iſland, where " they abide for the reſt of the Year, following each " his Buſineſs, without the Participation of a Wife. " The Women keep the Male Children till they are " twelve Years old, and then ſend them to their Fa- " thers: But the Girls they keep till they are of Age " to Marry, and then diſpoſe of them to the Men of " the other Iſland. It ſeems the Air of the Place will " not allow the Men to be always with their Wives, " becauſe they would dye. They have a Biſhop under " him of *Socotra*." *

---

* *Oltra de Cheſmacoran a 500 Miglia in alto mare verſo mezzo di, vi ſono due Iſole, l'una vicina all' altra 30 Miglia. Et in una dimorano gli huomini ſenza Femine, & ſi chiama l'Iſola Maſcolina: Nell' altra ſtanno le femine ſenza huomini, & ſi chiama Iſola feminina. Quelli che habitano in dette due Iſola, ſono una coſa Medeſima, & ſono Chriſtiani battezzati. Gli huomini van all' Iſola delle Femine & dimorano con quelle tre meſi*

continui

Nicolo di Conti has it, that they are obliged to retire after a three Months abode, or that otherwise they would dye by the malignity of the Climate. We can say nothing of these Islands, since it is so hard to find them out by such an imperfect Description. But what *Marco Polo* says, can never be true, with regard to the Time the Men cross over to the Women; for being Christians, the Discipline which still subsists in the Churches of the *Levant*, would have obliged them to have abstained from their Wives during Lent, which they keep much about the same Time we do. Nor is it an easy matter to understand how the Women could live on their Island without any outward Worship, which must have been suspended in the absence of the Clergy, who nevertheless might cross over at the Time mentioned by *Marco Polo*, which happens to be also the Season when they celebrate the Feast of *Easter*.

The Course they steered for China. [L]

It is very difficult exactly to trace out the Course the *Arabs* steered for *China*, as it is found in our Authors; not only because many Towns they mention have been destroyed, but also because the Ancients, who only coasted it along, held a different Rout from that now shaped by our Pilots.

The *Chinese* came as far as *Siraf*, but dared not stir beyond it, because of the foulness of the Weather, and the heaviness of the Sea, which their Ships could not live in. They did not then venture so far as *Madagascar*,

---

continui, cioe Marzo, Aprile & Maggio: & ciascuno habita in casa, con la sua moglie, & doppo ritorna all Isola Mascolina, dove dimorano tutto, il resto dell anno, facendo le loro arti senza femina alcuna. Le femine tengono suoi figlioli fino a dodici anni, & doppo li mandano alli loro padri: Se ella e femina, la tengeno fin che ella e da marito & poi la maritano negli huomini della Isola. E par che quel aere non patisca che gli huomini continuino a stare appresso le femine, perche moririano. Hanno il loro vescovo qual e sottoposto a quello del Isola di Socotra,

Hist. l. 6. p. 237. *dagascar*, as Father *Martini* pretends they did, because in the Bay of *Santa Clara* there is a People resembling the *Chinese*, and not unlike them in Speech. He offers nothing in Proof of this but the Report of some Seamen: But granting the thing to be as he would have it, these *Chinese* may have been driven thither by Tempest, and there have taken up their abode, because they could not possibly return back again to their Country. On the other hand, it is evident that *Navarette* is mistaken when he says the Straits of *Sincapor* were their *Ne plus ultra.*

Siraf was formerly a Maritime Town in the Gulf of *Persia*, 60 Leagues from *Shiraz*, according to *Abulfeda*, or 63 according to *Ebn Haukal.* They place it in 78 or 79 Degrees 30 Minutes of Longitude, and in the Latitude of 26 Degrees 40 Minutes, or 29 and 30. They say it was a Town of great Fame for Trade, but that the Country about it was bare and uncultivated, because of its sterility; quite destitute of Trees or Gardens; that the Heat was excessive; that the Town was well built, and that some of its private Inhabitants were so rich, as to have laid out thirty thousand *Dinars*, or fifteen thousand Pistoles *French*, in raising and embellishing their Houses; and in short, that most of them were built with Wood brought from the Country of the *Franks*, or *Europe.* The *Arabian Geographer*, also mentions this City in many Places, in the Description of the third Climate, as well as most of the other Geographers. Trade still flourished there in the Days of *Abulfeda*, or about the beginning of the fourteenth Century; but when it began to migrate to the Island of *Kis-Ben-Omira*, then *Siraf* soon fell to decay; but it made no long stay at *Kis*, but changed Seat for *Ormuz*, where it entirely settled.

Abulfeda *n.* 319.

P. 6.

Gol. in Alfrag. p. 117.

All the *Arabian* Ships put into *Siraf*, and especially when they came from *Bassora*, the chief Scale for the Merchants of the *Red Sea*, *Egypt*, and even the Coast of *Ethiopia.* The *Chinese* and *Indian* Merchants brought thither all the Commodities the East could furnish, whether from the *Indies*, the *Terra firma*, or the Islands then known.

They sailed from *Siraf* to *Mascat*, in the Country of *Oman*, by *Ptolomey* called *Omanum Emporium*, and by by *Arrian*, *Omana*. The Town also was called *Sohar*, or *Sohar-Oman*, or *Shihr Oman*. This Passage is pretty dangerous for the Rocks, Isles, and Flats which lye in the way. It is impossible to say what Places our *Arabs* mean, since they give us no Positions or Situations: But it should seem that *Kaucamali*, or *Kaucam*, is *Cochim*, or *Cochin*, which it was easy to reach in a Month's Passage, with the Wind aft; because of the Monsoons which are very regular. Immediately beyond *Cochin*, is the Sea of *Harkand*, as the *Arabs* call it; and in ranging along the Shore, they first touched at *Cala*, or *Calabar*, which is the same thing. An anonymous *Persian* Author, whose Abridgment, or Epitome of Geography, is in the King's Library, says, that this Town is in part inhabited by *Moslems*, or *Musulmen*, and that there are Trees here which yield *Camphire*, as may be proved by the Testimony of *Serapion*, by reading *Cala* instead of *Calca*.

In Peripl.

C. 144.

Our Author says, that *Cala*, or *Calabar*, is about a Month's sail from *Kaucam*, but this does not afford us much light whereby to discover its Position. *Abu Zeid*, the Author of the second Relation, seems to have better explained the thing, saying, that the Isle of *Cala* is in the mid Passage between *China* and the Country of the *Arabs*, and that it is eighty Leagues in Circuit. Thus according to his Notion, it comprehends an extent of Country under a Capital of the same Name, which must have been somewhere about the Point of *Malabar*.

From *Cala* in ten Days they reached a Place called *Betuma*: In *Syriac*, *Beit-Touma*, is the *House*, or *Church of St.* Thomas, which is upon the same Rout, and cannot be very far from *Cala*, or *Calabar*. The Ancients must have touched there, because they shaped their Course between the Coast and the Island of *Ceylon*; whereas at present Ships stretch to the Southward of the Point *de Gale*, and stand over for the Isles of *Nicobar* which must have been those of *Najabalus*, this Name, it is probable, being equally corrupted by the *Arabs* and by the *Europeans*. They are in eight Degrees of Northern Latitude, & consequently beyond *Cala* and *Betuma*; and thus there must be some Transposition in the Description of this Course, when they are

J. Davis ap. Purch. Vol. 1. p. 133.

are named before *Betuma* and *Katrange*, or *Kenerag*, according to *Benjamin* the *Jew*.

It is hard to ſay what Place this laſt was, if it be not the *Chitran* in our Charts, as well as to find the true Place of *Senef*, or *Sanf*, although the *Aromatic* Wood ſhipped there, was for many Ages known all over the Eaſt. *Serapion*, who ſpeaks of it, though it can hardly be known in the Tranſlation we have, which reads *Seiſi* inſtead of *Seneſi*, gives us ſome Direction towards finding this Place, by telling us it is but three Leagues from Cape *Comorin*, or *Ras Comri*, where the *Wood Aloes* is to be had, but it is not ſo good.

Clim. 1. p. 10. The *Arabian Geography*, printed at *Rome*, can reflect no Light upon this Obſcurity; for the Text muſt be ſadly diſtorted, ſince it makes two diſtinct Continents, of *Malai*, which ſhould be the Point of *Malabar*, and *Senef*, and ſince it is very likely we ſhould read *Kaukam-Mali*, or *Melai*, inſtead of *Mâlai*.

The ſame Author ſays, that from *Senef* they go to *Sandarfulat*, or, as it is in the *Arabic* printed at *Rome*, *Sandifulat*. The Word *Pulo* is frequently compounded by the *Malays*, to ſignify, that the Places whoſe Names have that Adjunct, or Affix, are Iſlands: And there is a great Number of theſe in the Sea from the Gulf of *Bengal*, quite home to *China*. *Fulat* muſt then be the *Pulo* of the *Malays*, and *Sandar Fulat* may be *Pulo Condor* which is the neareſt to *China*, and may for that Reaſon be the Place the *Arabs* ſteered for, when they were bound for the Sea of *China*. And as their Navigation was rather Coaſting than Sailing, and as their Ships were very handy and light, they might the more ſafely venture through the Straits of *Sincapor*, and keep the Shore aboard all the way: And thus they kept between that String of Iſlands and Flats, which ſtretches away from the Coaſt of *Cambodia*, quite home to the Mouth of *Canton* River; nor muſt we wonder they were five or ſix Weeks upon this Paſſage.

It is difficult to trace out the particulars of this whole Voyage by ſuch defective helps; and after all, that might be done towards it, nothing but a bare Curioſity could enjoy any Satisfaction in it; for our Seamen at preſent

present know more of those Seas, and how to steer in them better than the greatest Navigators of Antiquity.

The Sea of *Sanji* must be somewhere about the Gulf of *Cochinchina*, which however, as has been observed by several Authors, is not the true Name of the Country, but *Caochi*; and even this is a Name imposed on it by the *Chinese*; so that this diversity in the *Arabic* Name may borrow upon some ancient Name of the Country, we know not.

To a Place called Betuma. [M]

Betuma is a *Syriac* Compound, whose true Orthography is *Beit-Touma*, which both in *Arabic* and *Syriac*, is the House or Church of St. *Thomas*. In like manner the *Syrians* call the City of *Martyropolis*, *Bargamea*, or *Beit-Garmea*, and so of others. But as much as our Author leaves us in the dark as to the Course he steered; if we allow that *Kaukam*, or *Conkan*, as the *Portuguese* write it, is somewhere about the Gulf of *Cambaya*, and if we grant that their Navigation was no better than Coasting, which cannot well be called in Question; than need we not admire that the *Arabs* should reckon it a Month's Voyage from thence to *Betuma*. *Calabar*, *Senef*, *Kadrange*, or *Chitran*, are in the Neighbourhood of St. *Thomas*'s. *Marco Polo* and almost all the old Voyage Writers agree, that by the Tradition of the Country St. *Thomas* should be interred in this very Place; and this is confirmed by *John di Empoli*, *Barbosa*, *Corsali*, and almost all the other first Travellers. (P. 146. 312. 315.) This Tradition is still in force among the *Nestorians*; and one of their most famous Authors, having summarily touched upon the Preaching of St. *Thomas*, says, his Tomb was discovered upon the Sea Shore, in a Village famous for being the Scene of his Martyrdom. (*Amr. Hist. Ar. MSS. of the Nestorians.*) To this Tradition may be added that of the *Malabar*, and most of the other *Syrian* Churches, who all believe St. *Thomas* penetrated into the *Indies*, and that he there lies intombed: But this shall be treated more amply in the Dissertations on the the *Nestorian* Churches.

[N] *Atlas Sin. p.* 171.

Flying Fish.

It is called *Hoangcioqu*, according to Father *Martini*, who says it is a Yellow Fish, or rather a Bird; for in Summer time it flies upon the Mountains; and, Autumn over, plunges into the Sea again, and becomes a very excellent Fish. He speaks of another sort of Animal in the Sea of *Canton*, which has the Head of a Bird, and the Tail of a Fish.

[O]

Petrified Crabs.

The above cited Author describes these to the following Effect: "There are certain Sea-Crabs which " are taken alive, between *Quantung* and the Island of " *Hainan*, which differ little or nothing from the com- " mon Crab; but when they are out of the Water, " and are sensible of the Air, they harden like the " hardest Stone, though they preserve their pristine " Shape. The *Portuguese* use them in Fevers. There " are of this same kind in a certain Lake on the " Island of *Hainan*."

[P]

A Burning Mountain, or Vulcano.

There is a famous *Vulcano* in the greater *Java*, near the Town of *Panaoura*, which belched out a prodigious Quantity of Flames, Stones, and Cinders, in the Year 1586. There is another in the Isle of *Banda*, and another in the Island of *Sumatra*: In some of the *Molucca* Islands there are the like, particularly in *Ternate*, where there is a Mountain whose Top throws up Fire, and from whence issues many Springs of living Water. *Nucopora* which is either among the Isles of *Nicobar*, or else one of the small Islands about *Java*, has, according to *Barbosa*, a Burning Mountain also.

Varenii Geograph. p. 94. *& seq. Argentola. Hist. de Moluc. Barbosa, p.* 319.

The

There is a Mohammedan Kadi *settled at* Cansu. [Q]

This remarkable Fact is to be found in no Author older than this, and proves that the *Mohammedans* went first to *China* by Sea, allured thither by the Advantages of the Trade. This *Moslem* Judge or *Kadi* of the Merchants, was properly a Consul: By degrees he became Judge over all the *Mohammedans*; and even took on him the Religious Functions, presiding at their Religious Assemblies. But our Author observes it as something very extraordinary, that the Merchants from *Irak* were not against his performing the Spiritual Office; for it properly belonged to a Man of the Law, and a Merchant could not regularly act therein; and he was still less qualified to judge the Subjects of the *Kalif*, without Authority from him.

The Sermon, or *Cotbat*, was a Discourse with which the *Imams*, or Rectors of the *Moschs* commonly ushered in their *Friday*'s Prayers. These Discourses consisted of Praises to God, and to *Mohammed*, varied to the Circumstances of the Times; and therein the *Imams* affected to display their Rhetoric, but especially when the *Moslems* had obtained any Advantage over the Christians; and they concluded with a Prayer for the *Kalif*, as had been Customary after the *Kalif* had laid aside the Custom of Preaching the *Cotbat* in person, so that this was a kind of public Homage they paid him. This is the Ceremony so often mentioned in the History of the *Saracens*, and all the other Oriental Writings. The Person in whose Name the *Cotbat* was delivered, was thereby acknowledged Supreme: For which Reason the Princes of the Family of *Buiya*, the *Seljukids*, and the others of different Families, who revolted from the *Kalifs*, paid them the Honour of the *Mosch*; whereas the *Fatemites*, who usurped the Title of *Kalif* in *Afric* and *Egypt*, had the *Cotbat* in their own Name, without any mention made of the *Kalifs* at *Bagdad*, and thereby declared themselves Heretics. Towards the Extinction of the *Kalifat* at *Bagdad*, the *Kalifs* were mere Cyphers; and the Honour of the *Mosch*, the Right of Investitures, and that of coining Mo-

Emir. Cond. Hist. de Ali. MSS. Persico.

ney, were all they had left. The Descendants of *Buiya*, who seized on all that part of *Asia* which owned obedience to the *Kalifs*, ordered the *Cotbat* after this manner; the *Kateb* or Preacher, having offered up Praises to God and to *Mohammed*, began first to speak of the *Kalif*, and then of the *Soltan*; and the same it was in the matter of Coinage, for on one side was the *Kalif*'s Name, and on the Reverse the *Soltan*'s. The same was observed by the *Seljukids*: But as their Empire extended from *Cashgar* quite into *Egypt*, and almost to the very Gates of *Constantinople*, and comprehended a great many tributary Principalities; mention was first made of the *Kalif* out of Religion, then of the *Soltan* out of Duty as Sovereign, and then of the Prince himself, who by this Form acknowledged the *Kalif* his Superior in Spirituals, and the *Soltan*, in Temporal Concerns; and in paying this Honour, consisted the Devotion of the *Mahommedan* Princes, who adhered to the Sonnite or Orthodox *Kalifs*. So *Nuroddin* the *Soltan* of *Syria*, set up the *Cotbat* in the Name of the *Kalifs* all over his Dominions, and even in *Egypt* as soon as *Saladin*, who was general of his Forces, made himself Master of *Kahira* or *Cairo*. And their example was followed by all the *Mohammedan* Prices in *Mesopotamia*, *Syria*, and *Egypt*, in the Year of the *Hejra* DCXLVIII. and of *Christ* M CCL. after the Death of *Moadzam-Turan-Shah*, the last of the Family of the *Ayubites*, Successors of *Saladin*, who was killed by his own People while St. *Louis* was in Prison.

Abulfeda Ebn Chukna Mak. Hist. Egypt.

The *Tartars* who in the Reign of *Holaku-Khan* conquer'd all the East to the Frontiers of *Egypt*, and who murdered the *Kalif Al-Motaseim*, the last of the *Abassid* family, by tying him up in a Sack, and marching their Army over him, put an end to the *Kalifat*. After this the *Mohammedans* were without a *Kalif*, and the *Cotbat* was suspended for about four Years; at the Expiration of which Soltan *Bibars-Bondokdari*, the Fourth of the *Turkish Mamluks*, raised to that Dignity an unknown Person, who pretended to be of the Family of *Abbas*, in the Year of the *Hejra* DCLIX. and of *Christ* MCCLIX. But this new *Kalif*, who had a small Army committed to him by *Bibars*, attempting to drive the *Tartars* away from *Bagdad*, was slain five Months

Months afterwards with all that belonged to him. *Bibars* then sat up another called *Hakem*, whom the People nick-named the *Black Kalif*; and him *Bibars* kept a kind of Prisoner, close up in a Palace, and abridged of all Liberty; though honoured as *Kalif*, and particularly with the *Cotbat* or Sermon, which was delivered in his Name in the *Mosch*. The *Turkish* and *Circassian Mamluks* kept up this Custom, and the Princes, their Tributaries, did the same, in acknowledgment of the Pontificat and Soveraignty of the imaginary *Kalif*; and thus the thing stood, till the Defeat and Death of *Tumam-bey*, the twenty third and last *Circassian* Soltan, who was hanged by the order of *Selim*, the Emperor of the *Turks*, in the Year of *Christ* MDXV. Thus upon this second Extinction of the *Kalifat*, to which the Dignity of *Mufti* bears no manner of Relation, the Ceremony of the *Cotbat*, although as old as *Mohammedism* itself, was intirely laid aside.

Now the Origin of this Ceremony was such: *Mohammed* as Prophet and Head of his own Sect, addressed the People on the Days of their Assemblies; and that he might be the better understood, he was wont to mount an Estrade some steps higher than where the rest stood. He began with Praises to God, and particularly expatiated upon what Thanks the *Mohammedans* ought to return him, when they had gained any Advantage over their Enemies; and then opened to them the Business that was to come under their Deliberation. And in this was he imitated by the *Kalifs* his Successors, till the rise of the Family of *Ommiyah*, with the Addition only of the Praises of *Mohammed*. At the same time they communicated to the People the important Affairs of the Public; for in the beginning of *Mohammedism* the Government was not Monarchical, but the Tribes of the *Arabs*, as those of *Medina*, *Mecca*, *Basra* or *Bassora*, and some others, claimed a Share in the public Administration, which after public Prayers, as had been said, was brought upon the Carpet by the *Kalif*.

Elmat. Emir. Cond. &c.

The first *Kalifs*, and particularly *Ali*, who was very eloquent of Speech, affected to enrich their Discourses with all the Strains of Rhetoric and Poetry, which gave birth to the Custom of dressing them up with all the

the Pomp of Expression, and of mixing them with Verse and Prose; many Examples of which we have in old Histories, and particularly in the History of *Emir Cond*. Moreover the *Kalifs* upon solemn Occasions, and to stir up the People by a Remembrance of their Prophet, appeared sometimes in White, when they were to pronounce the *Cotbat*; which in the Sequel gave rise to the Custom of appearing in a particular habit; and in Imitation of *Mohammed*, the *Kalif* mounted a kind of Pulpit or Gallery, called *Manbar*. But the *Empire*, shortly after, increasing to a great degree, and the *Kalif* having altered the first Form of the Government, he abolished the old Custom, and then the *Cotbat* began to be given in his Name, by the *Mufti*'s, the *Molla*'s, and other Officers of the *Mosch*'s. And now to the Praises of God, and the Elogies of *Mohammed*, they added those of the *Kalif*: and when it was pronounced for the first time after the Elevation of a new *Kalif*, the People lifted up their Hands, and put them one upon the other, which was deemed as an Oath of Allegiance; their left Hand representing that of the *Kalif*, and by the right Hand laid thereon, they signified their old Form of taking an Oath.

The *Abbasids* having deprived the Descendants of *Ommiyah*, assumed the Black Garment, and when they spoke to the People, appeared always in Black: whence those who delivered the *Cotbat* in their Name, mounted the Gallery or *Manbar* in Black, which was the Dress of the *Katebs* in all the Parts where the *Abbassids* were acknowledged Supreme, either in Temporals or Spirituals. The *Manbar* itself was hung with Black; and in this manner was it that the Ceremony was performed. On the other hand the *Fatemite Kalifs*, who called the *Abbassids* Heretics, kept to the white Vest, and hung the *Manbar* with a White Carpet, because white was the Colour of *Ali*, whose Sectaries still wear white Vests, or Sashes, as we saw in the Ambassador of *Morocco* and his Train, who were of that Sect. Ever after then that the *Kalif* gave over his Function, he delegated it to the Doctors, the Men of the Law, or Dervises, nor could it be canonically done without a Mission from the Prince.

After

After all this, the Reader will perceive why our *Arabs* were in some sort astonished that the Merchants of *Irak* who traded with *China*, could bear to hear a private Man go through the *Cotbat* or Sermon, in the Name of the *Kalif*. For this Man had no Mission, he was no Doctor or Lawyer, and it must have seemed still more extraordinary to *Mohammedans*, that such a Ceremony should be allowed in *China*, which, to their way of thinking, seemed to erect the Spiritual and Temporal Authority of the *Kalif* in the Country where it was used.

Four Great Kings, &c. [R]

The Dialogue in the Second Part clears up what is here said, concerning the Account the *Chinese* made of Foreign Princes. We must not wonder that our two Authors, being *Arabs*, should give the *Kalif* the the first Place; but in so doing we must not tax them with Prejudice or Presumption, for, in reality, the *Mohammedan* Empire was then at its height. *Aaron Rashid*, known in our History by the Name and Title of *Aaron* King of *Persia*, taking Advantage of the Victories of his Ancestors, the first *Kalifs* of the Family of *Abbas*, had made himself Master of all *Asia*, from *Romania* to the *Transoxane*; and the Moors of *Afric*, *Spain*, and the *Mediterranean* Islands were Subject to him. In all this vast Tract, each way, the *Cotbat* was pronounced in his Name, and the Money was all coined with his Stamp; and about his Reign it was that the *Arabs* made their first Appearance in *China*. The *Mohammedans* of those Days were not only considerable for their Power and their Treasures heaped together from the Spoils of all the East, they excelled in the Sciences and the fine Arts; and their Translations of the *Greek* Books under the Patronage of and by the Encouragement of *Al-Mamun* the Son of *Aaron*, together with his Kindness to Men of Letters in general, made the Empire as great for Arts as for Arms.

But the Emperor of *China*, say they, reckoned himself the Second; this does not seem to square well with the *Chinese* Vanity, and we leave every one to paſs his own Judgment thereon.

The Balhara. This *Balhara* is dignified *Emperor of thoſe who have their Ears bored,* which is the common mode among the *Indians.* Moſt of the *Arabian* and *Perſian* Geographers ſpeak of this Prince juſt as our Writers do. *Abulfeda* treating of *Maabar,* which is Part of what we call *Malabar,* ſays, that *The Capital is three or four Days from* Coulam; and adds, that *the Mountains of this Country border upon the Land of the King of Kings, or Emperor of the* Indies, *call'd* Ilbara; where it is plain we muſt read *Balhara.* The Situations of all theſe Places are ſo very doubtful, that we can hardly even gueſs at them. The ſame Writer ſays elſewhere, that *The Country of* Chanbalig, *in its Southward extent, touches upon the Mountains of the* Balhara, *the King of the Kings of the* Indies. This Paſſage may be illuſtrated by our Author, who ſays, that *The Country under the* Balhara *reaches by Land from the Coaſt called* Kamkam, *to the Frontiers of* China. The

P. 62. *Arabian Geography* relates, that the Seat of this Prince is at *Nahalwanah* or *Nehalwarah,* a City which according to the Tables of *Naſſir Eddin* and *Ulug Beig,* is in the Longitude of 102 Degrees 30 Minutes, and the Latitude of 22, and therefore can have been neither *Calicut,* nor *Cochim,* nor *Viſapor,* nor yet any that have been in Reputation for ſeveral Ages laſt paſt.

What our Author tells us of the Power of this Prince, can ſeemingly ſquare with no others than the Anceſtors of the Emperor of *Calicut,* who by the Relations of the old Travellers, and as appears even by ſome Books of the Country, which were examined by the famous Hiſtorian *John de Barros,* had been inveſted with the Authority of Emperor and King of Kings, over all the *Indian* Princes.

The Commendations our Authors beſtow on the *Balhara* for being particularly kind to the *Arabs,* ſutes very naturally with theſe Princes; the laſt of whom, *Sarama Payrimal,* became a *Mohammedan,* and took Shipping to go and end his Days at *Mecca.*

The *Portugueſe* Hiſtories relate, that this Prince or Emperor of the *Indies,* tranſlated himſelf to *Calicut,* for the convenience of the Pepper Trade: It is therefore probable

probable that before he settled at *Calicut*, he resided somewhere in *Guzarat*, or in the neighbouring and more Northern Country; and so the Mountains of the Kingdom of the *Balhara*, or the *Cordillere* which runs all along *Malabar*, would have reached the Country of *Chanbalig*, that is, the Frontiers of *Turkestan*, then in the hands of the *Tartars*, as well as of a part of *China*; and hence *Abulfeda* calls them the County of *Chanbalig*.

By the first Relation or Account, we learn that the Country of the *Balhara* begins upon the Coast of the Province of *Kamkam*, which may give Strength to the foregoing Conjectures. For as *Barros* affirms; *All the Coasts which we reckon from the Mountain* de Gate, *and which is but a long narrow Slip, is called* Concan; *and the People are properly called* Conquenis, *altho' we call them*, says he, Canaris; *and the other Land which lies within* de Gate, *stretching Eastward, is the Kingdom of* Decan, *and the Inhabitants are* Decanis. So *Conkan*, or *Kamkam*, which is the same thing, must have been the Province where formerly the *Balhara* or Emperor of the *Indies* kept his Court, before he removed to *Calicut*; and this is confirmed by a *Persian* Geographer, who speaking of *Kamkam*, says it is the Pepper Country.

Dec. 1. l. 9. c. 1.

Notwithstanding it is no easy Matter to point out the City of his Residence, yet by the Tables of *Nassir Eddin* and *Ulug-Beig*, which place it in 22 Degrees of Latitude, we may conceive that this City was at the Entrance of the Gulf of *Cambaya*, and that it was to all Appearance the ancient *Barygaza*; for *Arrian*, says, *Near this City the Continent stretched down Southerly wherefore it was called* Dakinabades; *for* Dakan, *in the Language of the Country, signifies* South. Thus as according to the Moderns, *Decan* begins from the Coast called *Concan* or *Kamkam*; so according to the Ancients, the same *Decan* began from the most famous Scale, which was *Barygaza*. The Conformity of *Dakin* and *Decan* is self-evident, and the word *Abud*, with which *Arrian* terminates his Greek Name, signifies, moreover, a Country or inhabited Place, and is annexed to the Names of a great many Towns, as πολις in Greek, *Burg* in *German*, and *Ton* in English. *Conkan* according to *Teixeira*, begins from *Chaul*, and he says that *Visapour* is the Capital of that Province.

μετὰ δὲ Βαρυγάζα εὐθέως ἡ συναφὴς ἤπειρος ἐκ τοῦ βορέου εἰς τὸν νότον παρεκτείνει, διὸ καὶ Δαχιναβάδης καλεῖται ἡ χώρα· δάχανος γὰρ καλεῖται ὁ νότος τῇ αὐτῶν γλώσσῃ.

Al-

All this seems to evince that this Title of *Balhara* can be given to no other than the ancient *Samorin* or Emperor of the *Indies*, who resided at *Calicut* six hundred Years and more before the *Portuguese* arrived in those Parts. And it is very likely that those Princes, who from the very first were so kind to the *Arabs*, were the very same who brought them into Credit in the Kingdom, and suffered them to settle there. In History we do not read of any Settlement of the *Mohammedans* in these Parts before that of *Calicut*, from whence they spread to all the trading Cities in *India*: therefore till we meet with some History of the Country to afford us better Instruction upon this head, we may stick to this Conjecture.

The Kingdoms or Provinces of *Geraz* or *Haraz*, of *Tafak*, of the *Mouga*, of the *Mabed* or *Mayed*, as the *Arabian Geographer* writes them, must be somewhere on the Continent between Cape *Comorin* and *China*. It is well known that the Names of these Countries, as they stand with us, have been for the most part corrupted; and that they are hard to be expressed in *Arabian* Characters: It were then almost to no purpose to enter upon a number of Conjectures, which, at the best, must be very doubtful, from the little we know of the History of these Parts, and the great Revolutions which may have happened after the *Mohammedans* got good footing there. For being valorous, industrious, covetous, and great Meddlers, they have always fomented Disorders here, during which they have carved out for themselves by the utter ruin of the Princes, or by persuading them to embrace *Mohammedism* for Reasons of State.

Before we close up these Remarks, we will add that the *Thatarian Drachms*, mentioned by our Author, are not quite unknown; but we must take heed, lest, deceived by the Affinity of the Names, we imagine they are *Drachms*, or Pieces of Money of *Tartary*. For *Tatar*, which is the genuin Name of *Tartar*, is spelt with a *T*, and the other by two *Th*. These Pieces then may have been the ancient Coin of the Country, upon which the *Arabs* gained by the course of Exchange: or perhaps they were some of those old Pieces mentioned by *Arrian* to have been current at *Barygaza*: At *Barygaza*, says he, *they have old Drachms with Greek Letters and the Names*

Ἀφ' οὗ μέχρι νῦν ἐν Βαρυγάζοις παλαιαὶ προχωροῦσι δραχμαὶ γράμμασιν ἑλληνικοῖς ἐγκεχαραγμέναι ἐπίσημα τῶν μετ' Ἀλέξανδρον βεβασιλευκότων Ἀπολλοδότου καὶ Μενάνδρου.

Names of Apollodotus *and* Menander, *who reigned there after* Alexander.

If he will submit to a Proof by Fire. [S]

The same was for many Ages a Custom all over the greatest part of *Europe*, excepting *Italy*, where the Authority of the Popes, who never countenanced this Practice, prevented it from getting Ground. Upon this head you may consult the Passages and ancient Formularies, cited by *Juret* in his Notes upon *Yves de Chartres*, and several others in Monsieur *Du Cange*, on the words *Ferrum Candens* and *Judicium Dei*; together with some others in use with our Ancestors to denote this Practice. And so far was it from being thought a Superstition, that it was incorporated into the Rites and Ceremonies of the Church, and had peculiar Masses and Prayers to itself, whether the Tryal was to be by red-hot Iron, or Water, scalding or cold.

It has been observed that this way of Tryal was known to the Ancients, since *Sophocles* mentions it; but it is more extraordinary that it should obtain among such barbarous Nations, as most of the *Indians* are, as also as the *Cafres* of the Coast of *Mosambique*, who according to *Joam dos Santos* (*) oblige those they suspect of some capital Crime to swallow Poison, to lick a red-hot Iron, *In Antigon. v. 274.*

(*) *Ao Segundo juramento chamao os Cafres juramento de* Xoqua, *que o ferro de hua enxo metido nofogo, & despois de estar muy Vermelho, & abrasado, o tirao do fogo com hua tenaz, & o chengao a boca do que ha de jurar, disendolhe que lamba com a lingoa o ferro Vermelho, porque se nano tem a culpa que lhe attribuem, ficara sao & salvo do fogo, sem lhe quemar a lingoa, nem os beiços: Mas que se tem culpa, logo lhe pegara o fogo na lingoa, beiços & rosto, & lho queimara. Iste juramento he mais ordinario & usao muytas vezes delle nao somente os Cafres, mas tambem os Mouros que nestas partes habitao, & o que peor he, que tambem algums Christaos derao ja este juramento a seus escravos, sobra furtos que sospeitavao teremlhe feytos.* l. 1. c. 11. p. 17.

"or

or to drink boiling Water in which have been previously steeped bitter Herbs, aud which they cannot get down if they are guilty, but which they easily toss off if they are innocent. This is so extraordinary a Fact, that the Words of the Author himself, as to the second Method of Proof, may fairly claim a place here.

Lete de Ethiopia Oriental. c. 11. p. 17.

"The second Oath, which the *Cafres* called *Xoquia*, "is performed after this Manner: They take the Iron "of a Hoe, which they put into a Fire and make it "red-hot, and being all on fire and red-hot, they take "it out with a Pair of Pinchers, and hold it to the Mouth "of the Person who is to swear. They command him "to lick the red-hot Iron, for that if he is innocent of "what is laid to his charge the Fire will not hurt him; "that it will neither burn his Tongue nor Lips; but "that if he is guilty, it will set fire to his Tongue, his "Lips, and his Face. This is the most usual form of "swearing, and not only the *Cafres* use it, but the "Moors also of the Country: And what is worse, the "Christians have already administred the same to some "of their Slaves suspected of Theft.

Apud Purchas, 2. p. 983.

The Negroes of *Loango* and many others on the Coast of *Afric* have another Proof, by Water tinctured with a certain Root which makes it as bitter as Soot, as we are told by *Andrew Battle*, in his Account of *Angola*; where also the use of red-hot Iron is common, as also that of the Pot charmed and filled with Salt, among some other Negroes of *Guinea*. The *Siamese* have Proofs of the same kind, if we believe *Schouten*; as walking upon burning Coals, swallowing inchanted Rice, besides that of keeping a long time under Water.

P. 30.

P. 307.

Odoardo Barbosa relates that the *Indians* of *Calicut* have a Proof with Oil, or boiling Butter, into which they dip the Fingers of the Party accused: This done they bind them up for Examination on the third Day, and if they are scalded they kill him, but if there is no Sign of heat they put to death the Accuser. *Nicolo di Conti* writes to the same purpose, as well concerning this and the Custom of licking or else handling of red-hot Iron, as concerning what is commonly practised among all the *Indians* in general.

P. 344.

In

In Sarandib, *when the King dies.* [T]

The Author of the *Arabian* Geography, who has almost these very Words, says this was a Custom all over the *Indies*. Most of the Eastern Geographers, *Kazwini*, *Ebn Wardi*, and others, say the same. *Chin. 2. p. 8. p. 63. Edit. Lat.*

The Manners of the Chinese. [V]

The Chinese *are fond of Gaming.*] The *Arabic* Word signifies not only Gaming, but every other sort of Diversion; it may even be extended to Comedies and Shews which the *Chinese* are so pleased with, as well as the *Tonquinese*, the *Cochinchinese*, and some other neighbouring Nations.

They love not Wine because they have none, and because their Extraction of Rice, their Tea or *Chaw*, and some other Liquors serve them instead of Wine. The *Mohammedans*, who abstained therefrom, out of a Principle of Devotion, could not fail to make this Remark as well as some others, which referred to their own Customs. Hence is it our Authors take notice, that the *Chinese* did not circumcise; that they washed not after the manner of the *Arabs*; that they killed not their Meat by cutting the Throat, that the Blood might drain off; all which the *Mohammedans* most strictly observe.

Debauchery is at this Day very prevalent in *China*, not only as to Women, Polygamy and the Numbers of common Prostitutes, but also as to the abominable Vice, so much practised among the *Bonzes*. In the *Dutch* Embassy you have a Representation of their public Women as they are led about the Town veiled and upon an Ass; they are many in Number. Father *Martini* relates, that the Women sold themselves openly at *Yangcheu*. Debauchery runs to a great height in *Vancheu*, where they without Shame gratify the Rage of their Lust. *Fath. Gruber's Accoun, p. 7. 9. Atl. 129. p. 31.*

Lust, *Navarette* (*) informs us that Sodomy was punished formerly, and that those guilty of it were sent to serve in the Garrison of the great Wall.

REMARKS

ON THE

SECOND ACCOUNT.

[X] *The Ocean has a Communication with the Mediterranean.*

ABu *Zeid* observes it as a new and very extraordinary thing, that a Ship should be driven from the *Indian* Sea to the Coast of *Syria*. To find out this Passage into the Mediterranean, he supposes there may be a great Extent of Sea above *China*, which has Communication with the Sea of *Chozars* or of *Moscovy*. The Sea beyond Cape *Currents*, on the East Coast of *Afric*, was perfectly unknown to the *Arabs*, who did not dare to venture upon so unfavorable a Navigation; and besides the Continent that way was inhabited by such Savage Nations, that it would been a Task of great Labour to have reclaimed them from their Brutality, or to

(*) *Como aca condenan a Oran, y Galeras, condenave el Chino al muro, El pecado de Sodomia tenia este pena: Tambien pero si todos los que tienen este vicio la huvieran de pagar; juzgo quedaria despoplada la China, y el muro con demasiada guarnicion.* He mentions it again in the *Seventh Chapter* of the *Second Treatise*, where he says that, *En tiempo que reynava el Chino, avia tambiem en la corte de Pequin casa publica de muchachos; quitola el Tartaro, oy la ay en la civdad de Jangchen.*

have

have civilized them by the Intercourse of Commerce. The *Portuguese* found no Moorish Settlement on all the Coast, from the *Cape of Good Hope* to *Sofala*, as they did afterwards in all the other Maritime Towns quite to *China*. This City was the last their Geographers were acquainted with to the Southward, and they did not know that this Sea had Communication with that of *Barbary* round the Southermost Part of *Afric*; and accordingly they described no farther than the Coast of *Zinge* or that of the *Cafrery*. Therefore we cannot doubt but the first Discovery of the Passage into the *Indian* Ocean, by the way of the *Cape of Good Hope*, was made by the *Europeans* under the Conduct of *Vasquez de Gama*, or at least some Years before he doubled the Cape, if true it be, as is said, That Sea Charts have had the Cape by the Name of *Fronteira de Africa*, before that celebrated Voyage was undertaken. *Antonio Galvam*, relates from *Francisco de Sousa Tavarez*, That in the Year M D XXVIII. the Infant *Dom Fernand* shewed him, the said *Tavarez*, such a Chart, which was in the Monastery of *Alcobaça*, and had been drawn 120 Years; perhaps from that said to be at *Venice* in the Treasury of St. *Mark*, which is thought to have been copied from that of *Marco Polo*, which has the Point or Promontory of *Afric*, if *Ramusio* be right.

The *Arabs* knew no more of *Japan*, which they called *Sila*, than they learned from the *Chinese*, since by the Testimony of the oldest of our two Authors, no *Arab* had yet set foot there in the Year of the *Hejra* CC XXX.

The Metempsychosis. [Y]

This is very generally held among the *Chinese*. Their Histories say that one *Xekia* or *Shekia* an *Indian* Philosopher, who was about a thousand Years before Christ, was the first that taught this Doctrine of Transmigration; and our Authors add that the *Chinese* had it from the *Indians*. It over-ran *China* in the Year of Christ, LXV. and the Chiefs of this Sect have to this Day their Abode on or near the Mountain *Tientai*, in the Province of *Chekiang*. This *Xekia*, according to the *Chinese* Tradition, *Martin. Hist. Sinar. p.* 109.

Atl. p. 93. dition in *Navarratte*, has been born eight thousand times over, the last time, in the Form of a white Elephant. It is he that was called *Fohee*, after his Apotheosis. The Sect of *Xekia*, says the same Father *Martini*, hold the *Metempsychosis*; but this Sect is divided into two Branches; the one believing the exterior Metempsychosis, or that the Souls of Men pass after Death into other Bodies, and these worship Idols, and abstain from every thing that has Life; while the other Sect has faith in an interior Metempsychosis, which is the principal Foundation of their Morality, which consists in suppressing the Passions, which are as so many different Animals proceeding from Man: But neither the one nor the other expect Rewards, or dread *Trig. l.* 1. *p.* 94. Punishments in a Life to come. Father *Trigaut* acquaints us, that the *Chinese* have upon this Head some Notions not very unlike those of the *Pythagoricians*. Father *Grueber* avers that all the *Chinese* are Idolaters at Heart, and that in private they all worship Idols: That true it is they seem to be divided into three Sects; but that even their Sect of *Literati*, who profess to adore a superior Substance which they call *Xan-ti*, have these words written in Gold in all their Temples, and adulate them with Offerings of Paper, Wax Tapers, and Incense, purely by this form to distinguish themselves from other Sects, and particularly the *Bonzes*. These, says he, came from the *Indies* into *China*, and it is impossible to conceive what Veneration and Esteem was paid them on account of their Doctrine of the transmigration of Souls, altho' it differed somewhat from what was taught by the *Pythagoricians*. In a word, all the Authors who have written concerning *China*, agree with these. The *Indians* believed and to this day believe the Metempsychosis differently from the *Pythagoricians*; *In Abulfarg. p.* 135. and the *Arabs*, before *Mohammedism*, taught it after a particular manner, as Dr. *Pocock* will satisfy you. The *Chinese* will have it, that the Doctrine of *Fe* or the *Atl.* 198. Metempsychosis, came from *Kieo* in *Junnan*: but whence- *Trig. l.* 1. 94. soever it came, it is thereto owing, that they often murder their Children, when they think they cannot *M. Polo. l. c.* 26. maintain them, and that they butcher them with so little Regret.

Men

Men who devote themſelves. [Z]

The *Portugueſe* Hiſtories ſufficiently abound with Examples of Men who have devoted themſelves to certain Death upon great Occaſions; and this the *Portugueſe*, in their Hiſtories, term *Fazer ſe Amoucos*. It is a Cuſtom of very ancient Date; witneſs the *Ambacti* and *Soludurii* among the *Gauls*, who engaged to die with their King, as *Cæſar* and *Athenæus* will inform you.

The Inhabitants of *Ceylon* would do the ſame, and a Number of Perſons of Quality, ſtiled *Faithful to the King in this World and the next*, were wont, as *Marco Polo*
ſays, to burn themſelves when he died. *Odoarda Bar-* *L.* 3. *c.* 20.
boſa obſerved the ſame in the *Indies*, particularly among *p.* 302.
the *Naires*, who having engaged themſelves in the Pay *Ram. T.* 2.
of the King, or ſome great Lord, would, if he died, or *p.* 307. *de*
fell in Battle, ſeek Death by revenging his Fall, or lay *Id. T.* 1.
violent Hands upon themſelves to bear him Company. *p.* 330.

When the King of *Tonquin* dies, many of the Lords of his Court conſent to be buried alive with him; but for an ample Account of what the *Tonquineſe* obſerve upon theſe Occaſions, conſult M. *Tavernier*.

Indians *who burn themſelves.* [AA]

This is an ancient and univerſal Cuſtom in the *Indies*, where it has taken ſuch deep root, that it ſubſiſts to this Day. All Accounts, both ancient and modern, confirm this, and agree with what the *Greeks* and the *Latins* have written upon the ſame Subject. However it is but ſeldom now, that Men burn themſelves deliberately; and it is a long while ſince any *Bramin* has followed the Example of *Calanus*, and ſome other old Philoſophers, who, being ſick of Life, committed themſelves to the Flames: But it is ſtill common for the Women to burn themſelves with their deceaſed Husbands. And altho' the *Mohammedans*, at preſent Maſters of a great part of the *Indies*, where this Cuſtom chiefly obtains, endeavour all they can to ſuppreſs it, they have hitherto wrought in vain to eradicate this cruel Superſtition ſo much preached up by *Bramins*.

Pietro Alvarez in Ram. p. 120. Barthema l. 3. c. 10. Barbosa p. 302. The Processions our Author describes, are still the same when Women burn themselves; but as formerly those who burned themselves behaved with great Courage, Resolution, and apparent Contempt of Death in all Respects, the Custom is now to alleviate the Pain, and dispatch the Women by an extraordinary Fire. Our most famous Travellers have often beheld this terrible Sight in the *Indies*, and some of them have describ'd it, as *Bernier*, *Tavernier*, and others. *Teixeira*, when he was
P. 9. in the *Indies*, saw four hundred Wives and Concubines of the *Naique* of *Madura*, burn themselves along with his dead Body. *Marco Polo* mentions a Custom of
L. 3. c. 13. some of the *Indians*, who, being sentenced to die, kill themselves in honour of their Idols, and are afterwards burnt.

[BB] *The* Indians *have their Doctors.*

The Name *Bramin* is formed from that of *Brachman*; which was used by the *Greeks* and *Latins* to signify the *Indian* Philosophers, who are much mentioned in the
Geogr. N. 361. *Arabian* Writings. Our Author reports, that there was a great Number of them at *Kanuge*, a City, which, according to *Abulfeda*, is in 131, that is 141 Degrees 50 Minutes of Longitude, and in 29 or 27 Degrees of Latitude. It stands between two Branches of the *Ganges*, Eastward of *Multan*, in the furthermost Parts of the *Indies*, and is distant from this said Town of *Multan* about CCLXXXII Leagues, if *Alazizi* be right. The King here has two thousand five hundred Elephants; and the City is handsom, large, and a great Mart, like *Kahira* or *Cairo* in *Egypt*. The King himself is called *Kanuge*, and has many Mines of Gold in his Country, as is confirmed by the *Persian Geographer*. The *Indian* Histories make
Dec. 4. l. 9 c. 9. mention of the City of *Canose*; and *Barros* relates that it is near the Place where the *Ganges* meets the *Gemna*. But the ordinary Residence of the *Bramins*, and the University, as we may say, of all the *Indian* Doctors, is *Benares*, or, as others pronounce it, *Banarus*, or as it is called in the Tables of *Ulug Beig* and *Nassir Eddin*, *Banarsi*. *Bernier Tavernier*, and the best Travellers dwell much on this Place. *Kanuge*, or *Kennaug'*, is, in the abovementioned Tables marked for the Seat of the King of

of the King of the *Indies*, but is there placed in the 116th Degree of Longitude, and the 27th of Latitude, which it is impossible to reconcile with the Positions of *Abulfeda*.

All Histories and Accounts are full of what regards the penitent Life and Austerities of the *Fakirs*.

Caravansera's *built by Devotion*. [CC]

There are many Foundations of this sort in the *Indies*, as well as in *Turky*, *Persia* and *Mogulistan*, nor to mention the many Hospitals in the *Indies* for sick Animals. *Thevenot* observes, that the Charity of the *Indians* of *Cabul* consists in digging of Pits, or sinking of Wells, and in erecting a Number of small Receptacles on the Highways for the Accommodation of Travellers. *T. 3. p.* 69.

The Custom of Cock-Fighting. [DD]

This is remarked by *Nicolo di Conti*, in his Recital of the Manners of the *Javans*.

" Their most common Diversion is Cock-fighting. " They have many sorts of Cocks, which they carry " about with them in hopes of a Prize. They bet upon " their Cock and he whose Cock has the better, carries " off the Wager.*

The Cavalier *Pigafetta* says the same of the Inhabitants of *Pulova*, and others of the *Molucca's*. *John Davis* and *James Lancaster* observed the same at *Achem*, as appears by their Accounts in *Purchas*, *Vol.* 1. *p.* 132 and 156. *p.* 361.

Public Women in the Pagods. [EE]

This infamous Practice is of old standing in the East. *Herodotus* has a Story of this kind of the Women who prostituted themselves in Honour of *Mylitta*, who by the Analogy of the *Chaldee*, must have been *Venus*; and the *L.* 1. *c.* 131.

(*) *Il giuoco piu usato da loro, e di far combattre i galli, e cosi ve ne portano de piu sorti, ciascuno sperando che il suo resti vincitore. Fanno infra di loro delle scommesse sopra questi combattenti, & il gallo che resta superiore fa vincor li dinari.*

Tents or Tabernacles of these Women were much like
L. 2. *c.* 38. those describ'd by our Author. In *Marco Polo*, we read that the People of the Province of *Cainda* did the same thing; exposing their Women in honour of their Idols.
T. 2. *l.* 2, 5. *Tavernier* speaks of a Pagod near *Cambaya*, whither most of the Courtezans of the *Indies* repair to make their Offerings: And adds, that old Women, who have scraped together a Sum of Money, buy young female Slaves, whom they train up to wanton Songs and Dances, and all the Allurements of their infamous Calling: And that when these Girls have attained their eleventh or twelfth Year, their Mistresses conduct them to this Pagod, under a Notion that it is a Happiness for them to be offered, and delivered up to the Idol.

Again, we are told by *Marco Polo*, that there was a like Custom in the Province of *Camul*, where it was prohibited by *Mangu Khan*, whose Command was obeyed for three Years; but observing that their Lands did not produce as usual, they, at the Expiration of the aforesaid Term, sent Deputies to *Mangu Khan* to represent to him,
L. 3. *c.* 23. *Che da poi che mancavano di far questi piaceri & eleemosyne verso forastieri, le loro case andavano di mal in peggio.* The same Author, in another Place, speaks of certain *Indians*, who offer their Children to Idols, and
p. 302. go into their Temples stark naked. *Barbosa* tells of Numbers of Prostitutes, who took up their abode in Pagods; and adds, That, in *Tibet* the Custom is never to marry a Female who has not been exposed to some one, but especially to foreign Merchants. *L.* 2. *c.* 37.

[FF] *The Idol of* Multan.

This Idol must be very old, and, perhaps, gave name to the City and Country so called, which is a part of the
Abulf. n. 450. Province of *Sind*. The Capital is, according to *Abulfeda*, in 92 Degrees of Longitude, and 29 Degrees 40 Minutes of Latitude. According to *Ebn Haukal* it is twelve Days distant from *Almansur*, which is a greater Distance than is allow'd by our Author. *Abulfeda* speaks of this Idol, and says it is dressed in red Leather, and has two great Pearls for Eyes. The *Emir* who was Lord of this City, in the Days of *Abulfeda*, received the Offerings

erings of the *Indians*, who reſorted hither in Pilgrimage from the remoteſt Parts. This Idol is deſcribed juſt after the ſame manner in *Thevenot*'s laſt Voyage. *P.* 163.

The Iſland of Socotra. [GG]

This Story is told, in almoſt the ſame Words, in the *Arabian Geography* printed at *Rome*, as alſo in almoſt all the Oriental Geographers. They all imagine that the Diſcovery of the Iſle of *Aloes*, is one of the greateſt Incidents of *Alexander*'s Progreſs; and this they imagine from the great Account they make of this Drug, which is one of the firſt Ingredients in their *Materia Medica.* You may ſee what is ſaid of it by *Ebn Sina*, or *Avicen*, as we call him, and by the other *Arabian* Phyſicians, and, among the Moderns, by *Garcias de Orta*, and ſome others it were needleſs to cite.

Marco Polo relates of this Iſland, that its Inhabitants *L.* 3. *c.* 34. were Chriſtians, and that they had an Archbiſhop under a *Zatolic*, who reſided at *Bagdad*; that is, a *Catholico* or Patriarch of the *Neſtorians*. For the *Arabs* writing Catholic with an aſpirated Letter, which is of the ſame Power with our *J* conſonant or *G*, were it not for a Point underneath, many have ſpelt it *Jatolic*; whence *Marco Polo*, who was a *Venetian*, forms his *Zatolic*, pronouncing the *G* or *J* after the manner of his Country.

The *Portugueſe* Authors, on the contrary, will have *Barros*, them to be *Jacobites*, or ſubject to the ſchiſmatical Patri- *Dec.* 2. *l.* 1. archs of *Antioch* or *Alexandria*. When the *Portugueſe* *c.* 3. *Purch.* firſt came to this Iſland, the Inhabitants appeared to them *p.* 778. with Croſſes in their Hands, to ſhew they were Chriſtians: But *Odoardo Barboſa* ſays, that, in his time, they *P.* 292. had hardly any Notion of Baptiſm, and that they had nothing left to diſtinguiſh them as Chriſtians but the bare Name.

They have the Sonna *in* Arabic. [HH]

We do not ſee how this Paſſage can be otherwiſe underſtood, tho' the Tranſlators of the *Arabian Geographer*, who has copied it, underſtand it in a different Senſe, becauſe the Text is mangled a little:

Degit enim in ipsis natio quædam Arabum, qui diversis & antiquis utuntur linguis, Arabibus hac nostra tempestate ignotis. Thus is it the *Maronites* translate this Passage, wherein they are confessedly mistaken. For this Passage does not relate to two small Islands, but to that *Arabia* by the Ancients called *Libanophoros*, by the *Arabs* themselves *Shibr*, and by *Ptolomey* [illegible], where dwelt the old *Arabian* Tribes, *Ad*, *Hamyar*, *Jorham*, and *Thabateba*, who embraced *Mohammedism*. These *Arabs* had, besides the *Koran*, many Stories and Traditions touching the *Mohammedan* Religion, which they received from the Companions of their Prophet, and his Disciples. From these Traditions and Stories, they form the Body of their *Sonna*, which therefore is very different in different Places; so that not only the *Sonna* of the *Persians* differs from that of the *Arabians*, but that of the *Africans* varies from that of *Mecca* and the *Arabians* of the *Desart*. From this Variety a Number of Sects have arisen in the *Mohammedan* Profession; and these Sects have divided *Mohammedism*, and introduced several Variations in the Exposition of their *Koran*, and in their Jurisprudence. The Tradition of the old *Arabs* was the most authentic, and could not be mixed with so much Novelty and foreign matter as the Tradition of other Countries, where it was multiplied World without end.

This was the fundamental Principle of the Science the *Fakis* or *Arabian* Doctors professed. *Ebn Kalican* relates, in the Life of one of the most famous of them, *Abu Yacub Isaac*, the Disciple of *Kafei*, and the Head of one of their Sect; That he boasted of knowing by heart seventy thousand *Hadith*, or Stories, concerning *Mohammed* and his first Companions, and a hundred thousand others of less importance on the same Subject. They cite them in their Books with the Names of their Authors, and the Names of those these had them from, quite up to the first, as the *Jews* do in the *Talmud*.

We must not wonder therefore, if the Tradition was different from the Vulgar contained in the *Sonna* among the *Arabians* of the conquered Countries. In those Countries there are still old Copies of the *Sonna*, which are so different from the modern, that they have scarce any thing in common with them.

ON

ON THE HISTORY and CUSTOMS of CHINA.

FEW Eastern Writers have written worthily of *China*, although most of them are fond of dwelling thereon. But what they write is so confused, so inaccurate, and so stuffed with Fable that it is easy to see they knew next to nothing of the Situation and Remarkables of that Empire. The *Greek* and *Latin* Geographers, whom the *Arabs* perused in faulty Translations, could lend them no helping Hand in this Part of *Asia*, which was but little known to the Ancients; and our two Authors are, perhaps, the first that have written tolerably on this Head. By the Passages the *Nubian Geographer* copies from them, without naming them, it appears that in his Time there were no Memoirs of more Value for what concerned *China*; and if the other Geographers have made but little use of them, it is, seemingly, because they thought them Fabulous, as *Abulfeda* declares he did, in several Places. The Accounts of the late Travellers, and particularly those of Father *Trigaut*, and Father *Semedo*, and the several Tracts of Father *Martini* have more amply instructed us in the Geography, Natural History, Manners, and Customs of *China*, than all that had been written before. But as for the Illustration of History, it may be proper to compare the Ancient Accounts with the Modern, just as Father *Martini* has in many Places explained *Marco Polo*, whom the Ignorance of past times rejected as a Fabulist; it may be as proper to shew that our two Authors so often agree with our late Writers, that they for that Reason are to be had in particular Veneration, and especially as they went four hundred Year or more before *Marco Polo*, and our other earliest *Atlas Sin.*

earliest Travellers: And it will be perceived by the following Remarks, that, some Points excepted, which still want illustration, they abound with very judicious Observations, and such as are perfectly consonant with our latest Informations.

It were to no purpose to undertake a Justification of the lesser Circumstances to be found in our Authors, by a great Number of Citations. They may have been mistaken in some things, which new Discoveries may clear up hereafter; but if they sometimes happen to vary from the Modern Accounts, we must not at once conclude they are wrong; for *China*, as well as every other State, has been subject to great Revolutions, which must have wrought great Changes in the Government and the Customs; and perhaps the more we shall come to the Knowledge of the *Chinese* History, the more we shall be convinced of the Accuracy of the old Travellers.

The Name of China. Let us first examine into what our two Authors say of the Country in general. It seems they knew it by the Name of *Sin*, which the *Arabs* borrowed from *Ptolemey*. Thus it is that *Ebn Said*, *Yacûti*, *Abulfeda*, and most of the Eastern Geographers call this Empire. The *Persians*, however, pronounce it *Tchin*, much like the *Italians* and *Portuguese*; a Name which may have *Navar. l.* 1. been imposed by Strangers, either because the *Chinese* in their Salute say, *Chin Chin*, or *Ching Ching*, or from the Emperors of the Family of *China* as Father *Martini* thinks.

Father *Aleni* the Jesuit says, that in a *Chinese* Book *P.* 1. cited by *Navarette*, *China* signifies the *Country of Silk*; while others will have it that *China* signifies *to observe the South*; and the Merchants coming in from that Quarter, may also have given Birth to this Name; at least we may assure our selves it is of old Date among the *Lucen. l.* 10. *c.* 3. *Arabs*. The Name of *Cathay*, which is also much used, did properly belong to the most Western Parts of *China*, and probably derives it Origen from those *Scythians* beyond Mount *Imaus*, whom the *Greeks* called *Appendix ad Atlant. Sin.* Χαϊϑ. Father *Trigaut*, Father *Martini*, and, in a Word, *Golius*, have evidently demonstrated, that the *Cataï* of *Marco Polo*, and our ancient Travellers must not be sought for out of *China*: But they have not suffi-

ſufficiently explained this Diſtinction; and what *Golius* offers as a Proof (*viz.*) that *Misk Cataï*, and *Tcha Cataï*, ſignify Musk and Tea of *China*, makes good this Remark, ſince Musk comes from *Tibet* and the adjoining Provinces, and Tea alſo. But we do not find that the *Arabians* and *Perſians* gave the Name of *Cathay* to the Southern Provinces; yet, certain it is that all they report of the Magnificence of the *Khan* of *Cathay*, muſt be underſtood of the Emperor of *China*, and that the *Cambalu* or *Chanbalig* of the Orientals, can be no other than *Pekin:* And here let it be obſerved, that theſe Forms of Speech came from *Perſia*, and the Provinces of the Upper *Aſia*, conterminous with *China*; and that this Name was peculiar to the Weſtern and Northern Provinces only, which alone were conquered by *Jenghiz Khan*, the Emperor of the *Moguls*.

At the ſame time it may be pertinent to take notice that *Voſſius* is quite miſtaken, when, with his uſual Confidence, he is ſure the *Portugueſe* were the firſt that called the Country *China*, which he will have to be the ancient *Serica*, and that the *Chineſe* ſhould be called *Seres*, as he always calls them. For the *Portugueſe* were unacquainted with *China*, till the ſixteenth Century, and our *Arabian* Travellers wrote in the Ninth; and yet we muſt not ſuppoſe they were the Authors of this Name, which was in uſe long before them. The Appellation of *Seres* is equally unknown to the *Chineſe*, the *Arabs*, and the *Perſians*, nor is it an eaſy matter to prove that it bears any Relation to the Inhabitants of *China* properly ſo called, ſince *Ptolomey* diſtinguiſhes the *Seres* from the *Chineſe*, whom he calls Σῖναι.

It ſeems our Authors were but ſlenderly informed of the Limits of *China*, ſince they confine themſelves to the Sea-port where the Merchants traded, the Capital of the Empire, and the Provinces next to the Kingdom of *Samarkand*. They ſay that the *Sogd* of *Samarkand* is but about a two Months Journey from it, which ſquares with the Tables of *Abulfeda*, and the Author he cites, of *Ulug Beig*, and ſome others. They obſerve that the Kingdom of *Tibat*, *Tobit*, or *Tobat*, for ſo the *Arabs* pronounce it, is not far diſtant from the

ſaid

ſaid Provinces; and the County of *Tagazgaz*, or *Tabazaz*, if this Name is not corrupted, is conterminous therewith, on the Eaſt. By this Word we might be induced to think that we are to underſtand the People of *Laos*. Thoſe called *Mabed*, *Mujet*, and ſome others mentioned in the one and the other Account, muſt be placed between *Tibet* and *Bengal*; but it is a hard matter to know them again in a ſtrange Tongue, and after ſuch great Revolutions, whoſe Hiſtory we know not.

What our Author relates of the Number of Cities in *China* is conſonant with the Reports of the late Travellers; for our *Arabs* ſay, that in *China* there are above two hundred Cities, which have many others ſubordinate to them. Now, Father *Trigaut* reckons two hundred forty ſeven; Father *Martini* ſays, one hundred and fifty; and *Navarette* reduces the Number to one hundred forty eight of the firſt Order; but it is no difficult matter to believe that the Number of theſe Capitals may have increaſed and decreaſed according to the different Alterations which have happened in this Empire.

Canſu. *Canfu* was the City beſt known to the *Arabs*, becauſe it was the Scale of all the Commerce with the *Indies*, *Perſia* and *Arabia*. The Rocks called the *Gates of* China, in our firſt Account, muſt be the Iſles which lie between the Coaſt of *Cochinchina*, and the Mouth of *Canton* River. The *Arabs* required eight Days to ſteer through them, becauſe of the Dangers they ran of miſcarrying among them; a trouble they might have avoided by ſhaping their Courſe directly for the Iſland of *Hainan*, or *Ainam*, which is, probably, what they call *Alnian*. *Canfu* muſt be *Changcheu*, or *Quantung*, now commonly ſpelt *Canton*: *Fu* and *Cheu* are two Terminations, the firſt of which being added to the Name of a Place, denotes it to be a Capital City, and the ſecond is to denote a City only. *Canfu* was but a little way from the Sea, and ſtood upon a great River, which Ships entered with the Tide, and this Situation agrees perfectly with that of *Canton*.
N. 369. This City is mentioned in the *Nubian Geographer*, but both in the Original and in the Tranſlation the Name is very much corrupted, being written *Canaku*, and the

ſame

ſame Inaccuracy may be obſerved in *Abulfeda*, who ſays, this City was known in his time by the Name of *Canſa*. He places it in 164 Degrees 40 Minutes of Longitude, and 28 Degrees, 30 Minutes of Latitude; and adds, that "By the Accounts of ſome Travellers, " it is the greateſt trading City in all *China*. That " he had been informed by a Man who had been there, " that it ſtands to the South-Eaſt of *Zeitun*, half a " Day from the Sea, and upon the Branch of a River " which forms a Canal, navigable by the largeſt Veſ- " ſels. That it is extremely large, and that its incloſure ſurrounds four ſmall Eminences; that they there " drink Well-water; that it had very pleaſant Gardens, " and that it ſtood about two Days diſtant from the " Mountains." By this ſlender Deſcription it ſufficiently appears, that this Geographer was but poorly acquainted with the Situation of the capital Cities of *China*, and moſt of the others ſpeak with the ſame Obſcurity. But our two Authors leave no room to doubt of the true Orthography of this Name, and *Abulfeda*'s Conjecture cannot be borne, ſince, to all appearance, his City of *Canſa*, muſt be *Changcheu*, or ſome maritime City of Eminence for Trade in his time.

But it is a far more intricate Task to aſcertain what place our Authors may mean when they ſpeak of *Cumdan*, where they ſay the Emperor of *China* then reſided. This City they ſo often mention, that there is no ground to imagine the Text to be corrupted; and the *Chineſe* and *Syriac* Inſcription, found in the Province of *Xenſi* or *Chenſi*, in the Year MDCXXV, confirms what they advance; for in the *Syriac* words *Cumdan* is called *the Royal City*, and *the Capital of China*. Now the two Cities where the Emperors have for many Ages paſt reſided, are *Pekin* and *Nankin*; but the firſt which is thought to be the *Cambalu* of *Marco Polo*, and the *Chanbalig* of the Orientals, has not enjoyed this Dignity above CCCCL Years, or thereabouts; ſo that in the Days of our two Authors, *Nankin*, otherwiſe called *Kiangnang*, was the Capital of the Empire, and the place where the Emperors of *China* kept their Court.

Cumdan.

China illuſtrata l. 1.

Cumdan muſt then be *Nankin*, nor can we well doubt it, ſince the *Arabian Geographer*, ſpeaking of the

Cumdan *muſt be* the Nankin.

the greatest River in *China*, which certainly is the *Kiang*, calls it the River of *Cumdan*, because it flows through *Nankin*, the only City that crowns that River, which had for several Ages been the Seat of the Empire. Therefore is this Town called *Nankin*, or the *Southern Court*, whereas *Pekin* signifies the *Northern Court*. The *Syrians*, who wrote the *Chinese* Inscription, we just now mentioned, have another Title for it, and call it the *Eastern Court*; and thus this City may have been stiled by the *Chinese*, and, perhaps, the different Names of *Kingling*, *Moling*, *Kianle*, *Kiangning*, *Kiangnang*, and *Ingtien*, which it has borne under different Royal Families, may import what the *Syrians* have in their Inscription: But without entring into this Labyrinth, it is easy to perceive that it was natural enough for the *Syrians* to call it the *Eastern Court*; for of all the Royal Cities in *China*, it was the most Eastward from them who came from *Syria* by the way of *Tibet*. The magnificent Descriptions our Authors give of this City can agree with no other than *Nankin*; for *Pekin* was not yet the Seat of the Emperor, and even when it was thither transferred, *Nankin* did not fade much away till the last Wars, that it was entirely sacked by the *Tartars*.

Martin. Atlas, 129.

The Testimony of Abulfeda.

Abulfeda inthrones the Emperor of *China* at the City of *Biju*, or *Banju*, or *Bishu*; for this Name is so often varied in the Copies we have of this Author, who lays it down in 114, that is, 124 Degrees of Longitude, and 17 Degrees of Latitude; and adds, that it is the Residence of the *Fagfur*, who, says he, is the Emperor of *China*, otherwise called *Tumgage Khan*, that is, *Lord of the Country of* Tumgage, or *Tumgaz*; that it is an inland City, embellished with many Gardens, and that the Inhabitants have their Water from Wells; that it is some Days distant from the Sea, and five Leagues North-West of *Cansa*, and that it is incompassed with Walls, for the most part in Ruins. All this he says from the Information of a Traveller. *Golius* cannot settle upon what City this should be, and believes the Easterns may have meant *Pekin*, *Nankin*, *Quansi*, *Yamcheu*, or even *Pegu*. But the great Distance and Difference between these Cities evince, that *Ebn Said*, *Abulfeda*, and the other Authors cited by that learned Man, can have pointed at no other City than *Nankin*; not that the Positions *Abulfeda*, *Nassir*

In Alfrag. p. 75.

ſir Eddin, and *Ulug Beig* give their City of *Biju*, can be applied to *Nankin*, and even they differ among themſelves, ſome placing it in 124 Degrees, and others in 130; but we deduce thus much from the Situation of the City, which they ſay is ſome Days diſtant from the Sea, and not very far from *Canſa*, which, tho' it cannot be ſaid either of *Nankin* or *Pekin*, yet it may be more truly referred to the former than to the latter of theſe Cities. And this is the more to be regarded, inaſmuch as ſome very accurate Writers have evidently demonſtrated, that the *Cambalu* of *Marco Polo*, and the *Chanbalig* of the Orientals, can be no other than *Pekin*, the Poſition of the one and the other coinciding nicely enough.

Gol. Append. ad Atlantem Sin.

Among all the different Names of *Nankin*, we do not find it was ever called *Cumdan*, and it is very probable that this Name is not ſpelt exactly by the *Chineſe* Orthography: But it is enough for us that this Town was known by this Name among the Orientals; and the Conformity of the *Chineſe* and *Syriac* Stone, with our two Authors, as to the Name of this City, is well worthy our Obſervation, and may inconteſtably confirm what they write.

All that our Authors report of the Magnificence of this City is agreeable to the Deſcription of *Nankin*, in the Relations of the Fathers *Trigaut* and *Martini*.

The Government of China.

Our Authors ſpeak of the Government of *China* in Terms which prove them to have been been no Strangers thereto; for notwithſtandng the extraordinary Revolutions which have there happened within eight hundred Years paſt, what they ſay is, in its pricipal Circumſtances, confirmed by the Teſtimony of the later Voyagers.

They take notice that *China* was governed by an Emperor, who was ſupreme and abſolute over all the Governors of Provinces, whom they ſtile Kings. The *Arabic* Word, *Malec*, which they uſe, does not actually import a King, according to the Senſe and Meaning of thoſe who wrote contemporarily with our Authors, or in the following times. As the firſt *Mohammedan* Sovereigns aſſumed the Title of *Kaliſs*, or *Vicars of God upon Earth, and Succeſſors of* Mohammed; this ſtile was peculiar to his Deſcendants, or, thoſe who pretended ſo to be, in the Sequel. The *Kalif* enjoyed all Authority, both in Spirituals and Temporals, and no *Mohammedan* that erected himſelf

into

into a Prince, and particularly after the *Abbassids*, assumed that Title free from Schism; for the *Fatemites* of *Egypt*, and some other Princes of less Note, who presumed to take it on them, were guilty not of Defection only, but of Schism also, and were rejected as Heretics by the other *Mahommedans*. But those who adhered to the Bulk of *Mohammed*'s Followers, and remained in Subjection to the *Kalif* at *Bagdad*, and who to this Day call themselves *Sonnis*, pretended to no more than the Quality of *Soltan* or Prince. *Malec* was a Surname peculiar to the Branches of the Royal Family, and was granted, as an Honour, to tributary Princes, who acknowledged either the *Kalifs* or the *Soltans*. We must
L. 2. c. 68. Dutch *Embassy to* China.
not therefore wonder, that these Governors of Cities and Provinces, who ruled almost with a sovereign Sway, tho' at the same time subordinate to the Emperor, should be dignified *Maluc*, or Kings, by the *Arabs*; and especially since our later Travellers use the same Term. Thus *Marco Polo*, Father *Trigaut*, Father *Martini*, *Navarette*,
The Bagbun.
and the *Dutch* not only stile the Princes of the Royal Family by the Title of Kings, but the Governors also; and both the one and the other observe with our Authors, that
l. 2. *c.* 68.
these petty Kings are in Subordination to the Emperor, besides that *Navarette* reports the several Provinces of *China* to have been formerly so many Kingdoms.

The *Arabs* commonly write, that the Emperor of *China* is commonly called *Bagbun*, tho', according to the most ancient of our Authors, they in his Days pronounced it
Hist. Pers. In MSS.
Magbun. But others, as *Abulfeda*, and an old *Persian* Author, call him *Fagfur*, and pretend this and *Tumgage*, or *Tumgaz Khan* to be synonymous; and *Marco Polo* calls those Kings by the Name or Title of *Fansur*, who preceded the *Tartars*, under whom he went into *China*. They all agree that this Title signifies the *Son of Heaven*, and our last Accounts agree as to the Sense of this Word, but instead of it they give us another, *Tiençu*, to signify
Trig. l. 6. *c.* 16. *Navar. l.* 1. *c.* 9. *Mart.*
the same thing, and hence, perhaps, the *Arabs* formed their *Tumgage*, which is otherwise spelt *Timjage*, and after other ways.

We must not wonder that our two Authors tell us nothing of the Royal Family of the Emperors who reigned in their times; for we can reap no manner of Information from any other of the *Arabian* Writers, or the *Persian*, who

who did not begin to know *China* till towards the twelfth Century, when the *Tartars* became Masters of it. But the total Revolution, mentioned in the second Account, is the more remarkable, as it squares very exactly with what we read in the Beginning of Father *Martini*'s *Chinese Atlas*. He says, that from the Year CCXI before Christ, when the Family of *Hana* mounted the Throne, upon the Deprivation of the Family of *Cyna*; the Princes of the aforesaid Family of *Hana* reigned till the Year CCLXIV after Christ; and that then the Family of *Cyna* succeeded, and held the Throne till the Year CCCCIX of the same. Then five Kings rose up against each other, and commenced the War of the *Utai*, as it is called, which was carried on till four of these *Utai* being defeated, the fifth, of the Family of *Tunga*, seized on the Empire in the Year DCXVIII. That in a short time afterwards the Empire was rent into many Factions, the Chiefs of which were called *Heutai*: And that at last the Family of *Sunga* rose to the Empire, and kept it in Possession till the Year MCCLXVIII, when the *Tartars* quite subverted it, and then it was that *Marco Polo* entered *China*. It follows then, that in the Year CCXXXVI of the *Hejra*, which is in the Year DCCCLI of Christ; and that in the Year CCLXIV of the former, which is the Year DCCCLXXVII of the latter, and which are the two chief Dates of our Authors; the Empire of *China* was embroiled by these several Wars of the *Heutai*, and from these Factions must arise the Comparison *Abu Zeid* makes between the Division of the *Chinese* Monarchy and that of *Alexander*, which, however, happens to be as inaccurate as every thing else the *Arabs* and *Persians* write concerning that great *Macedonian*. This may be sufficient to evince that our Authors had been well informed of these great Events, and that they consequently may claim our Belief, in some other points, which cannot be so happily made out.

What our Authors write of the Government of *China*, as being a metropolitan City, or the Capital of a Province, is distinguished from others, by five Trumpets of extraordinary Size, is not altogether confirmed by our modern Accounts; but it is, however, a thing to be found in some Authors, and may, it is likely, have been observed when this Mark of Dignity was in being.

The

Drums. L. 1. c. 6. The Drums they relate to have been in each City, are to this Day Ensigns of Distinction. *Navarrette* writes, that at *Nankin*, then the Royal City, there was a Drum for each Tribunal; that it is beaten to call the Magistrates to Council; and that the Drum belonging to the supreme Council is covered with the whole Hide of an Elephant, and that they beat it with a great Piece of Wood which hangs by Ropes. *Martini* relates, that before each Governor's Palace, there are two small Towers with musical Instruments and Drums, which are beaten when the Governor goes out, or comes in, or takes his Seat. Father *Magalhaes* speaks of that at *Pekin*, as of unusual Bulk, being no less than thirty six Foot in Circumference.

All the Cities are square, as is observed by the Fathers *Trigaut*, *Martini*, *Navarette*, and many others.

Our Author tells us the Governors of the great Cities are called *Disu*; that those of the smaller Towns, which Father *Martini* calls Cities, are *Tusang*; that the Eunuchs are titled *Tukan*, and the supreme Judge of each City, *Lakshi ma-mak-van*; and confess that they know not how to delineate these Titles in *Arabian* Characters. Pinto. Now, we find Traces of these same Names in our late Purch. Vol. Relations; for *Trigaut* calls one of the principal Magi- III. p. 276, strates *Toutam*, the same the *Dutch* call *Tontang*, in their p. 319. Embassy. Father *Martini* observes also, that in *Junnan*, Atl. p. 195. there are certain Lords called *Tuquon*, who are invested with an absolute Power; and, according to *Magalhaes*, the Princes of the Province of *Junnan*, *Queichu*, *Quamsi*, and *Sutchuen*, are called *Tuquon* or *Tusu*. The supreme Magistrate of Cities and Provinces is still called *Lipu*, whence, to all appearance, the *Arabs* formed their *Disu*, or *Cisu*, which is still a considerable Dignity.

Eunuchs. In the same modern Writings, we read also of Eunuchs invested with the most important Posts, and particularly P. 129. employed to receive the Customs in Cities. Father *Mar-* l. 3. *tini* mentions him of *Nankin*, as a great Officer; and Father *Trigaut* mentions him of *Linsing*, who was sent to receive the King's Revenues, and of another who su- Purch. perintended the Shipping. Father *Diego de Pantoja* de- 353. scribes the Pomp of the Eunuch *Mathan*, in a Letter of his; and Father *Trigaut* informs us there is a great Number of Eunuchs, who are so made by their own Fathers; *Quos castrant quam plurimi, ut inter regios Famulos an-*

numerari

umerari queant, nam præter hos, alii Regi non famulantur, nec à consiliis sunt, nec cum eo colloquuntur, quin imo tota fere regni administratio in semi-virorum manibus versatur. In fine, Father *Martini* in his History of the *Tartar* Wars, says, that the Emperor *Tianki* raised his Eunuch *Guei* to so mighty a pitch of Power, that he ruled the Empire with an arbitrary Authority, putting to death, and depriving of their Offices all such as were not agreeable to him. *P. 64.*

What our Author adds of the little Bell hung in each Palace, for those who desired to be righted by the Emperor, or the Sovereign Magistrate, when they could not obtain Justice at the Inferior Tribunals, is grounded upon a very ancient Custom, which is to be seen in Father *Martini*'s Life of the Emperor *Yvu*, who reigned MMCCVII Years before *Christ*; "He lent a ready Ear "to all those who offered to advise him concerning "his Duty; and ordered a Bell, a Drum, a Table "of Stone, a Plate of Iron, and of Lead to be fixed at the "Gate of his Palace, causing Proclamation at the same "time to be made, That all Persons of understanding "and approved Character might strike upon any "of these Instruments, each of which was appropriated "to particular Cases. They rang the Bell for what regarded "Justice; they beat the Drum for what concerned "the Laws, or Religion; they struck upon the "Leaden Plate when they wanted to speak on Matters "of State; upon the Stone Table, for Wrongs "committed by the Magistrates; and on the Plate "of Iron, for Prisoners." * *Little Bell.* *Hist. Sin. p. 52.*

* *Eos qui officii sui admonitum reprehendebant non minori facilitate audivit, quam, ut Sinica phrasi utar, aqua densum fluit. Hinc ante fores Palatii campanam, tympanum, tabellam lapideam, ferream, & plumbeam appendi jussit, addito Edicto, quo doctis & probis viris, qui de re aliqua monendum Imperatorem ducerent, potestas fiebat, ex his instrumentis illud pulsandi, quod cuique causarum generi esset destinatum. Qui justitia consultum ibant, ære campana: qui legibus ac religioni, tympano edebant sonum: si regni negotia forent, tabellam plumbeam si injuriæ à Magistratibus illatæ, lapideam, si de carcere & vinculis querelæ, ferream pulsabant.*

He adds, that this Emperor one day rose twice from Table, and that another time he went thrice out of the Bath to give Audience to those who requested it by these Signals. This same Custom still survives in *China*, according to Father *Couplet*, who, in his *Chronological Abridgment* says of this same King, "He "erected a Drum and a Bell at his Palace Gate, at "the Sound of which he went out to give Audience "to his Subjects, and this same Custom subsists to this "Day."

P. 4.

Buildings. The *Chinese* still build much after the same manner described by our Author; for the Inside of their Houses is Wood, and they particularly make use of the *Bamboo*, or split Cane for their Partitions, which they do over with their Varnish or *Glue Cié*, the Composition of which they have hitherto kept to themselves; so that we cannot be sure our Author is not out, when he says they make it of Hemp-seed. Their Houses, says Father *Martini*, are not magnificent, but they are more convenient and neat than ours. They are not fond of several Stories, because of the Trouble of getting up Stairs; and the Emperor of *China* fell a laughing, when he was first shewn the Plans of the *European* Palaces, and could not conceive how our Princes did to live in upper Stories. Every Body is in the lower Part of their Houses, which is divided into Rooms and Chambers. The Outside of their Houses is but sparingly adorned, if you except the grand Entrance and others smaller in the Front, which are magnificent in the Houses of the Wealthy: But the Inside is more embellished; every thing is done over with their precious *Cié*, and shines to a wonder, all their Walls being varnished therewith. The Houses are commonly Wood, and even the Royal Palace is the same, but the main Walls are Brick, and serve to divide the other Rooms from the Chambers; for the Roof and Covering is supported by wooden Pillars, just as Father *Trigaut* had said before in almost the very same Words.

Trig. l. 4. *p.* 403.

L. 1. *c.* 2. *p.* 14.

Tympanum & campanam ad Palatii valvas erigit, cujus pulsu suos auditurus prodeat, qui usus hodieque viget.

The

The ancient Custom of keeping a Watch every Night upon a very lofty Tower, to beat a Drum as a Signal when they saw Fire break out in any House, is a Proof of the dread they have always had of Fires in their great Cities. It is even Death for the Person to whose Negligence a Fire is owing, because of the Danger of its spreading among so much Wood. *Marco Polo* takes Notice of this same Custom in his Description of *Quinsai*, and says, they there watch every Night for fear of Fire, because most of the buildings are of Wood; and that the Watch strike upon Basons [*Gongs*] or great Boards, to give Notice thereof to the City.

Watchmen to look out for Fire. *Atlas Sin. P. 17.* *L. 2. p. 476.*

Some Alterations may have happened in their Marriages, and we are not exactly informed of their Notions of Relation or Parentage. Father *Trigaut* reports, they are not very scrupulous in observing the Degrees of Consanguinity on the Mother's side; but they are very cautious of marrying any Person that happens to have their own Surname, tho' in no degree related to them; this is observed by the other Writers, and Father *Couplet* has not forgot it in his *Abridgment*.

Marriages. 2 Account *p.* 24. *P.* 48.

In our Author's days there were public Couriers in several Parts of the *Mohammedan* Empire. Some of these went on Foot, as the Custom still is in the *Othman* [*Ottoman*] Empire, where all the Soltan's orders are conveyed by *Olacs* or Footmen, who being fixed at certain Stations, make incredible dispatch. The same there were in *China*; and if we may believe Father *Martini*, there are still the same, disposed at each Stone, a Stone containing ten *Chinese* Furlongs, or one of our Leagues, who forward the Dispatches of the King and Governors.

Couriers and Horses. 1 Account *p.* 11.

Moreover, it appears by the Testimony of *Abu Zeid*, that they had Post-Horses, or at least Mules; for the word *Berid* has this signification, and has for a long while been very much in use, to signify Horse Posts. The *Arabs* made use of these upon many important Occasions, just in the same manner as in other Places, but with this difference, that as Posts were originally set up for Public Affairs only, they were applied to no other uses among the *Mohammedans*, and the same it was among the *Chinese*. Father *Martini* observes of *China*, that at every eighth Stone, which ends a Day's Journey,

Atl. p. 13.

Journey; there are Royal Public-Houses called *Cung-quon* and *Ycli*, for the Accommodation of Governors and Magistrates, who are there entertained at the King's Expence, if they send but a Letter before them; and that there they are furnished with Carriages, and every other Conveniency; which comes pretty near to the *Evectio* of the *Romans*.

l. 2. c. 20. *Marco Polo* says, that in his time, there were Posts in *China*, and that they were settled from three Miles to three Miles, which is much the same Distance allowed by Father *Martini*: that these Places were visited once every Month, and that the Notaries or Clerks wrote down the Name of each Messenger, the Days of their Departure, and such like Circumstances.

Administration of Justice. What is related concerning their Administration of Justice, the Severity of their Tribunals, and many other parts of the *Chinese* Polity, needs no particular Illustration. Those who have perused the Modern Accounts of *China*, will perceive that our *Arabs* are not much out of the way in what they write of the same. All Business is there transacted by Petition, and in Writing; and Justice was severely administred in former Days, a notable Instance of which we have in the Story of the *Khorassanian* Merchant, who demanded and obtained Justice against the Eunuch, though the Emperor's Favorite.

But it seems that this ancient Severity is ill observed in these latter times; for whereas, our Authors affirm, Robbers were punished with Death without any hopes
l. 1. c. 8. of Reprieve, Father *Trigaut* acquaints us, that, in his time, they were only condemned to the Gallies, even after many Repetitions of their Crime; and that for the first Commission they only branded them with a hot Iron and Ink.

The Bamboo. The Punishment of the *Bamboo* was also in his time, inflicted for the slightest Offences, and almost without any Form, quite the Reverse of the ancient Usages;
l. 1. c. 9. but our Authors agree with the Moderns, in what regards the Severity and Manner thereof; and that the Criminal was beaten upon the Buttocks with great Canes, to so
Mart. Hist. Sin. p. 335. violent a degree, that it often deprived him of Life. It was the Emperor *Venius*, who first appointed this kind of Punishment, instead of another infinitely more cruel, of

of cutting the Criminal into Pieces. And hence, possibly it is, that our Authors say, the *Chinese* are such as were executed, which we do not read in our modern Accounts, and seems to be quite inconsistent with the *Chinese* Politeness. We are told indeed, by Father *Martini*, that the Empress *Vibia*, Wife to *Kieu*, the *Nero* of *China*, who began his Reign 1818 Years before Christ, ate human Flesh; but it is unnatural to suppose so detestable an Example could prevail into a Custom, in a Country so abundantly productive of every thing good for Food. *Marco Polo*, however, relates that in the Province of *Xandu*, they had this horrid Practice, and that when a Person is sentenced to death, they dress him and eat his Flesh; and says also, that in the Kingdom of *Concha*, they eat the Flesh of those who die a violent death, and particularly of their Enemies slain in Battel.

l. 1. c. 48.

l. 1. c. 55.

The manner how the Emperor and the Kings or Governors, who represent him, appear in public, is pretty much like what we are told of the same by our latest Accounts, wherein are many Descriptions of the Procession of a *Mandarin*: His Train is very numerous, and he is attended by a great number of Officers under Arms. First he is preceded by some with large *Bamboos*, wherewith they make much such a Noise as the Christians of the *Levant* make with the Boards they use instead of Bells: Every body must stop to do him Honour, and those on Horseback must dismount; nay, according to *Trigaut*, every one withdraws into his House. * "Many "other Ensigns of Dignity there are, says he, to distinguish the Magistrates; Streamers, Chains, Censers, "and a numerous Guard, who, by the Noise they make, "disperse the Croud. So great a Veneration do they require, that these Noises are no sooner heard, even in "the most crouded Streets, but every Soul disappears, "every body withdraws." As for the Emperor and Viceroys, they agree with all our Travellers, that it is

l. 1. c. 9.

* *Sunt alia per multa dignitatis ornamenta, Magistratuumque insignia, vexilla, catenæ, thuribula. Satellitium frequens, cujus clamoribus arcetur in vicis turba, & tanta est eorum veneratio, ut in vicis etiam frequentissimis nemo compareat, sed secedant ad hos ejulatus omnes.*

seldom they appear in public, and that, not till they have put their Guards under Arms, and posted them in the Avenues of the main Streets; and that formerly they never stirred out but in close Litters, of which they carried many at a time, that it might not be known in which the Prince rode. This is an ancient Custom since, the Emperor *Hoai* set the first Example of it, MMXL Years before Christ. *Navarette* relates of the Emperor, that,
P. 20. * "When he moves they shut all the Doors in the Streets "through which he is to pass, that every body keeps "within Doors, so that not a Soul is to be seen, and "that the Person who should shew his Head, would be "most severely chastised."

Imposts and Taxes. Our Authors tell us that the Emperor's Revenues provene from a Poll Tax, which is levied only upon Men, from eighteen Years to eighty, and that, in proportion to their Wealth: That Salt and Tea pay Duty also to the King, and that Land is unburdened by any Tax.
Atlas Sin. But if you consult Father *Martini*'s Estimates of what each Province pays to the Emperor of *China*, you will perceive that Matters are very much altered; for they each pay very considerable Tributes in Silk, Cotton, Stuffs, Provisions for his Table, and his Stables.
Mart. Hist. Sin. Salt is still taxed in part, but Tea is clear; and this *Gabelle* or Duty must be of very old standing, since King *Venius*, who reigned 179 Years before Christ, took it
l. 1. c. 3. off; but it was soon put on again. Father *Trigaut* observes, that in his time it brought great Sums into the Imperial Coffers; but at present, according to *Navarette*, Commodities pay no Duties, and the main branches of the Revenue are the Land-Tax, Poll Tax, and the Duties upon Salt, Silk, Stuffs, and a Tax upon Houses.
l. 1. c. 11. He says the Imperial Revenue exceeds sixty Millions, clear of all charges; and Father *Martini* who descends to particulars, runs it up to a higher amount. These Exaggerations were the cause why *Marco Polo* was nicknamed *Messer Marco Millioni*, and even some old Co-
P. 26. pies of his Book, are intitled, *Il Millione*. *Navarette* talks of above a hundred Millions.

---

* *Las puertas de las casas por cuyas calles ha de passar se cierran de todas, y la gente se recoge; de suerte que niun alma se ve, y si se viera, recibiera gravissima castiga.*

All

All the Money current in *China*, is still Copper, and nearly of the Size of our *Liards* or *Farthings*, and shaped as our Authors describe. The *Arabs* call them *Falus*, which signifies their Copper Money, and is derived from *Follis*, which had much the same Signification in the lower Empire. It has a Hole in the middle that it may be strung, in which manner they make up their Sums. It is rather a made Metal than Copper, and for Colour is not unlike our *Sols* with *Chinese* Characters on one side only, that having one side quite flat, they may be the more conveniently strung. These Pieces are to be seen in many Cabinets, and you have a representation of them, in *Tavernier*'s Travels; but he has made the Hole round, whereas it should be square, which is better adapted to keep them steady. In our *Second Account* we are told, that a thousand of these Pieces are worth a *Dinar* of Gold, which is exactly equal, in Weight, to the half *Pistole* of *Spain*. It appears therefore that the *Arabs*, who have always been subtle Traders, and who had of this Money at *Siraf*, kept it down at a very low Value, and at much less than it ought to have been in proportion to the Standard of the *Chinese* Gold and Silver, as it is now allowed by our Merchants; the Gold at forty two *Livres* per Ounce, and the Silver at fifty nine *Sols*, eight *Deniers*. *Money.*

Both ancient and modern Authors are agreed upon the Prohibition, which prevents Gold or Silver from being coined in *China*; and Father *Martini*, in the Life of *Venius*, who reigned 179 Years before Christ, expresses himself thus. * "Their Kings have never allowed Gold or "Silver to be coined into Money, thereby to obviate "the *Hist. Sin.* p. 328.

d 4

* *Nunquam eorum Regibus placuit vel argenteam cudi vel auream monetam, fraudis quibus ista gens assueta, lucrique sagacissima, praecaventibus. Solo pondere argenti vel auri valorem expendunt, & quatenus quidque mistum purumve sit, accuratissime dignoscunt. Quanquam auro nunquam utuntur ad emendum, quippe quod non pecuniam sed mercem esse dicunt. Hinc autem fit ut argentum continuo quasi tormento subjaceat, & in minutissima frusta, ferrea forcipe ad hoc apta difringatur ---- Cupream vero monetam* à

" the universal Frauds of the Nation, so greedy of Lu-
" cre. They take Gold and Silver by Weight, and
" know perfectly well whether it be fine or not. Ne-
" vertheless they sometimes purchase with Gold, but
" then it is reckoned as a Commodity, not as Money;
" whence it is that Silver is perpetually chopped to
" pieces, with a kind of Sheers contrived on purpose.
" But they have a long time had Copper-Money, which
" this Emperor brought to a better and more commodi-
" ous Form; and allowed it to be coined all over the
" Empire, provided it was good. For till this time it
" was struck no where but in the Palace, to the great
" Gain of the Emperor, but to the great Inconvenience
" of the People, because of the difficulty and length of
" the ways. He ordered it into a round Form, with a
" square Hole in the middle, that it might be strung
" the more conveniently. It is commonly marked with
" four Characters, which tell the Name of the Empe-
" ror, and the Value of the Piece." Father *Trigaut* writes to the same Purpose, and adds, that the same thing is observed to this Day; and the same is repeated by *Martini* in the beginning of his *Chinese Atlas*.

Porcelane. The fine Earth mentioned by our Author, must be that wherewith the *Porcelane* is made, particularly in the Territory of *Yaocheu*, the second City of the Province of *Kiangsi*; and is brought from the City of *Hoiecheu*, in the Province of *Nankin*, where they cannot work it up, as much as they have of it, which is thought to be owing to a difference in the Waters. Almost all this Ware in *China*, is made in the Town of *Feuloang*, by clumsy Country Fellows. They make some of it yellow, which is set apart for the Emperor. Great

---

à multo jam tempore habuere, quam hic Imperator ad meliorem commodioremque formam revocavit, ac concessit insuper ut ubique, modo sine fraude, in toto imperio cuderetur. Nam ante hæc tempora fiebat hoc in sola regia, magno quidem Imperatorum quæstu sed majori populorum incommodo, propter difficultates itinerum & distantiam locorum. Monetæ formam rotundam esse voluit, & in medio quadratum foramen, quo facilius filum insereretur. Insignitur quatuor plerumque literis, nomen Imperatoris, & impositum valorem significantibus.

Quantities

Quantities of it are also made in the Province of *Kiamsi*, according to *Trigaut* and *Martini*. Among the Articles *Macrizi* of a noble Present sent to *Nuroddin* by *Saladin*, soon *MSS.* after he became Master of *Ægypt*, mention is made *Arab.* of a Service of *China* Ware, consisting of forty Pieces.

Merchants What is in the same place said of their way of treating the Merchants they admitted into their Dominions, is not altogether conformable to the present Practice; but by our last Accounts, and particularly by the *Dutch Embassy*, we may perceive they have been very cautious how they suffered Strangers to enter among them. *Trigaut* insinuates that in his time it was customary to send the Emperor whatever was most curious in the Country. And their manner of visiting and stopping the Goods, and even the Presents the *Dutch* carried with them into *China*, is very agreeable to what we are told by our two Authors.

Funerals. As for their Funerals, they are almost still the same as formerly. *Martini* relates that they still mourn three *Hist. Sin.* Years for the Death of their Fathers, during which they *p.* 43. abstain from all public Business, and the Magistrates from their Employs. That they express their Grief, not by the coarseness of their Dress only, but that they also change their Table Service, their Bed, their Place, their Food, their manner of writing, their ways of speaking, their Paper, their Ink, and their Name; and then they put on white. They mourn three Years by way of Acknowledgment to their Parents, who administred to all their Wants and Imbecilities, during the three first Years of their Infancy, and Father *Trigaut* has the very same Customs described by our Author. * "Children oftentimes keep the dead *l.* 1. *c.* 7. "Bodies of their Parents three or four Years, shutting "them up in Coffins, which they do over with their "Varnish in such a manner that no offensive Smell can "come forth; and during all this time they set Meat "before them just as if they were alive."

---

* *Non raro filii parentum cadavera feretro inclusa ad tres quatuorve annos domi asservant, suo enim illo pellucido bitumene ita rimas ilinunt, ut minime fœtorem transmittant. Quo tempore in singulos dies, cibum illis potumque offerunt, non secus ac si superessent.*

This

This Custom of setting Meat and Drink before their Dead, which *Abu Zeid* harps upon; is to this Day the Practice; and, by *Tavernier*, is a Custom still in force with the *Chinese* at *Batavia*.

Trig. p. 78. The Expences the *Chinese* are still at in burying their Parents, are very extraordinary; for they put them into Coffins of a precious Wood, which sometimes cost two thousand Crowns. They invite all their Relations and Friends to pay their last Duties to the departed Person, during the time the Body is in the Coffin, and expend great Quantities of precious Perfumes, Flowers, and other different Things, which those who come, offer as a Sacrifice to the Soul of their deceased Friend or Relation. They light up Tapers, and they sometimes burn rich Stuffs, under a Notion of sending them to the dead Man: All this must naturally cause a vast Expence, without reckoning the Funeral Procession, when they have always a great Number of Bonzes, Minstrels, and Mourners.

Writing common. All the *Chinese* can write and read; this is confirmed by the common Concurrence of all Authors, ancient and modern; and what is said afterwards, that all Business is transacted in Writing, is, to all Appearance, the chief Reason thereof. *Martini* attributes this to the Emperor *Sivenius*, who began his Reign 73 Years before Christ, and the Reason he alledges for it, was to the end that Judges might the more maturely weigh the Cases brought before them, and might not be confounded by the Noise and empty Babble of the Parties concerned. All Accounts agree in what is said of the great number of their public Schools, which is so much the greater, as one Master cannot instruct above three or four Scholars.

(l. 9. p. 390.)

Alms. What our Authors observe of the Subsistance the poor receive from the Emperor's Granaries in times of a general Dearth, is very remarkable, and *Marco Polo* expresses himself in almost the same Terms. He says that at such times, the Emperor claims no dues, but, on the contrary, administers to the Wants of his Subjects, and supplies them with Corn for their Subsistance, and to sow their Ground. That to this purpose the great *Khan* in times of Plenty, buys up great Quantities of Corn, which he keeps in Store-Houses for three or four Years together

together, and that in times of Dearth, he ſells it out at ſo low a rate, that he gives four Meaſures at a Price, which would purchaſe but one of the ſame at Market.

In the ſame Author you may read alſo of the very extraordinary Alms, the great *Khan*, who was then Emperor of *China*, gave to the Poor, which as *Navarette* avers, drew on a Debt, many Millions of which, do ſtill ly heavy upon the Emperor's Houſehold.

Manner of receiving Merchants

What is ſaid by our Authors, of their Behaviour to foreign Merchants, may have been formerly the caſe, and their Cuſtom of ſearching all their Goods, and of taking them as a Pledge, is obſerved by ſeveral Writers. *Joſeph Barbaro*, who met a *Tartar* from *China* at the Court of *Perſia*, ſays, that the Merchants, immediately upon their Arrival, carry their Effects to Ware-Houſes, and thoſe, whoſe Buſineſs it is, coming to ſearch them, and finding any thing that may be acceptable to the Prince, take it and pay for it in other Goods. *P. 107.*

ILLUS-

ILLUSTRATIONS

ON THE

NATURAL HISTORY

Contained in the Foregoing Accounts.

OUR two Authors agree with the most sincere Travellers, as to the great abundance of every thing necessary for Life, or that can administer to Luxury in the Country of *China*. It produces Wheat, Rice, and many other sorts of Grain; it produces Apples, Pears, Quinces, Lemons, Citrons, *Mousa's* or *Indian* Figs or *Banana's*, Sugar-Canes, Figs, Grapes, Cucumbers, *Citruls*, Walnuts, *Pistachio's*, Plumbs, Abricots, Services, Coco-Nuts, and even Almonds, according to our Author; but therein he varies from *Martini*, who observes that there are no Almonds in *China*, nor Olives, which is confirmed by other Authors.

Trig. l. 1. c. 3. They have all sorts of Cattle, and particularly Beasts of Service. Many Horses they have, but, formerly they were not to compare with the *Arabs*; and indeed till the last Conquest by the *Tartars*, who brought great numbers of their Horses into *China*, the *Chinese* Cavalry was of no worth; for their Horses could not bear the sight, nor even the Neighing of the *Tartar* Breed.

Our

Our Authors say there are no Elephants in *China*, which must be understood of the Provinces they knew, where, in truth, there are none. Father *Martini* writes, that they begin to be met with at *Nanning*, in the Province of *Quangli*, where the Inhabitants use them for War and for Carriage. Some there are also in the Province of *Junnan*; nor is it a wonder that these Creatures, who so swarm in the *Indies*, and in *Tungkin* or *Tonquin*, should straggle hither. *Atl. Sin. p. 183.*

All our Travellers report with our Authors, that there are no Lions in *China*; this, *Trigaut*, *Martini*, and many others, affirm: But as it would be endless to insist upon every particular of this kind, the following Remarks shall be confined to what our Authors say of two very rare and extraordinary Animals, the Unicorn, and That which yields Musk.

The Unicorn.

By the Word or *Appellative* Unicorn, we understand a Creature, which the *Arabs*, and other Orientals, call *Karkandan*, the same with the *Monoceros* of the Ancients. Our Author says he is much smaller than the Elephant; that from the Neck downwards he is not unlike a Bufflar; that his Hoof is not cloven; and that his fore Legs are all of a piece and jointless, which seems incredible, and to contradict what both Ancients and Moderns have told of his Swiftness. He adds that the lowing of the Unicorn, is between the lowing of the Ox, and the Cry of the Camel. Now Father *Jeronymo Lobo*, and other Jesuits, who have lived some Years in *Ethiopia*, aver they have seen of these Creatures in the Province of *Agaos*, in the Kingdom of *Damota*, and describe them to this Effect: This Creature is about as big as a middle-sized Horse, of a dark brown, with a black Tail and Main, the Main short and thin. They add that in other parts of this same Province, they saw others with a thicker and longer Main, and with a strait Horn of five Palms in length, and of a whitish cast; and that they are eternally in the Woods, being very timorous, and never venturing themselves abroad in open places. Father *Lobo* relates that many of the *Portuguese* had seen them also in *Ethiopia*, and that from the tops of Rocks, they discovered them passing along in Herds in the Valleys of the Province of *Nanina*: and this he attested to Mr. *Toinard*, who saw him at *Lisbon* in the Year

MDCLXVII

This whole Account is to be found in the 4. vol. of Thevenot's *Collection of Voyages.*

MDCLXVII. He told him that some were white, and others Bay, with a white Horn in the Forehead a Yard long; and that he had a Colt of this same kind that lived but eight or ten Days, for want of its Dam to suck.

What the *Nubian Geographer* writes of this Animal, is almost wholly taken from our two Authors, with some Additions, as the Custom is with the *Arabs*, who seldom transcribe a Passage exactly, but are for ever adding what they find elswhere. Most of their Authors tell wonders of this Creature, though perhaps from a very slender Knowledge of him. The Testimony also of *Cosmas* the Monk, in his *Christian Topography* must not be omitted. This Writer owns he never saw the Unicorn himself, but assures us he saw four Brass Figures of him in the King of *Ethiopia*'s Palace, called *the four Towers*; that they told him this Creature was terrible and untractable; and that when he was closely pursued by the Hunters, and on the brink of falling a Prey to them, he would throw himself down Precipices, and fall upon his Horn, which stood all the Shock of the Fall. To this Creature he applies many passages in Scripture.

In Thevenot's *Collect. vol.* 1.

In *Anselm de Boot*'s Treatise, you have the chief of the Observations made upon the Unicorn by the Ancients. He remarks that the Name *Monoceros*, which corresponds with the Name *Unicorn*, is common to five different Animals; the *Indian Beeves*, described by *Pliny*; the *Rhinoceros*, an Animal of a particular *Genus*; the *Monoceros* of *Pliny*, of the size of a Horse, with the Head of a Stag, the Feet of an Elephant, and the Tail of a wild Boar; the *Indian* Ass of the same *Pliny*; and the *Oryx* with a split Horn, often mentioned by *Aristotle*, *Ælian*, and the other Naturalists.

All these several Creatures have but one Horn, and what the curious preserve under the Denomination of the Unicorn's Horn, may be the Spoil of one or other of these kinds; but to these we may also add, the Horns of the Nothern Fish, called *Morss*, which are of extraordinary length; and the Horns also of the *Sea-Cow*, who sometimes comes to land, and is described by *Martini*. Most of our modern Writers will have it that the Horns in our Cabinets are not of the Unicorn, but the Teeth of this Fish, in the North particularly; or else some of those

those fossil Horns described by *Anselm de Boot*; whence many have pronounced there are no true Unicorns Horns, and that we must search the Sea for these long-horned Creatures, rather than the Land. In *de la Pereyre* Account of *Greenland*, you have on this Head many curious Observations, which were communicated to him by *Wormius*. By them it is demonstrated that these Horns have all the Marks of the Teeth of a Fish the *Ice-landers* call a *Narhual*, the same, perhaps, our Author calls a *Wal*; that they are carious at the Root, almost like rotten Teeth; and that the Sea throws up great Quantities of them upon the Shores, a plain Proof that they come from an Inhabitant of the Water. In the same Book you have a Representation of the *Cranium* of this Fish, and those who have treated of *Ice-land* concur with the Observations of *Wormius*. But all this can only prove, that most of the Horns supposed to come from the Unicorn are the Spoils of a Fish, not that there is no such Creature as we have a Notion of when we mention the Unicorn, in Scripture called *Reem*; where also he is frequently set forth as an Animal rare to be seen, vigorous, and wonderfully fleet and strong. Thus almost is it that the *Arabs* and *Persians* express themselves of their *Karkandan*. *Louis Barthema* P. 151. says he saw two at *Mecca*, sent thither as a Present from the King of *Ethiopia*; Since therefore we have some credible Authors, who profess to have seen this Creature, and since our *Arabs* even say that they have eaten of his Flesh, we seem to want something more than bare Conjecture to satisfy us, with some of the Moderns, that there never were any other Unicorns than the *Narhuals*; for this Fish is as uncommon in the East, as the Unicorn is in the North and the West.

Those who would be more amply informed of what the Ancients have written concerning the Unicorn, may find their Words most faithfully cited by *Bochart* in his *Hierozoicon*, as also some Passages from *Arabian* Writers concerning the same, and particularly from *Damiri*, whom he calls *Demir*, who being but a late Author, seeing he died in the Year MCCCCV, has compiled all that had been said by those who went before him. You have also a great Number of curious Observations upon the same Subject in *Thomas Bartholinus*'s Dissertation, printed at *Padua* in the Year MDCXLV, as well as in that of *Deusingius*, printed at *Groningen* in the Year MDCLX.

Our

Amber. Our Authors thought, with some of the ancients, that Ambergreese grows like a Plant at the Bottom of the Sea, and that it is thrown on the Shore by the Swell; and that pieces of it are to be found in the Belly of Whales. The oldest of them having first observed, that among the *Maldives* they found Lumps of Ambergreese of extraordinary Size, adds, that it was also found in smaller pieces, almost in the Form of Plants torn up; that in Storms it was forced up from the Bottom; that the Wave washed it to the Shore, and that there it is found in the Form of a Mushroom or Truffle. The other says, that the best of it is found upon the Coast of *Barbary*, or the Country of *Zinge*, that is of the *Cafres* on the East Coast of *Afric*, and even on the Coast of *Arabia*; That the Negroes train up Camels to go along shore with them by Moon-light; That these Camels know the Amber, and when they discovered any, bend their Knees, that their Master may pick it up; That there is another sort of Ambergreese, which floats upon the Surface of the Sea; That a great Fish of the Whale-kind swallows it, and immediately dies; and that when the Negroes see him dead upon the Water they know that he has Amber in him, and that they go off to him, and find it in his Belly; both of them adding, that the best Amber is of a whitish Colour.

Vid. Barbos. p. 313.

Serapion, *Avicen*, and others since them, concur with the principal Observations of our Authors. They say it comes from the Sea, but not as a Plant, according to *Avicen*, but in Veins, which does not seem at all likely. He confirms, that Quantities of it are collected on the Coasts, and that That called *Shelaheti* is the best; this, in the old Translation, being rendered *Selachitum*, the learned *Garcias de Orta* imagined that *Ceylon* was thereby pointed at; for the Sea is very liberal of this precious Substance to that Island: But it was thus denominated from the Sea of *Shelahet*, which, according to our Authors, is beyond Cape *Comorin*, and divided from the Sea of *Harkand*, by those great Islands, which must be *Java* and its Neighbours.

L. 2, *c.* 143. *p.* 233. The Commentator upon *Avicen*, cited by *Plempius*, assures us that Amber grows in the Sea like a Plant; *Serapion* will have it to grow upon Rocks: *Simeon Sethi* relates

lates that it rises in Springs like Pitch and Bitumen; but is mistaken when he adds, that it is found ἐν τινι ἰνδι-χῆ πόλει σελάχετον ὀνομαζομένῃ *In an* Indian *City called* Selachet; for, as we have observed it is the Name of the Coast washed by the Sea of *Shelabet*. These Passages in *Avicen* and *Simeon Sethi*, shew that the Sea of *Shelabet* was not unknown in their Days. The Town of *Arabia the Happy*, which he calls Σύγχριον, is *Sichar*, where also, according to our Authors, it is washed on Shore by the Wave.

The Opinion of those who believe Amber is found in Whales, or in other great Fishes of the Cetaceous kind, is, by most of the Moderns, rejected; because there is no where less Amber found than on the principal Coasts of the *Whale-Fishery*; and because the *Basques* and the *Bretons*, who are almost always out a Fishing, confirm not the Testimony of the Ancients. Again, by the Dissections that have been made of several Whales, it is proved that their Throat is not wide in Proportion to their Body; tho' possibly Amber may have been found in some of the great Fish of a voracious Nature, as well as many other foreign Substances, which they greedily snap at and swallow. But this amounts not to a Proof that they have any particular Gust for Ambergreese, which is by no means a food proper for them; and it is still less to be supposed they would seek after a Thing that must prove fatal to them, a very Poison, if true it be, as our Authors take it, that the Fish dies upon swallowing this Amber; for the natural Instinct of Animals prompts them to such Things as are good for them, and deters them from such as are hurtful. It is therefore more likely that Ambergreese is found naturally in the Sea; that it is not voided as an Excrement by the Whale or any other of the cetaceous Tribe; and that if at any time they are found to have Amber within them, which at present is very seldom, it must be considered as a mere accident against the common Course of Nature, and the Instinct of Animals.

Garc. de Orl. l. 1. *c.* 1. *Scalig. Exerit.* 204 *n.* 10.

There are two other Opinions, which carry a greater Air of Probability with them, and seem to confirm each other. The *First* is that Amber is not a Plant at the Bottom of the Sea, but is generated thus;

Upon the East Coast of *Afric*, and in some Parts of the *Indian* Ocean, there are craggy Rocks or Precipices, which swarm with wild Bees, who there make their Honey in Clefts as in natural Hives. Now they say that this Honey, either dissolved by Heat, or blown away by Winds, or washed down by Rains, drops into the Sea, where it assumes a new Form, and changes its Nature; for that the Saltness of the Sea elaborating the whole Mass, hardens it, purifies it, and gives it the agreeable Scent of Amber. That hence it is it smells somewhat like Honey when it happens to be picked up soon after it comes from Sea, and that the Spoils of Bees are found in or upon it; and to crown all, this is a pretty generally received Opinion among the Inhabitants of the Coasts most favored with Presents of this kind. Thus thinks *Not. in Guilst. p. 542. l. 2. c. 23.* *Gentius* a learned *Dutchman*, who herein agrees with what other Authors write, as that it comes from Rocks, or Islands, and that it is perfected in the Sea.

It is not without Ground that *Gentius*'s Opinion appears so probable to some of the Learned. The Whiteness of Amber, inclining to the Grey, borders somewhat upon the Colour of Honey; and certain it is, that the Spoils of Bees and the Bills of small Birds which are sometimes found in Bits of Amber, are far from weakning this Conjecture. All the Difficulty is how to conceive, that Bees should be able to make Combs of such extraordinary Size as to be equal to some Lumps of Amber that have been formerly found upon the Shore, and even in our own Days. For it is not very natural to suppose that these Combs, falling into the Sea, should combine into Pieces of fifteen, twenty, and thirty Pound Weight; or into Heaps of such Bulk that a small Vessel might have been laden therewith; nay, a Number of Ships, if we can add Faith to the *English Edition. 168. l. 1. p. 20.* Report of a *French* Captain mentioned in the History of the *English* Royal Society.

Teixeira writes that in the Year 1696. a Piece of Amber was seen, near *Brava* on the East Coast of *Afric*, of so unusual a Size, that a Man mounted upon a Camel could not be discovered behind it.

A ship from *Mosambique*, once dropped an Anchor upon a great Piece of Amber, and the same Thing hapned to another near Cape *Currents*.

The same Author speaks of a Piece of Amber of twenty Pounds Weight thrown up between the Rivers *Linda* and *Quilima*; of another washed on Shore u on the Coast of *Malabar*, which the Inhabitants mistaking for Pitch payed their Barks with. Captain *Keeling* was told by the Moors at *Delisa*, that upon the Coasts of *Monbaça*, *Magadoxo*, *Pata*, and *Brava*, there were Pieces of Ambergreese of twenty Quintals. *L. 1. c. 28.* *Purch. Vol. I. p. 193.*

Tavernier confirms what our Authors advance, saying, that great Quantities of Ambergreese are gathered on the Coast of *Melinda*, and that the Governors of *Mosambique* negociate it with *Goa* to the Amount of great Sums. He relates also that it has been found in Lumps of extraordinary Size, and gives you two Instances thereof, of one that weighed twenty Pounds, and of another that weighed Forty-two. *Vide. T. 2. l. 2. c. 23.*

In the History of *Saladin* we read that among the Presents he sent to *Soltan Nuroddin*, there were two Pieces of Ambergreese, the one of Twenty, the other of thirty Pound weight. Many Examples we have of Pieces of Amber of very great Bulk like that found towards Cape *Comòrin* in the Year MDLV. which weighed three Thousand Pound; but what *Rabbi David de Pomis* advances, that Amber was found in the *Jordan*, and that it was an Ingredient in the Perfumes of the old *Law*, is a meer Fable; for unless we grant that Amber was there found by a Miracle we must reject what he says in this respect, especially as he has not the Concurrence of one single Author to support him. The *Jews* say, that the Word *Kifat*, in their *Talmud*, signifies an odoriferous Plant, and not Amber, as the Moderns have thought. It does not appear that the Ancients had any Knowledge of this Perfume. *Dict. Hebrai.*

Joam dos Santos has many particulars concerning Amber, and most of them confirm what our Authors say; he reports it to grow at the Bottom of the Sea, whence it is torn up by Storms; and that at such times the *Cafres* never fail to be along Shore in quest of it, to sell it to the *Portuguese* and the *Moors*. Moreover, that there are three Sorts of it, the first very white, *Hist. de Ethiop. Orient. l. 1. c. 28.*

the ſecond of a greyiſh caſt, and called *Maxueyra*, and the third black like Pitch, ſoft, and often ill ſcented, becauſe as the Inhabitants report, Wales and other Fiſhes, and even Birds ſwallow it as often as they ſee it floating on the Surface. The *Cafres* called *Fumos*, near the Land of *Natal*, ſeeing ſome of the People belonging to a *Portugueſe* Ship called the St. *Thomas*, who was loſt in her homeward-bound Paſſage, cryed out to them to throw away what they had picked up, ſaying it was a Poiſon which dryed up thoſe who collected it ſo that they dyed.

Of Musk. *Abu Zeid* the Author of our ſecond Account, is particular enough in his Deſcription of the Creature which affords Muſk. He ſays he is like the Roe-buck; that his Skin and Colour is the ſame; his Legs ſlender; his Horn ſplit and a little bending; that he has two ſmall white Teeth on each ſide, of the Length of half a Finger, or a little leſs; that they are ſtrait and riſe above the Muzzle of the Creature, almoſt like the Elephant's Teeth; in ſhort, that this it is that diſtinguiſhes him from other Roe-Bucks. This Deſcription does not much vary from what we read in the beſt Authors; for *Avicen* ſpeaking of Muſk, according to the Tranſlation of *Plempius*, ſays, *Eſt Cyſtis ſeu folliculus animalis, ipſi capreæ non abſimilis caninos duos dentes candidos exertos gerentis & introrſum reflexos, inſtar cornuum.* You have two Repreſentations of this Animal, the one in the Fragment of *Coſmas*, printed in the firſt Volume of *Thevenot*'s Collection, the other in the ſecond Volume of *Tavernier*'s Travels. Theſe are exactly alike, but they differ in two Articles from the Deſcription *Abu-Zeid* gives us; for they put no Horns on the Head of this Creature, and make the two Teeth which diſtinguiſh him from the Roe-Buck to turn downwards, inſtead of pointing upwards like the lower Teeth of the Elephant, according to *Abu-Zeid*'s Compariſon, in which he is ſupported by the Teſtimony of *Avicen* and *Serapion*, cited by *Matthiolus*. *Marco Polo* deſcribes the Muſk-creature to this effect; " His Skin is very coarſe like that of " the Stag; in his Feet and Tail he reſembles the " *Gazelle*, and, like her, has no Horns. He has " four Teeth, two above, three Fingers long, fine, and

" as

"as white as Ivory; two that rise up, and two that "turn down; and he is beautiful to the Eye. In the "full of the Moon he has an Imposthume which takes "him on the Belly near the Navel; and then the "Hunters go out and cut this Imposthume *".

Barbosa writes, that he nearest resembles the *Gazelle*, but differs from the others in saying his Coat is white; for these are his Words; *Musk is found in small white Creatures like* Gazelles, *with Teeth like an Elephant but smaller. These Creatures are subject to a Kind of Imposthume under the Belly and the Breast, and when the Contents are ripened, they are taken with such an Itching, that, for Relief, they rub themselves against the Trees, and what falls in small Drops or Grains is the most perfect and the most exquisite Musk.*

Thevenot's Description is still wider from the rest, he writes that *in those Countries there is a Creature with the Muzzle of a Fox, and not bigger than a Hare. For Colour he is like the Stag, and has Teeth like a Dog; and produces the most excellent Musk. He has an Excrescence or Bladder under the Belly, full of corrupted Blood, and and it is this Blood which makes Musk, or rather that is the Musk itself. They take this from him, and immediately clap a Piece of Leather upon the Mouth of the Bladder that none of the Scent may evaporate; but the Creature dyes soon after this Operation. Antony Pigafetta*, who says that Musk is the Cuttings of a Cat, cannot be allowed to agree with the rest foregoing. *Par.* 3. p. 149.

Father *Philip di Marini*'s Description is also different from what the others write; for he reports this Creature to have the Head of a Wolf, and Father *Kircher* in the Figure he gives, represents him with the Snout *Chin. Illustr.* p. 191.

* *Ha i peli a similitudine di cervo molto grossi, li piedi & la coda a modo della Gazella, no ha corne como la Gazella: ha quatro denti, cioe due della parte di sopra, lunghi ben tre dita e sortili, bianchi come avolio, e due ascendono in su, e due descendono in giu, & e bello animale da vedere. Nasce a questa bestia quando la Luna e piena, nel umbilico sotto il ventra un apostema di sangue, & i cacciaori nel tondo della Luna, escono fueri a prender de ditti animali, e tagliano questa postema.*

of a Hog, which may be the Ingraver's Fault, who furnishes him with Claws also, whereas he has a cloven Hoof. *Simeon Sethi* errs still farther from Truth, by representing him to be as big as the Unicorn, and to be even of that Genus or Tribe; but hear his Words *. *The baser Sort Musk is that which is brought from the Indies, which is blackish; and the worst of all is that which comes from* China. *All this Musk is formed in the Navel of a very large Creature which has but one Horn, and is like the Roe-Buck. In rutting time a Quantity of thick Blood gathers about his Navel, and causes a Tumor, attended with such anguish that, during the Time, he can neither eat nor drink. He rowls himself upon the Ground, and frees himself of this Tumor, full of turbid Blood, which clotting a considerable Time afterwards, aquires a good Scent.*

All Authors then agree as to the Manner it is formed in the Excresence or Bladder, or in the Tumor which gathers about the Navel of the Creature in rutting time; and there are few that do not confirm what is said of the Way the *Chinese* have of sophisticating it, by mixing therewith the Blood of the Creature, or some other Things which debase the Substance of it, or by putting little Bits of Lead into the Bladders or Cods, that they may weigh the heavier.

It seems that the Musk which runs from the Wound of the Creature when he rubs himself against the Stones, was prized by the Ancients at the highest Rate, as is observed by our Author, *Serapion,* and some others. That what was found in the Tumor itself before it was

* Τούτου δὲ ἥττων ὁ ἀπὸ τῆς Ἰνδίας μετακομιζόμενος· ῥέπει δὲ ἐπὶ τὸ μελάντερον, καὶ τούτου πάλιν ὑποδεέστερος ὁ ἀπὸ τῶν Σινῶν ἀγόμενος. Πάντες δὲ ἐν ὀμφαλῷ ἀπογεννῶνται ζώου τινὸς μονοκέρατος μεγίστου, ὁμοίου δορκάδι. Οἰστρεσμα ἐς γὰρ τὸ τοιοῦτον ζῶον ὀγκοῦται τὸν ὀμφαλὸν παχυμεροῦς αἵματος ἐν τούτῳ συναγομένου καὶ τηνικαῦτα νομῆς καὶ πότου ἀπέχεται, καὶ κυλίεται ἐπὶ γῆς, καὶ ἀποβάλλει τὸν ὀμφαλὸν αἵματος πλήρη βορβορώδους, ὅπερ πηγνύμενον, μετά τινα καιρὸν ἱκανὸν ἐπικτᾶται εὐωδίαν.

broken,

broken, was reckoned of least value, because not perfectly ripe; and the Merchants of our times always make this Distinction.

Father *Martini* speaks thereof to this purpose; *to the End that you may no longer be at a Loss to know what Musk is, I will declare what I have more than once seen with my own Eyes; it is a Lump at the Navel of a Creature like a Purse, made of a very delicate Pellicle, and covered with very fine Hair.* The *Chinese* call this Creature *Xe* from whence the Word *Xahicang*, that is the *Odour* or *sweet Scent* of this Creature *Xe* which signifies Musk. He is a Quadruped, and is not very unlike a little Stag, except that his Coat inclines more to be black, and that he has no Horns. *Teixeira* says, he is like a *Gazelle*, and that his Coat is like the Tiger's. *Atl. Sin. p.* 58.

A great Quantity of Musk is found in the Province of *Xensi*, at *Hangchung*, at *Cungchang*, at *Queichu* in the Province of *Suchuen*, in the Province of *Junnan*, and in some others, particularly in those conterminous with *Tibet*, where these Creatures most abound. *p.* 110.

According to our same Author, the Musk of *Tibet* is the most exquisite of all; because of the aromatic Pastures this Creature finds in *Tibet*, and not in *China*. *Probatissimus* say *Avicen, si regionem spectes, est Tebetius, sive Tumbascinus*, that is, the Country of *Tumgage* which the *Arabs* take to be a Province of *China*. *Simeon Sethi* for want of understanding the Geography of these distant Parts, says that the best Musk is that which comes from a City a great Way to the Eastward of *Chorassan* and called *Toupat*. A *Greek* Author, cited by *Lambecius*, calls it ταπὰτ; for thus is it the Orientals commonly pronounce what we write *Tibet*. From this Text *Ruellius*, who understood it not, has read τȣ̃ πὰτ, and writes that the best Musk is called *Pat*. *Serapion* observes also that the best Musk is from *Tibet*, for the very same Reasons already alledged.

All the Ancients then and Moderns agree, that the most exquisite Musk is that of *Tibet*, or as others call it *Tumgage*; and this because of the *Aromatic* Pastures in that Land, such as are no where else to be found. That the *Indian* Musk comes next in degree of fineness, if so we may term what was brought to *Cabul*, and the other trading Towns of the *Indies*, by Merchants who trafficked with it by Land from *China*, and dispersed it all over the East. That the *Chinese* Musk is the worst of all, not only because the *Chinese* adulterate it several ways, but also because what is produced naturally in that Kingdom, is not comparable to what is in *Tibet*. All this is confirmed by the Testimony of the learned *Golius*, and Father *Martini*. *Teixeira* says, the Musk that does not come from *China*, is always the best; and that the reason is, because *no llega a las manos de los Chinas, cuiyo animo no sufre dexar alguna cosa en su pureza*.

Not. Afragan. p. 865.

At present the Kingdom of *Boutan* is the greatest Mart for Musk: This must have been a part of the ancient *Tibet*, or Country subject to the *Khan* of *Tibet*, and thence it is that the *Indian* Merchants fetch the best sort of this Perfume, whether in the Bladder or Cod, or out of it.

Tavernier vol.. 2. l. 2. c. 24.

Tea.

Our Author is the oldest and almost the only *Arab* that mentions the *Chinese* Drink, so universal in our Days over *Europe*, and known by the Name of *Tea*. But this is not the Name he gives it; for he calls it *Cha*, which comes nearer to the true *Chinese* Name, *Chah* or *Chaw*, than the Name we have for it. He says that it is an Herb or Shrub, more bushy than the Pomegranate-Tree, of a more taking Scent, but somewhat bitter to the Taste. That the *Chinese* boil Water and pour it scalding hot upon this Leaf, and that this Infusion preserves them from all Distempers. This, we own, is an imperfect Description, but is plain enough to evince that nothing can hereby be meant but the Plant we know by the Name of *Tea*, the same with the *Tcha Catayi*, or *Sini* of the Orientals. The Tree which bears this Leaf is but small, and must be classed with Shrubs, being no bigger than a small Pomegranate Bush; and even the Leaf of the one and the other are not much unlike. It has a pleasant kind of a violet Scent, is bitter to the Taste, and it is common for those who are fond of it, to imagine it does them good, and keeps them in Health. It is certain then, that Father *Trigaut* is mistaken when he imagines it is but of late date among the *Chinese*, because there is not, as he says, any Character in their Tongue to signify this Drink; for by the Testimony of the oldest of our Authors, who does not speak of it as any new thing, but as an Herb very much in vogue with them, nay, to that degree,

L. 1. p. 16.

degree, that the Emperor thought fit to lay a Duty upon it, and to reſerve all the Profits of it to himſelf; by this Teſtimony I ſay, it appears that the *Chineſe* have been addicted to it above eight hundred Years; nor is it poſſible to believe with *William Piſo*, that it grew a long time wild and uncultivated, or that the *Chineſe* and *Japaneſe* have been but lately acquainted with its Vertues and the manner of preparing it, and with all the Advantages it is of, Advantages which are diſcovered daily more and more. This he ſays he was told by ſome *Dutch* Commanders, who had been a long time in the Country.

Father *Martini*, who has written more accurately of *China* that any other Perſon whatſoever, has no ſuch Obſervations upon the uſe of this Leaf, which muſt make the reſt look very ſuſpicious and doubtful. He ſays it grows particularly in the Province of *Kiangnan* or *Nankin*, where the beſt of it is. It is, adds he, a ſmall Leaf perfectly like that of the *Rhus Coriarius*, or *Sumac* of the *Curriers*. I believe it is even of the ſame kind therewith; however, it grows not wild, but is domeſtic and cultivated: Nor is it a Tree but a Shrub which ſpreads out in little Branches, with a Bloſſom very much like that of the *Sumac*, except that the former inclines more to be yellow than the latter. It blows firſt in Summer, when it emits no great Scent, then follows a Berry which is firſt green, and aftewards blackiſh. In the Spring it is that they gather the Leaf to make their *Cha*, for then it is the moſt ſucculent and tender. The Preparation of theſe Leaves conſiſts in gathering them, drying them by a ſlow Fire, rolling them upon a Cotton Mattreſs, and in packing them up in Tin Cheſts or Boxes, for the ſake of preſerving them, and the convenience of tranſporting them. This Deſcription does not exactly ſquare with that of Father *Alexander de Rhodes*, and Father *di Marini*, in their Accounts of *Tonquin*, and ſtill leſs with thoſe of *James Bont*, and *William Piſo*, in his Additions to the fifth Book of his Hiſtory; for he relates from what he was informed by the Sieur *Caron*, who was a conſiderable time in *China* and *Japan*; *That this Plant grows no where but in* China, Japan, *and* Siam, *ſprouting up to about the Height of the Roſe-Buſh of* Europe. *That the Stem and all the Branches*

Branches are covered with Blossoms, and little peeked Leaves indented all round, all in the same form, but of different size, so that they are of five different sorts. The greatest grow on the lower Branches, whence they diminish upward to the very top of the Bush. The smaller the Leaves are the more they are worth; so that a Pound of the largest shall sell but for five Pence, while that of the second size shall be worth fifty, those of the third size five Florins, of the fourth size, fifteen, and the fifth and least size of them, shall sell from one hundred to one hundred and fifty Florins the Pound. The same Author has it, that the Blossom of this Tree is white, and not unlike to the *Eglantine*, except that it has a different Scent. But it were a fruitless Task to insert other Descriptions on this head, which vary from these. This Leaf is now so well known in *Europe*, that we may judge for our selves, that it bears no likeness to the *European Sumac*, whose Leaf and Flower are extremely different. The several sizes of this Leaf according to which the Price is regulated, are by no means peculiar to this Shrub: but the difference of the Value is according to the time when it is gathered, whether when it first sprouts out, or after it has been some time upon the Stalk. Of the budding Leaf is the most exquisite Tea made, very little of which comes to us in *Europe*; the Flower is what is most universally esteemed, and is properly the *Chaw*. The fineness of Tea diminishes as the Leaf grows bigger and bigger, and also according as it is gathered in Season, or out of Season. It may be observed also, that as Tea grows not only in *China*, but in *Japan*, *Tonquin*, and even in the Kingdom of *Siam*, it is natural for Merchants to purchase at the cheapest Markets, whence we have but little of it that is really fine. Now, as the *Chinese*, *Japanese*, and even several Nations of the *Levant*, not to mention the *Europeans*, make a great Consumption of Tea; they, it is probable, keep the best for themselves, which is very dear even in *China* itself, and as it easily loses its Flavor upon the least Accident, the Merchants must be unwilling to run the Risque of transporting it, except they are sure of turning it to a good Account. Most of them, therefore, buy it at *Japan*, where the *Dutch* have exported great Quantities; but in *Japan* it is not comparable to what grows in the

Province

Province of *Kiangnang*. You have the Figure of this Bush in *Piso*, in the *China Illustrata*, and in the *Dutch Embassy*. It is mentioned in *Ramusio*'s Illustration on some Passages in *Marco Polo*.

Coco-Nut Tree.

What our Travellers report of the Coco-Nut Tree, is confirmed by all Accounts, ancient and modern, and you have a very minute Description of it in *Pyrard*, *John de Barros*, and in many others. They all declare that this Tree alone, affords wherewithal to build a Ship, and to lade her when she is finished. The Trunk supplies them with Plank, Masts, Anchors, and Oars; the Fibres about the Nut itself, make a very valuable Cordage, because it never perishes in the Water. The Anchors made of the Wood of this Tree, are well enough for small Craft. The Nut itself affords a sweet, pleasant and milky Liquor, which, fermenting, becomes a Wine, a Vinegar, a Sugar, and even a kind of Brandy: Its Oil is sovereign in cases of the *Erysipelas* or St. *Anthony*'s Fire, Tetters, and many other Ailments. In fine, this Tree alone supplies with Food, Habitation, Cloathing, and Commodities to export, if true it be, that the chief Trade of the *Maldives* is in the Articles they reap from the Coco-Nut. The *Arabs* call both the Nut and the Tree *Nargil*, whence the modern *Greeks* have ἀργέλλιον, the word used by *Cosmas* the Monk, in his *Topography*. Besides the Authors we have cited, you may consult others who have dwelt on this Tree, as *Marco Polo*, *Lodovic Barthema*, *Barbosa*, *Garcias de Orta*, *A Costa*, *John Davis*, and others.

Decad. 3. l. 3. c. 7.

AN INQUIRY

Into the Origin of the CHRISTIAN RELIGION in *CHINA*.

The Chinese *had a Knowledge of Christianity before the Close of the ninth Century.*

OUR two Authors supply us with a very ancient Testimony of the Existence of the Gospel in this vast Empire, before the close of the Ninth Century; for they observe that on the Revolution of the Year CCLXIV. of the *Hejra*, or the Year DCCCLXXVII. of *Christ*, when the City of *Cansu* was taken and sacked, a great Number of Christians were there put to the Sword, together with the Inhabitants of the Place. It appears also by the Dialogue between the Emperor of *China* and the *Arab*, in the *Second Account*, that they had a knowledge of *Jesus Christ* and his Apostles, and the Doctrine of the Gospel; since among the Images the Emperor shewed him, *Jesus* was represented with his Disciples, just as when he went up to *Jerusalem*:

rusalem: And what this Prince observed to the *Mohammedan Traveller* of the shortness of our Saviour's Days, here upon Earth, assures us he had some glimmering Light into the Gospel History; but it is a Matter of Intricacy to settle the Time when, and the Manner how Christianity made its way into *China.*

The Opinion of those who believe St. Thomas *preached there.*

Those who first attempted this obscure Point, have, upon a very suspicious Foundation, advanced that the Apostle St. *Thomas* having planted the Gospel in the *Indies* transferred it thence into *China.* Father *Trigaut* who wrought on the Memoirs of Father *Matthew Ricci* one of the first Missionaries that went to *China,* started this Notion from a Passage in the *Beit Gaza,* or *Breviary of the* Syrian *Churches,* where are these Words; *By* St. Thomas *the Error of Idolatry has been confounded in the* Indies. *By* St. Thomas *the* Chinese *and* Ethiopians *have been converted to the Knowledge of the Truth. By* St. Thomas *the Kingdom of Heaven hath taken its flight, and ascended quite up to* China. To this he adds another Authority, taken from a Collection of Canons, among which there is one that speaks of the Metropolitan of *China,* and this is all. Father *Kircher* has repeated the same, drawn the same Inferences therefrom, and has carried the Thing to that length, as to trace out the Way he went into *China,* and the Way he returned again into the *Indies,* where, accor-ding

Chin. *Illustr.*

ding to the Tradition of the *Malabar* Churches, he suffered Martyrdom.

This Tradition very uncertain, and unknown to the Orientals.

Had the same Church any Tradition to commemorate that *St. Thomas* preached also in *China*, we might hearken thereto; but we have no such Testimony, nor do we find any Thing to confirm the same either in the Greek or Latin Authors; no, not even in the *Synaxaria* of the Greek Church, or of the Christians of the *Levant*, whose Authors have made no scruple to admit every Sort of Fable. That there have been Christians in *China* is not to be doubted, and as the Light of the Gospel was conveyed thither by the *Syrians* who were converted in the earliest Times of the Church, either by *St. Thomas* or some of his Disciples, this was sufficient to derive on him those Praises in the *Malabaric* Breviary; seeing he was, in some Sort, the Author of their Conversion, because he preached the Faith to those, who afterwards planted it in *China*. The Passage taken from the Collection of Councils is of no weight, and can only prove that there has been a Metropolitan in *China*, not that St. *Thomas* himself preached the Gospel there.

It has been embraced as indubitable by the Moderns. Mem. de la Chin. T. 2. p. 195.

Yet most who have touched on this Matter in our times, do, upon no other Testimony than *Trigaut* has offered, lay it down as an indubitable Truth, that St. *Thomas* himself preached in *China*; *it is not doubted*, says one of the last of them, *but St.* Thomas *preached the Faith in the* Indies,

Indies, *and it is certain that in those Days the* Indians *were perfectly acquainted with* China, *whither almost all of them sent some Kind of Tribute. It is then very probable that this Apostle, who had this new World in charge, would not have neglected the finest Part of it, at that Time as renowned in the East as* Italy *was in* Europe *when the* Roman *Empire was in its Meridian. Therefore it may have been that he travelled thither in Person, or, at least, that he sent some of his Disciples thither. This Conjecture, which has all the Strength of an authentic Proof, has received an additional Force, from what has been remarked in the* Chinese *History of those Times; for it declares that a certain Man came into* China *and taught a heavenly Doctrine; he was not, according to the same, an ordinary or common Man; his Life, his Miracles, and his Vertues, attracted him the Admiration of all that knew him.*

The Tradition concerning the Mission of St. Thomas *in the* Indies *is most certain.*

It is true, indeed, the common Tradition of the *Malabar* Churches has it, that St. *Thomas* preached in the *Indies*, and the same has been admitted into the *Roman* Martyrology, where it is said he suffered Martyrdom at *Calamina*; but there is no Memorial left of any City so called in those Parts, and the Conjectures which some of the Learned have advanced, concerning this Name, are quite intolerable. Father *Kircher* pretends we must read *Calurmina*, instead of *Calamina*, and that the Word signifies *upon a Stone*; because in that Country they still shew a Stone figured with

with ſome Croſſes, and other Enſigns of Chriſtianity, and upon this Stone, the *Malabars* tell you, he was pierced through with a Lance by a *Bramin*. Now although this Tradition is not altogether certain, it nevertheleſs carries ſome air of Authority with it, inaſmuch as the Name of *San Thome*, which is impoſed on the City of *Meliapor*, has, for many Ages paſt, been known not only among the *Europeans*, but alſo among the *Arabs*, both *Chriſtian* and *Mohammedan*. For our two Authors ſpeak of *Betuma* or *Batuma*, as of a Place known upon the *Indian* Shores, and this Word ſignifies the ſame with *Beit-Thoma*, the *Houſe* or *Church*, of St. *Thomas*, juſt as the *Arabs* and *Syrians* write and pronounce *Bazbadi* for *Beitzabdi*, *Bagarmi* for *Beitgarme*, and ſo on. But we are no where told that this Apoſtle reached *China*, and ſuch Points of Antiquity are not to be aſcertained by Probability, when backed by no poſitive Authority; for by this Rule of Conjecture a *Portugueſe* Writer has taken on him to prove that the ſame Apoſtle croſſed over to *America*, and particularly that he was in *Braſil*, a Thing no Body had ever thought of before.

Simaon de Vaſconcellos Noticias do Braſil. l. 2.

The Proofs offered by the modern Writers are dubious.

We are to the full as unwilling to grant what the Author of the *Memoirs* ſo poſitively aſſerts, namely, that the *Indians* who were taught by St. *Thomas*, and who were of *Malabar*, were perfectly acquainted with *China*, or, conſequently, that they were Tributaries to that Country; for

for we are quite ignorant of the History of those Countries. But what is infinitely more probable, and what the *Chinese* themselves acknowledge, and what our two Authors and almost all the *Arabs* jointly confirm, is that the *Chinese* had their Idolatry, and their Doctrine of Transmigration from the *Indians*, with almost all the Superstitions which prevail among the *Bonzes* and among the People. So that this Conjecture has not even Probability for Foundation; wherefore its Author reduces it to a bare Possibility; *perhaps he went thither himself*; which is not a whit more likely to have hapned. For the Life of Man had been unequalto such long Traverses, almost without Respite; nor would have allowed of the Delays necessary to catechise such Numbers of Nations and Tribes, to found Churches sufficient, and to go through all the other painful Functions of the Apostolat, which must have required St. *Thomas* to sojourn a very considerable Time among them.

The Chinese *History says nothing of St.* Thomas.

Now tho' we could discover any Passage, in the History of *China*, to favor this Notion, it would be but of little Weight; but, quite to the contrary, Father *Couplet* has often declared that the *Chinese* History says not the least Thing concerning the Gospel in that Country, no, not even of the Mission recorded in the *Chinese* and *Syriac* Inscription we shall come to hereafter. In his *Histroical Abridgement* he only observes, that the Emperor *Mim-ti* who reigned about sixty-four Years before the Birth of Christ, had a Dream wherein he beheld a golden Figure of a Man, of Gigantic Stature; and that this Emperor calling to mind, as they pretend, that saying of *Confucius, the Saint is in the West*; sent Embassadors to the *Indies* to enquire after the true Law; instead of which they brought back with them the pernicious Sect of the Idol *Foee*, and the Doctrine of the Metempsychosis *.

There is no Proof of Christianity in China before the seventh Century.

Nor can we suppose St. *Thomas* is meant by the Preacher the Inscription calls *Olopuen*, who came into *China* about the Year of *Christ* DCXXXVI. nor had any body done it before the Author, or Editor rather, of the last *Memoirs*.

We have no Proof then, that the Gospel was preached in *China* before this Epoch: For what many have written concerning the ancient Name the *Chinese* had for Christians, that it signifies the *Worshippers of the Cross*, is of no positive Validity, since they may have thus called the Christians in the neighbouring Countries, tho' at the same time there had been none in *China*. *Hoei hoei*, which they say was their other Name, was equally applicable to

* *Occasione somnii quo oblata fuerit species aurata viri gigantei, & memor dicti, ut putatur, a Confucio prolati, in Occidente extitit sanctus, quaeri jubet Imperator per suos legatos, veram legem ex Indiis. At enim Idoli Foë pestifera secta cum Metempsychosi (proh dolor) invecta est.*

the

the *Christians*, *Jews* and *Mohammedans*; and as for the Name of *Tersai*, it is not *Chinese* but *Persian*. The first Appearance then of Christianity in *China*, that we know of, was in the Year of *Christ* DCXXXVI; and this is what we gather from an Inscription, which, in the Year of *Christ* MDCXXV, was found at *Signansu*, the Capital of the Province of *Chensi*, delineated in *Chinese* Characters, with several Lines of *Syriac*.

This is proved by the Chinese *and* Syriac *Inscription.*

As this *Chinese* and *Syriac* Inscription is a Monument of very great Importance, and the only certain Thing of the kind hitherto discovered in this Empire, it may not be amiss to explain the principal Passages of it, tho' that is what we hope to do more amply elsewhere. You have a representative Copy of this Inscription and Stone in Fath. *Kircher's China Illustrata*, which he assures us is very exact, as indeed it seems to be; and *Hornius*, and some other Protestants, who would have had it a Forgery, without any, the least, Ground, have been refuted by some of their Brethren, who have cooler Heads, and more Understanding. It was in the Year MDCXXV that it was discovered in the Province of *Chensi*; and Fath. *Semedo*, Fath. *Boim*, Fath. *Martini*, and some other Jesuits, took notice of some Passages in it; but it was most unhappily explained.

Muller de Monum. Sinic.

In the Year MDCXXXV, when Fath. *Kircher* published his first Essay upon the *Coptic* Tongue, he inserted the *Syriac* Words, and gave a Translation of the *Chinese* Matter; but he was vastly out in his Reading

Prodrom. Copt.

and Interpretation of the *Syriac*; for mistaking a Word which signified *Priest*, and starting another which signified *Ethiopian*, he pretends to discover a Mission of *Coptic* and *Ethiopian* Priests, a Notion of the wildest sort. For they would have made use of their own Languages in this Inscription, or, at least, of one of them, seeing they are so distant from each other; and not of the *Syriac*, which was foreign to both. Again, neither *Copts* nor *Ethiopians*, who are *Jacobites*, would have preached up *Nestorianism*, which they abominate; and nothing is more certain than that all the Christians, for many Ages, in the *Indies* and the *Upper Asia*, have been *Nestorians*. Father *Kircher* also is mistaken upon the Word *Patriarch* in the *Syriac* Inscription, and leaves his Reader in the dark, unable to determin whether it should be the Patriarch of *Alexandria*, or the Patriarch of *Antioch*, when it happens to be neither the one nor the other.

The Second Explication Kircher *has given, no better than the first.*

When the same Father publishes his *China Illustrata*, he makes mention of *Ethiopians* only; but his Translation, tho' different from the former, is not at all more conformable to the Original, which runs to this Effect: *In the Year of the* Greeks MXCII. Mar Isdabuzid, *Priest and* Chorepiscopus *of* Cumdan, *the Royal City of the East, otherwise called* Milis, *or* Melecius, *Priest of* Balk, *a City of* Turkestan, *erected this* Stone Table, *whereon is described the Mystery of the Life of our Saviour, and the preaching of our Fathers*

to

to the Kings of China, *in the time of the* Father of Fathers, Hananjashuah, *Catholic Patriarch.* Father *Kircher*, in his first Version, renders it, *Dominus Isdbuzad Sacerdos & Archiepiscopus*; in his *China Illustrata*; *Sacerdos & Vicarius Episcopi Cumdan*; and in a third Version *Sacerdos & Vicarius Episcopus.* Other Words he read wrong, as *Belch* for *Balk*, *Taburstan* for *Tokarestan*; and of the Word which signifies a *Stone*, he makes *Papa*, incoherently translating it, *erexit hanc tabulam Papa.* He would have it also, that *Hananjashuah* is *Johannes Josue*, and that by the Title *Catholic* we are to understand the Patriarch of *Alexandria*, or him of *Antioch*, or him of *Babylon*, by whom he imagins this Title was peculiarly affected, and so he leaves this Point undecided; tho' if the Priests who erected this Monument, acknowledged the Patriarch of *Alexandria*, who never was styled *Catholic*, they were either *Orthodox* if the Patriarch was the *Greek*; or *Jacobites*, if he was the *Coptic*; or if him of *Babylon*, they were *Nestorians*; and this is all the Light he reflects upon this Obscurity. *Muller*, who examined this Inscription, had no Fault to find with the Version, and adds nothing but Commendations on the Author; tho' it requires nothing but a tolerable Skill in *Latin* to perceive that many Passages of the Translation are lame and senseless; and with a very slender Stock of *Syriac*, it were easy to see that the Interpreter understood it not; but his Inacuracies against History and Geography are still more conspicuous.

The Explication of of this Inscription. It appears that this Inscription is of the Year of *Jesus Christ* DCCLXXX, which corresponds with the Year MXCII of the *Greeks* or *Seleucidæ*, and that Father *Kircher*, who makes it the Year of the same MLXXXII. is ten Years out in his Account. He that speaks, was originally a Priest of, or, at least, came from *Balk*, a famous City, which many Geographers place in *Tokarestan*, or in *Turkestan*, two Names, tho' often confounded together, belonging to two distinct Provinces. He was at that time *Chorepiscopus* of *Cumdan*, *the principal City of the Eastern Kingdom*, or *of the Eastern Court*. The *Chorepiscopi* are very well known in the Eastern Church, who has several Offices for their Consecration; and the Word being distinctly expressed in the Table, it is hard to conceive why Fath. *Kircher* translated it either *Archbishop* or *Bishop's Vicar*.

What we are to understand by the City of Cumdan. *Cumdan* is certainly *Nankin*, at that time the imperial Seat of *China*, as well as when our two *Arabs* were in the Country. This City has had several Names, as Father *Martini* observes; the *Arabs* called it *Cumdan*, as appears by *Yacuti*, *Ebn Wardi*, and the *Nubian Geographer* tho' scarce to be known in the *Latin* Translation. For the *Maronites*, who undertook that Work, so unequal to their Strength, imagined *Cumdan* to be the Name of a River, whereas the *Kiang* is meant, which the Author sufficiently gives us to understand, saying, It

Geograph. Nubi.

It is the largest River in China, and calling it the *River of* Cumdan, because it passes through that City. This Name is so very often repeated in the one *Account* and in the other, that we can have no Doubt concerning, and especially as we find it in the old *Arabian* Geographers. For, if *Abulfeda*, and some other Authors mention it not, but have a different Name for the Capital of this Empire, and cannot even settle upon that among themselves; it is because they wrote after the Throne was translated to *Pekin*. They say *Nankin* signifies the *Southern Court*, and in the *Syriac* Inscription *Cumdan* is called the *Eastern Court*; the reason is plain, for, to those who came from *Mesopotamia*, *Nankin* was not only the most distant, but the most Easterly also. Ebn Wardi, Yacuti.

The Catholic Patriarch, *Hananjashuah*, was certainly the Patriarch of the *Nestorians*, as may be proved by History, which has two Patriarchs so called; the first consecrated about the Year of *Christ* DCLXXXVI; the second about the Year DCCLXXIV. Now the Inscription was cut in the Year DCCLXXXII, and, consequently, in the Life-time of this last, or a short time after, if, as the same History records, he sat but a little more than four Years. We shall however take a time professedly to demonstrate that the Date of his Consecration ought to be put some Years backward; but tho' two or three were wanting to make it quadrate with this Inscription, it would not at all lose of its authenticity; *Who was the Catholic Patriarch in the Inscription.*

for the Patriarch may have been dead at *Bagdad*, and they have known nothing of the Matter in *China*. Acts and public Writings are, every Day, drawn up in the *Indies*, and in *America*, with the Years of the Popes and Kings, after they are dead; because the News thereof cannot reach them in time, but these Writings are genuin nevertheless.

Of the Title of Catholic.

The Title of Catholic, added to that of Patriarch, was never assumed but by the *Nestorians*, and when *Kircher* says the Patriarch of *Alexandria* did the same, and *Muller* applauds his Conjecture, adding, "there never was any one of the *Oecumenic* Bishops that did not take this "Title upon him," they are greatly in the wrong. For what can *Muller* mean by *Oecumenic Bishops?* If he conceived them to be the Bishops of great Sees, none but the Patriarchs of *Constantinople* ever styled themselves Oecumenical Patriarchs since *John the Faster*; and those of *Alexandria*, *Antioch*, or *Jerusalem*, whether Orthodox or not, never assumed this ambitious Title at all. But it seems *Muller* took *Catholic* and *Oecumenic* to have the same Import, whereas they are of very different Meaning; it was in the Days of *Justinian*, that they began to give the Title of Catholic to those Prelates who were superior in Dignity to Metropolitans; and who had Authority over several of them, and might consecrate them without Recourse had to the Patriarch of *Antioch*. At first they were two; him of

Catholici Patriarchæ titulum nemo non Episcoporum Oecumenicorum sibi ab olim sumpsit.

of *Persia*, and him of *Armenia*, who are still retained in the *Jacobite* Church; but the *Nestorians* of *Seleucia* and *Ctesiphon*, witdrawing Obedience from the Orthodox they succeeded, and divesting them of their Authority, under the Countenance of the last Kings of *Persia*, arrogated to themselves the Style of Catholic, and have kept it ever since, adding Patriarch thereto, as they were the Heads of all the *Nestorian* Communion. From this same Word the *Arabs* have formed their *Jatelik*, the two Letters being the same but for the Position of the diacritic Point, while *Marco Polo*, conforming to the *Venetian* Pronunciation, has expressed it by *Zatolic*. In short, it became so very peculiar to the *Nestorian* Patriarchs, that the *Jacobites*, out of Hatred to them, tho' they themselves had real Catholics in their own Church, have for five hundred Years past given them the Title of *Mofrian*.

Muller's *Mistake upon this Head.*

Muller, and those, who, with him, imagined that the *Catholic*, mentioned in the Inscription may have been the Patriarch of *Alexandria* did not so much as dream of one thing, which should nevertheless have first presented itself to the Consideration of those who had but the least Acquaintance with the Eastern Churches; and this is Why any Ecclesiastics of the Church of *Alexandria* should have made use of the *Syriac*, which was of no Predominance in *Egypt*, either in common Discourse, or in the Offices of the Church. They never could have assigned a Reason for this, and consequently they should have had

had some Thoughts of the Patriarch of *Antioch*, and him of the *Nestorians*; and accordingly have fixed upon this last, seeing the former never assumed the Title of *Catholic*, and that those who, in his Church, were distinguished thereby, were subordinate to him.

A Proof from the Date. The Date of the *Grecian* Year should also have suggested to these learned Men, That the Inscription could not have been ordered by Ecclesiastics sent from the Church of *Alexandria*, nor from that of *Ethiopia*, with whom this Epoch was not in use, but that of *Dioclesian*, or of the *Martyrs*.

The Names plain. There is no Obscurity as to the Names of the Persons, except what *Kircher* has raised by his faulty Reading. The Names are perfectly *Syrian*, and common enough among the *Nestorians*; a Bishop, *Chorepiscopi*, *Papas*, who have the same Authority; Priests and Deacons, who, very probably, did at that time constitute the Christian Clergy of *China*. *Muller*, who has compared these Names with those in the *Prodromus*, might have spared himself the Trouble; for all the Difference arises from some Names, in the first Work, ill read, and not in the Original.

Examination of the Chinese Inscription. Let us now examin the *Chinese* Part of this Inscription, according to the Translation of some able Jesuits, more to be relyed on far than *Muller*, who, in some Places, presumes to restore the *Chinese* Text, and to alter the Version. This, is a sort of an Article we will not dwell on;

on; tho', by the way, it is hard to conceive how a Man that has never been out of *Europe*, should be able to play the Critic upon a *Chinese* Inscription, only by the Help of a few Lexicons; to have done with this, we will take notice of what is most essential in each Column.

The first Article which has Regard to the Existence and Name of God.

The first lays down the Ground-work of the Christian Faith, the Existence of a Godhead, in three Persons, Creator of all Things. It is remarkable that these *Syrians* use the word *Aloho*, which they, most certainly, did because they could find no word in the *Chinese* Tongue to convey the Idea the Christians have of the true God: But *Muller*, who fancies he knows more than any body finds you out four others, which he pretends will answer the end, *For we must not imagin*, says he, *the* Chinese *have no adequate Name to signify God, tho' they have not the ineffable Name of Jehovah.* And yet *Ricci*, *Martini* and many others were of a contrary Opinion, while those, of our Days, who side with *Muller*, have not been able to prove what they say. His turn upon the ineffable Name is quite puerile; for without knowing the Pronunciation it may have had among the *Hebrews*, we have, through Mercy, an Idea of the Sovereign Entity. It is astonishing, That after so many learned Men, even Protestants, have unveiled the Absurdity there is in the Pronunciation of *Jehovah*, there should still be People to stickle for it.

Capell. de *Nom. Elohim*, &c.

Now

Now for the Remark he afterwards makes upon the Name of God expressed in *Syriac*, and which he modestly offers as a Conjecture: *It is likely then*, says he, *the Author of the* Inscription *was of a Church that spoke* Syriac. Nothing in the World more certain; and hence it might naturally have been inferred that the Patriarch, therein mentioned, could never have been him of *Alexandria*. But the date, and so many *Syrian* Names might equally have convinced him, not only that the Church of this Clergy, that is, of the Christians of the Country, spoke *Syriac*, but that it was also the sacred Language in which they celebrated divine Service, and drew up their Ecclesiastical Writings.

Of the second and third Column. The second and third Column continue to explain the Mystery of the Creation, the fall of the first Man by the Seduction of the Devil, who is called *Satan*, a Name quite foreign to the *Chinese* Tongue, and the general Corruption of Mankind by Sin and Wickedness.

Of the fourth concerning Jesus Christ. The fourth explains the Advent of Jesus Christ by his Incarnation, to the following effect: *Donec Personarum trium una communicavit se ipsam clarissimo venerabilissimoque* Mixio, *operiendo abscondendoque veram majestatem, simul homo prodiit in sæculum.* These words sufficiently express the *Nestorian* way of expounding the Mystery of the Incarnation; they rejecting the Union of the Word and Man, except by Inhabitation, by a Plenitude of Grace, superior to that of all other Saints. This conformity of of Creed is easily comprehended, by comparing the Passages in *Elias* the *Catholic*, and other Divines who have been cited upon several Occasions.

Elias Nisib. MSS. Arab. Amruf. Mathæi.

In the same Column are these words: *Spiritus de cælis significavit lætitiam*, which means the Annunciation by an Angel. *Virgo fœmina peperit sanctum in* Tacin, which must here signify *Judæa: Clarissima constellatio anunciavit fælicitatem*, *Potu* (Reges ex illa terra orientali) *viderunt claritatem, & venerunt offerre munera subjectionis completa, bis decem quatuor sanctarum*. This plainly points at the Appearance of the Star to the Wise Men, and the Adoration they came to pay to *Jesus Christ:* but as what follows is very dark, let us see how the Interpreters have commented thereupon: *ut lex & prophetiæ viginti quatuor Prophetarum adimplerentur*; according to *Kircher*, *This alludes to the four major, and the twelve minor Prophets, to which if you add* Abraham, Isaac, Jacob, Job, Moses, Samuel, David, *and* Zachary, *the Father of* St. John *the* Baptist, *you will have the twenty four Prophets complete*. *Muller* likes this Exposition, and only remarks that some have thought the *Chinese* Word might signify *Prophecies* as well as *Prophets*. This is trifling enough, except we lay hold on it to shew how little we are to depend upon Versions from the *Chinese* Writings; for this Diversity may produce very different Meanings, and no one can be fond of so odd an Interpretation. This number of twenty four Prophets

Other Mysteries therein noted, and the Completion of the Prophecies.

Chin. Illust.

Twenty four Prophets.

Prophets is equally unknown to the Synagogue and to the Church, as well as that of the twice twelve Prophecies, nor ever did any Man name among the Prophets the Persons *Kircher* has introduced.

The true Explication of this Passage, and Muller's *Mistake.*

It is easy to perceive that by the Completion of the Prophecies, or of what the Prophets foretold, these *Syrians* understood the Predictions in the Old Testament: this is evident by what follows of the twenty seven Books the Apostles left behind them, which make up the New Testament; and so the number of twenty four must relate to the Books of the Old. The *Syrians*, whether *Orthodox*, *Jacobite*, or *Nestorian*, have their Version from the *Hebrew* Text, which contains twenty four Books, commonly by the *Jews* called the *Twenty four*. This is the mighty Mystery our Critic could not unfold; at the same time that he is mightily disturbed at the twenty seven Books of the New Testament, because, truly, *Kircher* reckons fourteen Epistles of St. *Paul*; for my part, says *Muller*, I can make out but thirteen, and there is some doubt concerning that to the *Hebrews*. We very well know the *Lutherans* make a doubt of it, but the *Syrians* and all the other Eastern Christians are satisfied it is canonical, as appears not only by their Copies of the New Testament, but also by the Enumeration their Divines and Canonists make of the sacred Books. If *Muller* was ignorant of so common and certain a Fact, he

was

was but ill qualified to talk of the Religion of the Orientals.

In the sixth Column mention is made of Baptism, which cleansing the Body purifies the Soul. and then according to the Translation word for word; *Dispersi in quatuor partes mundi*; we are not sure whether these words have reference to the Apostles or to the whole Body of Christians; but it is most likely they are meant of these last, by what follows; *Ad congregandos & pacificandos sine labore pulsant ligna, timoris, pietatis, gratitudinisque voces personando.* Here we have an instance of the Imperfection of the *Chinese* Tongue; for very able Translators have been at a loss to determin, whether these Words relate to the preceding, or to the succeeding. But it is beyond Dispute that they intend the Ceremonies of the Christians, by this time in subjection to the *Mohammedans*, as they were in the Days of *Hananjashuah*, seeing he was appointed by the *Kalif Mahadi*, who dyed in the Year of the *Hejra* CLXIX, and of *Christ* DCCLXXXV. At this time the Christians were not allowed the use of Bells, but were obliged, as they are at present, to strike upon wooden Instruments instead thereof; and this is most likely to be Sense of the *Chinese* Words.

Of the sixth Column.

But *Muller* discovers a more exalted Meaning; he will have it that *Mo*, which the Jesuits render *Ligna*, signifies the Devil, and that so it must be altered, *sine labore pulsant Diabolum*; and that this Expression

Muller's Conjecture intolerable.

preſſion is to be underſtood of Exorciſm. We have already declared, That thoſe who fancy they have acquired the *Chineſe* Language by poring in their Cloſets, deſerve not to be heard in oppoſition to ſuch of the Learned as have patiently and painfully ſtudied it a long time in the very Country. To ſay no more of this, I would ask if any Chriſtian, in any Language whatſoever, has made uſe of an Expreſſion like that of *beating* or *ſtriking upon the Devil*, with a view to the Exorciſms of Baptiſm.

The Ceremonies and Cuſtoms of the Chriſtians ſpecified in the Inſcription.

The next Columns mention the ſeveral Ceremonies practiſed by the Chriſtians, That they ſacrifice with the face to the Eaſt, that ſeven times a Day they pray for the Quick and the Dead, that they offer Sacrifice upon the firſt Day of the Week, and that they purify the Heart by the Remiſſion of Sin. Then as to their exterior, That they wear long Beards, that they ſhave the upper part of the Head, that they have no train of Slaves, and that they hoard not riches, but that they beſtow great Alms, and that they faſt. We may plainly diſcern all the Practiſes of the Eaſtern Chriſtians amidſt the enigmatical Expreſſions of the *Chineſe*; the Paſſages *Muller* heaps together from ſeveral Authors, are by no means to the point, and the leſs as none of them are Orientals, who, as it happens, are thoſe he ſhould have conſulted.

Muller's *Animadverſion upon the Euchariſt.*

He makes a moſt grave Remark upon the Word Sacrifice; ſaying there is no *Chineſe* Word to ſignify the *Sacrifice without Blood*. I

I do not find, continues he, *that they made Use of the Word* Sacrifice, *or that they believed they offered the real Body and Blood of* Jesus Christ,* *into which the Bread of the* Eucharist *was converted by Transubstantiation.* If this Inscription had been a Theological Tract in form, we might have required it to be more explicit and circumstantial, as well upon this Head as upon all the rest; the Matter is, what the *Syrian* Clergy believed concerning this *Sacrifice.* Fath. *Kircher* had cited three or four *Oriental* Passages from *Ecchellensis*, to prove these Christians believed a real Mutation of the Bread and Wine into the Body and Blood of *Jesus Christ*: But *Muller* cannot discover either the *Sacrifice without Blood*, or *Transubstantiation* in the *Chinese* Tongue, adding, That he cannot perceive this Doctrin to have been authorised by Liturgies, or by the Testimonies exhibited by *Kircher.* And yet there are above fifty *Oriental* Liturgies, not to mention other Books of public Devotion, where the Term of the *Sacrifice without Blood*, is often and often repeated; but we do not there meet with *Transubstantiation*; by the same Rule it may be proved, that the *Roman* Church disclaims it; for the express Term is no where in the Canon of the Mass. To be plain, it is evi-

* *At quod Sacrificum appellaverint, quodque putarint se ita verum Corpus & Sanguinem obtulisse, ut Eucharisticus Panis per Transubstantiationem talis evaserit, equidem non invenio*, p. 58.

dent by *Muller*'s Way of talking of the Liturgies, that he never ſaw any of them, much leſs the Works of the Theological Writers. Thoſe who have written in *Syriac* and *Arabic*, could not uſe the Word *Tranſubſtantiation*; becauſe there are no Compounds in thoſe two Tongues; but they have declared this Transformation to be *from Subſtance to Subſtance.* Theſe are the Terms in the Expoſition of Faith by *Elias* III. of the Name, Patriarch of the *Neſtorians*, and one of the Succeſſors to the Perſon mentioned in the *Syriac* Inſcription. Now as theſe *Syrians* who went to *China*, did moſt certainly believe, as their Patriarchs did, *Muller* ſhould have turned over the Writings of the *Neſtorian* Church, to have informed himſelf of their Creed, and not have been ſatisfied with the dark Expreſſions of the *Chineſe* Monument, where not a Word was ſaid of it.

Concerning the Work Muller *promiſes, in order to prove that the* Eaſtern *Chriſtians did not believe the real Preſence,* &c.

But having thus decided the Caſe, he ſtops ſhort; becauſe he was to diſcuſs the Point in a Work apart, to be penned by Order of his Superiors. It is not known that he ever committed this intended Work to the Preſs; but without ſo much as ſeeing it, we may pronounce it a Piece of no vaſt Depth; a Man who was a Novice to the moſt common Things relating to the *Eaſtern* Chriſtianity, who approved the groſſeſt Miſtakes of the firſt Tranſlator, and who imagined that three or four Paſſages, contained all the Proof the Catholics could produce, touching the belief of *Orientals* upon the

the *Eucharist*; ſuch a Man I ſay, was but ſlenderly prepared for the Task, by far more difficult than the Hiſtory and Geography neceſſary to illuſtrate our Inſcription, concerning which, he has advanced nothing but has been demonſtrated to be falſe.

Of Olopuen *the first Preacher of the Goſpel in* China.

In the Sequel of this Inſcription, there is ſome Talk of the firſt preaching of the Goſpel in *China*, and it is ſaid, that in the Time of *Taizan-ven*, a holy Man called *Olopuen* or *Lepuen*, *came from* Tacin, *conducted by blue Clouds, and by obſerving the Courſe of the Winds.* Thoſe who have laboured at the *Chineſe* Chronology, make this Date to correſpond with the Year of *Jeſus Chriſt*, DCXXXVI. *Kircher* has it, *That he guided himſelf by the Winds, with the help of Sea-Charts*, a Thing more eaſy to ſay than to prove; adding, that *Tacin* is *Judæa*, though he himſelf, and the reſt agree it is a Name which belongs as well to *Syria* in general as to *Paleſtine*.

The Teſtimony of Couplet.

Father *Couplet*, in his *Chronological Abridgment*, ſpeaking of this King, delivers himſelf to this Effect, * "The Hiſtories of "the Country report, that in the XIII.

* *Memorant Chronica anno Imperii* VII. *perveniſſe ex longinquis Regionibus variarum gentium legatos, oris habitu corporiſque admodum peregrino, & nunquam antea Siris viſo: quin adeo gloriatum fuiſſe Imperatorem quod ſuis primum temporibus, homines capillo rufi, oculiſque viridibus, glaucos interpretor, ditionem Sinicam adiiſſent. Certum videtur eos ipſos fuiſſe, quos lapideum in Provincia Xenſi Monumentum, effoſſum Anno* 1625. *ætati noſtræ*

" Year of his Reign, there came Ambassa- " dors from very remote Parts, and from " several Nations; and that they were of a " very extraordinary turn of Countenance, " and of a very foreign Appearance, such " as had never till then been seen in *China*. " That the King accounted it a Glory for " him, that in his Time there should ap- " pear Men with sandy Hair and green " Eyes, blue, *that is, says the same Fa- " ther*, who continues: It seems evident, " that these are the same mentioned by " the *Chinese* Monument, found in the Year " MDCXXV. in the Province of *Chensi*, " concerning which, you may consult *Kir- " cher*, and an *Arabian* Manuscript in his " most Christian Majesty's Library, where- " in it is expresly said, That about that " Time, certain Missionaries were sent to " *China* by the Catholic Patriarch of the " *Indies* and *China*, who resided at *Musol*."

Couplet's *Confession*. It is of Importance to note, that by the Testimony of even *Couplet* himself, there is no such Mention made of this Mission in the *Chinese* History, and that he owned to me and to others, That what he had inserted in his *Chronological Abridgment*, was borrowed from the Inscription. What he afterwards says, of an *Arabian* Manuscript,

---

prodidit. - - De hoc consule Kircheri *Sinam Illustratum, & vetus MSS* Arabicum *quod asservatur in Regia Galliarum Bibliotheca, ubi diserte scribitur circa idem tempus, missos esse Evangelii præcones in Sinam a Catholico Patriarcha Indiæ & Sinæ qui in urbe Mosul degebat*, P. 55.

which

which is no where to be found, and never was in the King's Library, he had from the late Mr. *Thevenot*, who how he came to dream of such a Thing is more than can be told. There is a Manuscript indeed, but it does not say that the Catholic of *Musol* or rather of *Bagdad*, sent Missionaries to *China*, tho' you therein find the Name of *Hananjashuah*, in the Series of the *Nestorian* Patriarchs, and are told that he lived nearly about the Time mentioned upon the *Chinese* Stone. It is a Mistake also, to call him Catholic Patriarch of the *Indies* and of *China*; for Catholic was the usual Title to which Patriarch was annexed; and the Metropolitans of the *Indies* and of *China* were subordinate to him, as may be gathered from the *Notitia* of the *Nestorian* Churches.

MSS Arab. *in Biblioth. Colbertina.*

But to return to the Inscription, it alone acquaints us, that so early as the Year DCXXXVI. the Gospel had been preached in *China*, by Priests from *Syria*, whose Chief was *Olopuen*. This is all we know of the Matter; the *Chinese* History has no Words concerning it, and it is no hard Matter to perceive, that this Name is *Chinese*, and that it was imposed on this Preacher of the Word, as the Custom still is in our Days, for all those who go to *China* to receive new Names. *Muller*, full of his Conjectures, fancies these Preachers were Christians of *Persia*, who fled the Persecution of the *Arabs*; but long before *Mohammed* there were Christians in *Persia*,

We have no Authority to rely on but the Inscription itself.

 and

and in the *Upper Asia*, protected by the last Kings; and no sooner was *Persia* conquered, than the *Nestorians*, who were almost the only Christians of that Country, obtained very ample Privileges at the Hands of the Kalif *Omar*, together with the free and entire Exercise of their Religion, all which is expresly recorded in History.

Hist. Nest. in MSS. Arab.

We learn nothing in the Ara-bic *Writings concerning* Olopuen, *who cannot have been St.* Thomas.

It must be confessed then, that we are furnished with no Light in *Arabian*, *Syrian*, or *Chinese* Authors, to shew us who this *Olopuen* may have been; we can only say that he entered *China* in the Seventh Century. He cannot then have been St. *Thomas*, as some have thought: And yet *Kircher* and many others, account it an indubitable Fact, That this Apostle beamed out the Rays of the Gospel there, after he had preached in the *Indies*. This Father has even traced out the Track he must have followed in his Journey thither from the *Indies*; but his Notions as to this Matter are quite intolerable, and can never be brought to quadrate with the Geography of those Parts.

The Track Kircher *will have St.* Thomas *to have followed.*

In the first Place, he brings St. *Thomas* to a Town of *Persia*, called *Soldania* or *Soltania*, which is known to be in the Province of *Beladaljebel*, or the *Country of Mountains*, and to have been built by *Muhamed* the Son of *Argun Khan*, in the Year of the *Hejra* DCCX. and of *Jesus Christ* MCCCX. Thence he conducts him to *Cabul*, a City famous for Trade; and thence to another he calls *Cafurstan*, or *City of Infidels*, because

cause inhabited by Christians only, whom the *Mohammedans* call *Kafars* or *Infidels*. No *Arabian* Geographer or *Persian*, has taken Notice of this Town, so that *Kircher* for this depends only on the Authority of *Benet Goez* a Brother *Jesuit*, who came by Land from *China* to the *Indies*; but by the Manner of spelling this Name, as it stands in the *China Illustrata*, it seems evident that this *Casurstan* is owing to a Mistake in reading the Name of the Province of *Curistan*, or *Cuzistan*, which is a Part of the ancient *Susiana*, which was usually crossed by the Merchants of *Mesopotamia* and *Persia*, who went by Land to *Tibet*. The Matter, however, was not to exhibit a Diary of St. *Thomas*'s Travels this Way, tho' the Road pricked down, had been as plausible as this is not.

All the Proofs hitherto offered to persuade us St. *Thomas* preached in *China*, are founded upon mere Conjecture only, whereas this Monument, whose Authority cannot well be contested, assures us, the first Knowledge the *Chinese* had of the Evangelic Faith, was not before the VII Century; nor is there the least Footstep of the contrary in Ecclesiastical Antiquity. It remains now, that we enquire who these first Missionaries may have been, a Point as yet not sufficiently cleared up.

The Observations already made upon the *Syrian* Words, at once declare, that this Mission consisted of *Syrians*, that they were of the same Church with those who erect- *This first Mission consisted of* Syrians.

ed this Monument to commemorate the first Appearance of the Gospel in *China*, seeing they call them *their Fathers*; and that they professed Obedience to the *Catholic*, and that his Name was *Hananjashuah*.

Again, there is not the least Room to imagin these first Preachers were not *Syrians*, seeing that the Date which is as the Seal of what is contained in the Inscription, as also the Signatures, which have an absolute Affinity with those still in Use with the *Eastern* Churches in all Writings of Record, are in the *Syrian* Tongue, the holy Language, wherein they celebrated Divine Service, and transacted all Church Matters. If the Priests and others mentioned in the Body of the Inscription had been of *Egypt*, the Date and their Names had been written in *Greek*, or in *Coptic*. They were then of the same Church with the first Preachers, and subordinate to the same Patriarchs, a Thing of the plainest Visibility, seeing they looked on their Predecessors as *their Fathers*.

The Syrians *of different Communions; and those who went to* China *were* Nestorians.

In former times there were *Syrians* of different Sects, as at this day, *Melchites*, or *Orthodox*, *Nestorians*, and *Jacobites*: Now if we can discover the Seet of the Person styled Patriarch, we shall be infallibly guided to the Communion of the Clergy who acknowledged him their Superior. The very Title therefore of Catholic, to which Patriarch is annexed, is a demonstrative Proof, that he was the Catholic of the *Nestorians*, who was Patriach in re-

spect

spect of them, as being subordinate to no other; and the rather, as neither the Patriarch of *Antioch*, nor him of *Alexandria* ever assumed the Style of Catholic. But the dispute is incontestably decided by the Testimony of the *Nestorian* Church her self, who acknowledges an *Hananjashuah* among her Catholics, or Patriarchs, and declares he lived about the time this Monument was erected. Several of the Names which fill up the Margins of the Stone, are compounded of two Words, a Custom more prevalent among the *Syrians* of *Mesopotamia*, and the *Nestorians*, than with any of the rest; and this added to the Arguments before offered, confirms these Preachers to have been of their Communion. And what still proves it more and more, is the manner of explaining the Mystery of the Incarnation; for through the Clouds of the *Chinese* Style, we discern the Doctrin of this Sect, which admits the Union but by the Inhabitation of the Word, and the Communication of his Dignity and infinite Power.

The Chinese *part of the Inscription alone contains what is said of the Progress of Christianity.*

This is all we learn from the *Syriac* Inscription; but the *Chinese* Words contain a more minute Detail of the Progress of this Mission. It is there said that this *Olopuen* from *Tacin*, that is, from *Syria* or *Judæa*, did in the Year which coincides with the DCXXXVI of *Jesus Christ*, in the Reign of *Tai çum-ven*, promulgate the Law of the true God; that this Prince approving of it, commanded it to be proclaimed all

all over *China*, and the Emperor's Edict to that End is summarily referred to, bearing Date DCXXIX; that at the same time a Church was built in the Royal City of *Ininfan.* That some Years afterwards, in DCLI. under the Emperor *Cao-ſun*, the Christian Faith was known in every Province of *China.* That in the Years DCXCIX. and DCCXIII. the *Bonzes*, or idolatrous Prieſt, raiſed ſome tumult againſt the Chriſtians; but that the ſame was quelled by the Authority of the Emperor *Yven-ſun-ci-tao.* That in the Year DCCXLVII. there came from *Tacin* another Prieſt, called *Kieho*; that the Emperor *So-cum-ven-mi* had built ſeveral Churches in the Year DCCLVII. that his Succeſſors were, in like manner, Friends to Chriſtianity; and that at length this Stone was erected in Commemoration of all theſe Facts in the ſecond Year of the Emperor *Tam*, and DCCLXXXII. of *Chriſt.* You may read it at length in *Kircher*'s *China Illuſtrata*, but this is a Summary of the whole.

Whereupon it is ſaid the Chineſe *Hiſtory concerns not it ſelf with Foreign Matters.*

What *Couplet* relates in his *Hiſtorical Abridgment*, is borrowed from this Inſcription, and he himſelf confeſſes there is no Mention at all made of the Event in *Chineſe* Hiſtory; and the reaſon is, becauſe it concerns not itſelf with what belongs to Strangers. But this Reaſon is liable to ſome Confutation; for this ſame Hiſtory records the Embaſſy ſent into the *Indies* in queſt of the Saint pretended to have been

been foretold by *Confucius* ; it reco ds also the evil Result of this Inquiry, whence sprang among them the worship of *Foee*, Idolatry, and the Doctrin of Transmigration. The knowledge of Christianity, the Root it took over the whole Empire, and the Imperial Edicts in Favor thereof, were not in the least more Foreign to the *Chinese* Affairs, than the new Religion of *Foee*. It is then on all Hands agreed, that the *Chinese* History, and that also of the *Nestorian* Patriarchs, is totally silent upon this Head: Wherefore we are reduced to the Necessity of wholly relying on the Incision upon the *Chinese* Stone ; but particularly upon the Date the Translators have fixed to the Year of *Christ* DCXXXVI. for the Appearance of the first Preacher of the Gospel in these Parts, who is *Olopuen*.

It is rational to think that Olopuen *was a* Syrian *of the same Church with those who ordered the Inscription.*

We have heretofore remarked that we have no Assistance, whereby to get acquainted with this *Olopuen* ; and that to all Appearance it is a *Chinese* Name, imposed on him in the Country, as the Custom still is in Cases of the like Nature ; for this Name is by no means *Syriac*, nor has it any Affinity therewith. All therefore we can deduce from certain consequences, is, that this same Preacher, and the other mentioned after him in the Inscription, were of the very same Church with those who erected this Monument, seeing they call them *their Fathers*. They then paid Obedience to the Catholics, or Patriarchs of the *Nestorians*, the Predecessors of *Hananjashuah*,

ashuah, and were consequently of Communion with him; and as certain it is that he was a *Nestorian*, the others must have been so likewise, the Title of Catholic prefixed to that of Patriarch, being quite peculiar to the *Nestorians*.

A Series of the Nestorian *Patriarchs of those Times.*

From the Year DCXXXVI. the first Epoch noted in the *Chinese* Inscription, down to *Hananjashuah* the second of the Name, under whom this Inscription was dated in the Year DCLXXX. or two Years afterwards, according to the Computation of those who translated the *Chinese*, the History of the *Nestorians* has the following Patriarchs, *Jashuaiab*, *Mar-Amba*, *Jashuaiab*, *Gregory*, *John*, *Hananjashuah*, another *John* intruded, *Selibazaba*, *Phiton*, *Mar-Aba*, *Surin* or *Surenas*, *James*, and *Hananjashuah* the second of that Name. At first they resided at *Seleucia* and *Ctesiphon*, which were considered as one and the same City, by the *Arabs* called *Modain*. He who stands foremost in this List, was consecrated in the Reign of *Siroes* the *Parricide*, who died towards the Year DCXXXIV. *Ardeshir*, who succeeded him, reigned but one Year; and *Buran* the Daughter of *Cosroes*, who according to the *Persian* Historians, was the only Survivor of the Royal House, ascended the Throne. The *Nestorians* have it, that she sent *Jashuaiab* in quality of her Ambassador to the *Greek* Emperor, and charged with considerable Presents; that he met with a very gracious Reception; that he made his Con-

fession

fession of Faith, and that he celebrated the Liturgy in presence of the Emperor, who received the Sacrament at his Hands: A Circumstance worthy of just as much belief, as is due to many of the same Stamp in their History. By the Testimony of the *Greek* Authors, and particularly of *Theophanes*, it is certain that this Queen maintained Peace with the *Greek* Emperors, and that she ruled with great Wisdom. They call her *Buran* as doth the *Nestorian* History. The *Persians* call her *Turan*, and *Turan-docht*, and exhibit a Series of Kings and one Queen called *Arzemi-docht*, before *Isdejerd*, under whom *Persia* fell a Conquest to the fortunate *Mohammedans*, whereas the *Nestorian* Accounts, make her the immediate Successor to *Buran*, or *Turan-docht*, in consideration that the intervening Princes sat but a short time, and in the midst of great Commotions. The *Persian* History before the Conquest is extremely intricate, whether we consult the *Persians* themselves, or the *Arabs*, and the several Copies are not of one Mind, as to the Name of this Queen *Turan-docht*, by others called *Buran*, as in the History of the *Nestorians*. *Touan* is a Name *in nubibus*, for which we stand indebted to *Schikard*'s mistaken reading; all that he says in his *Tarich Regum Persiæ*, so much famed, vanishes away to nothing, or is reducible to very Trifles, if we except what he borrows from *Teixeira*, and the *Jukhassin*; but we cannot dwell longer upon this Head, without wandering into

Emir. Cond. deb. Tarik. Kozid. Teixeira. p. 208.

into a Digression, which would lead us too far astray.

What is to be found in the History of the Nestorians *touching the last Kings of* Persia.

We will insist therefore on no more than what the History of the *Nestorian* Churches adds concerning the Patriarch *Jashuaiab*. It informs us that he lived in the Reign of the last King *Isdejerd*, and that he survived under the *Kalif Omar*, the Son of *Al Kittab*, the third *Kalif*, at whose Hands he obtained an ample Protection, as well as an Exemption from all manner of Taxes for himself and his. The same History has it, that, while *Isdejerd* was yet living, he sent Presents and Letters to *Mohammed*, or, as others express themselves, to the General of the *Arabian* Army, to request his Favour, a Step, which though it had like to have cost him his Life, procured him the injoyment of his wish. *Omar* began his Reign, as *Kalif*, in the thirteenth Year of the *Hejra*, and *Modain* was taken in the Years DCXXXIV. and DCXXXII, of *Jesus Christ*. This last Date therefore quadrates with the Date of the *Chinese* Inscription, and the arrival of *Olopuen* in *China*, if the Supputation of the Translators be right. And yet the *Nestorian* Writings make no mention of Ecclesiastics sent to *China*, or into the Provinces of the *Upper Asia* about these Times; and very hard it is to comprehend, how amidst the Broils which then distracted *Persia*, and the very extraordinary Revolution upon the Conquest of the whole Kingdom by the *Mohammo-*

hammedans, the Catholic ſhould have been able to ſend a Miſſion into *China*.

Muller thought the Chriſtians fled from Perſecution into the neighbouring Provinces, and that thence they might have penetrated into *China*; and indeed this Conjecture might paſs, was it not repugnant to Hiſtory, which moſt explicitly declares, that the *Neſtorians* enjoyed themſelves in Peace, from the Reign of *Siroes*, that they were countenanced by Queen *Turan-docht*, and that the *Mohammedans* from the very beginning, were ſtill more kind to them. *Mohammed* himſelf had recommended them to his Captains, and had granted them Protections, which were confirmed by *Omar* the third Kalif, and which, as the Hiſtorian aſſures us, were preſerved, and afterwards ſtill farther confirmed by *Othman* an *Ali*. The Chriſtians had nothing to compel them out of the Country, or to take Refuge elſewhere, and leaſt of all the *Neſtorians*, who were more numerous than the reſt, and by no Means obnoxious, as being proſcribed and expelled the Provinces under the *Greek* Emperors. Again they had a ſolid Claim to the *Mohammedan* Friendſhip, they being the firſt that made Advances towards a Submiſſion to the falſe Prophet, whom the *Neſtorians* alone have applauded as the *Extirpator of Idolatry*, nor have their Divines ſcrupled to quote the *Koran*, in ſpeaking of the Myſtery of the Incarnation: Their Hiſtory acquaints us, that ſeveral Chriſtians of this ſame Communion, were

The Christians did not remove out of Perſia *to avoid the Perſecution of the* Arabs.

Amruſ. Matth. Ele. Niſib.

were much considered at the Court of *Bagdad*, and particularly in the Reign of *Almamun*, who imployed them in the Translations he ordered of the ancient *Greek* Books into *Arabic*; they were valued also for the Skill some of them had in Physic, as *Honain* the Son of *Isaac*, and his Son. *John* the Son of *Massowia*, known by the Name of *Mesvus*, *Boctjashuah*, *George*, and *Gabriel*, mentioned by *Abulfaragius*, as well as those who penned the Lives of the Physicians. So *Muller's* Conjecture must fall to the Ground, and the rather, because the Christians could not withdraw from the Provinces late in Subjection to the Kings of *Persia*, without exposing themselves to very great Dangers, in the Midst of barbarous and mostly irreligious Nations, as those were, who inhabited the *Transoxane* quite to *China*.

We know nothing of this Mission but by the Inscription on the Chinese *Stone.*

We must be contented therefore, with what we are told by the *Chinese* Inscription, whose Authority cannot well be contested, tho' the History of the *Nestorian* Patriarchs does say nothing of any *Syrian* Missionaries sent to *China*. For this History is so imperfect that no Wonder it slips over the Concerns of so distant a Country, seeing it omits many Facts of the same Nature, which we know from other Hands. The other Histories, as well Printed as in Manuscript, are by no Means more complete, and the Aversion the Orthodox or *Melchites*, as well as the *Jacobites*, have ever had to the *Nestorians*, is the Reason they

they ſcarce name them; beſides, it is probable they knew but little of what paſſed in a Communion they had nothing at all to do with.

These Miſſionaries were Neſtorians.

Suppoſing then the Contents of the *Chineſe* Inſcription to be true, and we have almoſt all the Reaſon in the World to admit it; Chriſtianity was firſt taught in *China* in the Courſe of the ſeventh Century, and the firſt Miſſionaries were *Neſtorians*, of the ſame Church with thoſe who erected this Monument, one Hundred and forty-ſix Years afterwards, to commemorate this firſt Miſſion. Nor can we doubt but that, in Conformity to the common Diſciplin of all Chriſtians, the Catholics or Patriarchs of the *Neſtorians*, erected the uſual Hierarchy, ſending one or ſeveral Biſhops thither, without which, this infant Church could not ſo long have ſubſiſted; accordingly in the *Syriac* Signatures, you have the Names of a Biſhop, a Chorepiſcopus, Prieſts and Deacons; and it is altogether probable, that as faſt as there was a ſufficient Number of Converts, they appointed Paſtors over the new Chriſtians: But tho' Hiſtory nor this Inſcription is particular as to this Point, there is an important and collateral Teſtimony which makes it almoſt certain.

Their Notitia *has a Metropolitan of* China.

We have a *Notitia* of the Metropolitans of the *Neſtorian* Church, which cannot be queſtioned, the ſix firſt of them being the ſame as are in the *Office of the Conſecration of the Catholic*, publiſhed by Father

De Sanct. Ordin. *Morin*, as the Chief in Dignity, and the ſame as are often mentioned in Hiſtory, as are moſt of the reſt. The Order theſe *Metropolitans* ſtand in, ſeems at firſt to be confuſed; and it might be thought, they are not named according to the Rank they held in the Church. For the Metropolitan of *Jeruſalem* is but the twenty-ſecond, tho' there are but twenty-four in all, which is contrary to the Uſage of other Churches, and to the Canons of the Council of *Nice*, which dignifies him next after the four Patriarchs. And hence is it that he, for many Ages, has been conſidered as the fifth Patriarch in the *Greek* Church, and in the *Latin*; tho' the ſame was not allowed him by the *Coptic* Church of *Alexandria*. But it may be readily underſtood that this Order, the *Neſtorian Metropolitans* ſtand in, was not regulated by the Dignity, but the Antiquity of each. Now this Antiquity was not deduced from the Rank theſe Metropolitan Cities may have enjoyed under the Chriſtian Emperors; for in thoſe Days they were ſcarce known, and deſtitute of Biſhops, nay, ſome of them were not built.

They erect a new Hierarchy. The *Neſtorians* then erected a new Hierarchy, whoſe general Metropolis, and, as it were, the Capital of their Patriarchat was *Seleucia* of the *Parthians*, and *Cteſiphon*, which have been deemed as one and the ſame City. *Simon*, by the *Neſtorians* called *Barſabai*, who ſuffered Martyrdom in *Sapor*'s great Perſecution, and whom they

they number with their *Catholics*, was, according to *Sozomen*, Archbishop of *Seleucia* and *Ctesiphon*, Royal Cities of *Persia*. The *Nestorians* there settled, and rose to great Authority under *Cosroes Nushirowan*, who protected them in Opposition to the *Greek* Emperors, and compelled the other Christians to embrace their Communion. In this State of Favor they remained under the last Kings of *Persia*, and the same was secured to them, as has already been said, by the first Kalifs. As they well knew, and as was the Belief of all Christians, there could be no such Thing as being of the Church without an Apostolical Succession, that is, if the principal See had not been founded by some of the Apostles or Disciples of *Jesus Christ*, a Prerogative they wanted, they sought for one which they thought sufficient. They began then with the holy Bishops of *Seleucia*, whom they would have to be the Predecessors of their *Catholics*, but fraught with no other Proof than that of possessing the same Churches, wherewith they had been invested by infidel Princes. Then as, according to the Tradition of the *Mesopotamian* Churches, St. *Thadæus* preached the Gospel at *Edessa*, a See they had also usurped, as well as the ancient School of the Holy Scripture, whence they were driven by *Heraclius*, but which they were restored to by the *Arabs*; by the help of this and many Figments at the beginning of their History, they persuaded their

Ἀρχιεπίσκοπος Σελευκείας, καὶ Κτησιφῶντος τῶν ἐν Περσίδι βασιλευουσῶν πολιῶν.

Sozom. l. 2. c. 8. *Cedren.* T. 1. p. 415.

People, that St. *Thadæus* had founded the Church of *Seleucia*, and the Dignity of *Catholic*. Thus is it that they fixed their Patriarchal See at *Modain*, the ancient *Seleucia*, and when that City was partly ruined, and *Almansur* the Kalif had built *Bagdad*, they transferred it thither.

The Erection of their new Metropolitane.

The Foundation of this new Hierarchy being laid in *Persia*, their first Metropolitan City was *Jundaisabur*, built by *Sapor Ardshir* King of *Persia*, and which before had not so much as a Bishop. The second was *Nisibis*, after they had expelled the Orthodox from that City and School there, which they did to honour their Sect by the Commemoration of St. *James*, and many other Saints. The third was *Bassora*, the fourth *Hazza*, the ancient *Arbela*, by the *Arabs*, *Erbel:* The fifth was *Bajarmi*, or as the *Syrians* pronounce it *Beitgarma*, the ancient *Martyropolis*; the sixth was *Halwan*, a City of *Irak*, five Days from *Bagdad*, but unknown to Antiquity. These six first Metropolitan Cities, accounted such by the *Nestorians* only, were either in *Mesopotamia*, or the *Irak Ajami* or the *Persian Irak*, it being in these Provinces that they first began to spread. After this they erected a Metropolitan of *Persia* that is of the Country comprehended under the Name of *Fars*, or *Persia* properly so called, they being admitted by the last Kings. From thence they penetrated into the *Upper-Asia*, and the ninth Metropolitan was that of *Maru* in *Chorassan*; the tenth

Abulf. n. 291.

was

was *Aract*, the *Aria* of the Ancients; the eleventh *Katarba*, but little known. To conclude, the twelfth was that of *China*, the thirteenth that of the *Indies*.

According to what we have noted above, this Order or Series of *Metropolitans*, acquaints us with the Seniority of each; and thence it follows that *China* being, in the *Notitia*, named before the *Indies*, must have been the elder of the two. It may be said these two were but one, and it may seem that *Trigaut* supplies us with a Proof thereof; for speaking of the two last Bishops sent to the *Indies* by the *Nestorian* Patriarch, at the Time that *D. Alexis de Meneses* was labouring to reform the *Malabar* Churches, he says, *they called themselves* Metropolitans *of the* Indies *and of* China. It is true, that in the latter Ages these two Titles were put together, but formerly they were distinct; and in the History of the *Nestorians*, we read of several Examples of two Bishoprics in like Manner united, even of two Metropolitan Sees in one Person. So the Catholic *Shebarjashuah* who is the LXV, and was consecrated towards the End of the eleventh Century, united the Bishoprics of *Cashgar* and *Waset*, in the Person of the Priest *Hormisdas*, a Native of *Siraf*. Another called *Stephen*, was appointed Bishop of *Elsan* and *Bowazije*. The Metropolis of *Halwan* was united with that of *Rai*; *Hazza* or *Arbela*, and *Musol*, two of the six Principal, were held by the same Metropolitan *Jabalaha*.

They were ranked according to Seniority.

Gov. *Hist.* of Menes.

There are many Examples of the same kind that occur among the *Nestorians*, and the Abuse sprang from these Sources; for, *First*, notwithstanding the ancient Canons, they admit in Concurrence with other Christians, no Sect has more daringly infringed them, and especially in the Translation of Bishops. Most of their Catholics and Patriarchs were Bishops or Metropolitans of other Churches, which not only was no Obstacle in the Way of their Election, but they were also consecrated a new, much in the same Form with Bishops. The *Coptic* Church of *Alexandria* never gave way to this Abuse, and down to these latter Times she has observed it as a Rule, never to elect any Man her Patriarch, if by Consecration he was wedded to any particular Church. The *Jacobite* Church of *Antioch* adhered a long Time to the same, and two of her Metropolitans chose rather to lay down their Lives, than consent to the Election of *Isaac* Bishop of *Harran* into the Patriarchal See of *Antioch*. The *Greeks* have a long while forgot this holy Institution, nor can we ourselves decently reproach them therewith. It may then have hapned, that the *Nestorian* Patriarchs, presuming upon the full Power they arrogated, thought they had Authority to make these Unions; but to deal ingenuously by them, they may have had this; *Secondly*, To excuse them, that their Sect dwindling considerably away in the second and third Century

Elmac. p. 98.

tury of *Mohammedism*, by means of the Privileges the *Melchites* and *Jacobites* obtained of the *Kalifs* and *Soltans*, it hapned that in many Cities where the *Nestorians* had been the only Christians, they were not a number sufficient to constitute an Episcopal Church or a Metropolitan. Hence some came to be joined with their Neighbours, others were totally extinguished, as in process of Time hapned to that of *China*, when Christianity was there no more, as was the Case when the *Portuguese* first arrived there. Then it became a mere Title like those *in Partibus Infidelium.*

The Patriarchs of Antioch *sent no Missionaries to* China.

The *Greek* Patriarchs of *Antioch* have pretended that their Jurisdiction reached all over the *East*, whence it is said in the *Notitia* of *Nilus Doxapatrius*, *That his Authority extended over all* Asia, *the* East, *and the* Indies, *whither he sent a Catholic called of* Romogyris. This Title may have been kept up together with some others assumed by the *Greek* Patriarch of *Antioch*: But we find not the least vestige in History since the seventh Century at least, of *Catholics* or *Metropolitans* sent to the *Indies*, either by the Orthodox or *Jacobite* Patriarchs of *Antioch*, much less to *China*, where the Christians were always of the *Nestorian* Persuasion.

Κατεῖχεν ἅπασαν τὴν Ἀσίαν καὶ ἀνατολὴν αὐτήν τε τὴν Ἰνδίαν, &c

Allat. l. 1. c. 9. p. 166.

These first Missionaries went to China *by Land.*

There is Reason then to believe, that those who went thither to spread the Light of the Gospel, obscured as it was by the darkness of Errors, took the way of the Provinces conterminous with *Chorassan*,

 and

and that they travelled thither by Land. For that enigmatical Expreſſion, *contemplando ventorum regulam, & a nubibus cæruleis directus*, is far from proving, that this *Olopuen* ſailed thither by Sea, and by the help of the Compaſs. We want ſomething more than *Chineſe* Hiſtory to perſuade us they knew any thing of the Magnetic Needle, but if we grant the *Chineſe* to have uſed it, we are pretty ſure the *Syrians* did not; the Courſe they ſhaped for the *Indies* is a plain Demonſtration of their Ignorance in this Particular. But, indeed as they had vaſt Deſarts to croſs before they could reach *China*, they might have had recourſe to the Needle to guide them, juſt as they do in the vaſt Wilderneſſes of *America*, when they were out upon any Diſcovery. Others, as thoſe mentioned in the Sequel of the *Chineſe* Inſcription, may have gone thither by Sea, ſteering the ſame Courſe laid down by our Authors; and it is likely they went much about the ſame Time, the Metropolis of the *Indies* being immediately named after that of *China*.

How long Chriſtianity laſted in China.

We may conclude, then, from what we are told by the Inſcription, that Chriſtianity which was firſt preached in *China* in the Year DCXXXVI, ſubſiſted there till the Date in *Syriac*, that is, till the Year of Chriſt DCCLXXX and even a conſiderable time afterwards, ſince *Abu Zeid*, the Author of the ſecond *Account*, ſpeaking of the general Revolution which happened in

China

China, and particularly of the Deſtruction of *Canſu* in the Year of the *Hejra* CCLXIV, or of *Jeſus Chriſt* DCCCLXXVII, relates that a great Number of Chriſtians was there ſlaughtered. He ſays nothing of thoſe in other Cities, whence it ſeems that in this City, which was the principal Scale, there were none but Merchants.

But we are told by another Author, whom we know but by the means of *Golius*, in the Margin of one part of his Notes upon *Alfraganus*, that the Chatholics ſent ſome Eccleſiaſtics into *China*, above an hundred Years afterwards. This is the Tranſlation. "*Abulfergius* relates, from the "Teſtimony of a Monk of *Najaran*, theſe "very Words, That he returned from *China* in the Year CCCLXXXVII, that is in "the Year of *Chriſt* DCCCCLXXXXVII "whither he had been ſent, ſeven Years "before, or thereabouts, by the Catholics, "together with five Perſons more; and "that the Name of the City, he had been "at, was *Tajuna*.

Hence we infer, that towards the end of the tenth Century, the Catholics or *Neſtorian* Patriarchs continued to ſend Miſſionaries to *China*, after the Example of their Predeceſſors. But from that time we are on all ſides left in the dark concerning theſe Miſſions, whence it ſhould ſeem that Chriſtianity was ſoon after wholly loſt in that Country by ſome Cauſe to us unknown. We do not diſcern that there was any Perſecution, like the laſt in *Japan*, one

We know nothing further of the Chriſtians of this Country ſince the tenth Century.

one of the moſt cruel the Church ever underwent; nor could the Revolutions, brought upon *China* by the *Tartar* Conqueſts of *Jenghiz Khan* and his Succeſſors, have been fatal to the Chriſtians; for we know that *Jenghiz Khan* himſelf had a love for them; his principal Wife was the Daughter of *Ung Khan* whom he deſpoiled of Empire, and who was a Chriſtian, as were many of the Hoards of *Tartars* that paid him Homage. His Succeſſors were to the full as well inclined towards the Chriſtians; and in the Life of *Jahabalaha*, which ends the Hiſtory of the *Neſtorians*, we read very remarkable Inſtances to prove it. It is therein related that this Catholic was originally of *Cathay*, and that he was ſent by *Abaſha-Khan*, great Emperor of the *Tartars*, to viſit the holy Places at *Jeruſalem*, there to lay certain coſtly Robes upon the Sepulchre, and afterwards dip them in the *Jordan*: That afterwards he was made Metropolitan of *Tangut*, by his Predeceſſor *Danha*, who had inveſted him with a plenary Authority over the Hoards of Chriſtian *Tartars*, and that at laſt he was choſen Catholic. He ſat thirty ſeven Years; but when the *Tartars* were driven from *Bagdad*, the *Mohammedans* deſtroyed a part of the *Neſtorian* Churches, added to the former Tributes, and things put on quite another Face.

From that time Hiſtory ſays nothing of the ſubject we have been upon, and we are

are left barely to guess at what may further concern it. This last Revolution fell out a little before this Catholic dyed, who departed this Life in the MDCXXIX Year of the *Seleucidæ*, or the Year MCCCXVII of *Jesus Christ*. We find no Name that succeeded him, and very probable it is, that Chistianity dwindled away by Degrees in *China* for want of Pastors, or for some other reasons we know not. For when the *Portuguese* sailed to *China* in the Year MDXVII under the command of *Fernand Perez d'Andrade*, who was the first that went to *Canton*, there was not the least Footstep of Christianity to be traced out; and the first Missionaries of that Nation as well as the *Castilians*, who crossed over from the *Philippine* Island, met with none that were not Idolaters. Some Crosses and other Signs, which have been since discovered, being naked of all Date or Inscription, could afford us no certain Light, till the Year MDCXXV, when the Monument we have had under consideration was discovered.

Barros. T. 3. l. 2. c. 6. 7, 8.

A N

AN

INQUIRY

Into the Time when the *Mohammedans* first entered into

CHINA.

OF the many curious Particulars to be found in the *Two Accounts* we have presented to the Public, the Entrance of the *Mohammedans* into *China*, before the third Century of the *Hejra*, is not the least considerable. All their Historians are very obscure upon their Travels or Voyages to this part of the *Upper Asia*; and their most famous Geographers differ so widely from each other, that we may believe they were as ignorant of those Parts, as we were in *Europe* before the Nautical Attempts of the two last Ages. *Abulfeda*, the most accurate of their Geographers, speaks of *China* merely by what he heard from some Merchants. The rest are full of Fables, such as *Alexander*'s Travels to *China*, his Conference with the Emperor there, and the like: Their Copists have but added to the useless Lumber by fresh

fresh Stories, which have thickened the Mist, and may convince us of their thorough Ignorance: And, indeed, our Authors seem to be the first, and almost the only Writers that have dwelt on those Parts with some tolerable exactness. They first told us the *Mohammedans* had a considerable Settlement in the principal Port of *China*, and that they had there a *Kadi*, who acted both as a Judge, and a Spiritual Director. In a word, that great Numbers of *Mohammedans* were in the Imperial City before the great Revolution, mentioned in the second *Account*.

Our own Ancient Authors take Notice, that in the vast Provinces, known formerly by the Name of *Cathay*, they met with *Mohammedans*, who had been there a long while; and the Accounts of the first *Jesuits* that went to *China*, confirm what they say. They, in every City, found *Mohammedans*, in Number sufficient to evince That they must have been of very old standing in the Country. But since nor the Ancients nor the Moderns give us any Circumstances, or inform us when or how they came into this Country, it may not be unacceptable if we make some Inquiry into this Matter.

Whether the Mohammedans *went thither by Land.*

It is the Belief of many that the *Mohammedans* went first to *China* by Land, and that the Track pursued by some modern Travellers, ought to point out to us the Road the Ancients may have taken: *Marco Polo*, say they, went into *China* by the

the way of *Tartary*; *Mandeville* almost trod in his very Footsteps; *Jenghiz Khan*, the first Emperor of the *Moguls*, conquered a Part of *China*, and marched thereto from the ancient *Mogulistan* or *Turkestan*; we have a *Persian* Account of an Embassy from a *Tartar* Prince to the Emperor of *China*, and this Ambassador went also by Land; at the beginning of this Century, *Benet Goez*, a Jesuit, travelled also from the *Indies* to *Pekin*; the Fathers *Grueber* and *Orville* did a few Years ago perform the same Journey the *Moscovite* Ambassadors do when they go to *China*, and they even assure us, this Rout, which is not always the same, is pretty well frequented by the Caravans of the Merchants of the *Upper Asia*. These different Routs are pricked down in the Map of *Cathay*, published by *Kircher* in his *China Illustrata*; and Father *Couplet* had another, which pretty much confounded us, tho' the Names of the Places were written in *Persian*.

Voyages de Thevenot. T. 4.

All these Instances sufficiently prove that we may go to *China* by Land, and there is no doubt of it; but the Way held by a small Number of Travellers does not seem to prove, That for certain the same was held by the Caravans and Merchants, which ought to have been the Case, for such a Number of *Mohammedans* to get into *China* that way. For, according to the old Method of travelling in Caravans, it was a very hard matter for the Merchants of *Persia* and *Mesopotamia* to go thither by Land,

Land, unless the Track was well frequented; and it seems not only certain that it was far from being so, but also that it was considered only as a By-way, a Short Cut.

The better to clear up this Difficulty, which, well explained, may let us into many Points of Eastern History and Geography, we must first survey the Extent of the *Mohammedan* Empire in the third Century of the *Hejra*, and at the same time consider what Bounds the Eastern Geographers set to the Provinces of the *Upper Asia*, nearest the Borders of *China*.

To clear up this matter we must examin what were the Limits of the Mohammedan *Empire in the third Century.*

Mohammed made himself Master of a part of *Arabia*; and *Abubecr* his Successor conquered the rest of this Province, with the greatest part of *Syria*: *Egypt* also was subdued in his Reign, and these Conquests were ensued by others Westward, which are foreign to our Subject. In *Asia*, the *Mohammedans* had two potent Enemies to cope with, the *Romans* and the *Persians*: the former were Lords of the greatest part of *Syria* on this side the *Euphrates*; the latter were Supreme over the rest, and their Empire extended far away into the *Upper Asia*. The *Romans* were driven out of *Syria* in the Reign of *Heraclius*, by *Omar* the third Kalif, who possessed himself of *Damascus*, and all the *Holy Land*. The Empire of the *Sassanian* or *Cosroid Persians* expired at almost the same time, by the Defeat of *Isdejerd*, the Son of *Shah-Riar*, the last of these Princes, who being forced out of all the *Persian Irak*, retreated into *Chorassan*, where he was

was almost instantly attacked by the King of *Turkestan*, and at last slain in the Year of the *Hejra* XXXI, of *Christ* DCLI. At this same time the *Arabs* made a Conquest of the greatest part of *Chorassan*; and *Abdallah*, the Son of *Amar*, who commanded the Troops on that side, advanced quite up to the *Oxus* or River of *Balk*, before the Death of *Isdejerd*.

The civil War which broke out in the Reign of *Ali*, the fifth Kalif, and which blazed till the Settlement of the Family of the *Ommiyads*, put a stop to this mighty Progress: But in the Year of the *Hejra* LXXVI, and of *Jesus Christ* DCXCV, they made an irruption into *Tabaristan* or *Tabrestan*. In the first Century also they made some Conquests in *Armenia*, and and in the Country of the *Turks*; but as the *Arabs* bestowed this Name promiscuously on several Provinces of the *Upper Asia*, which they knew not, it is impossible to say how far they advanced in their first Wars with the ancient People of *Turkestan*.

Elmac. p. 70.

Walid, the thirteenth Kalif, who began his Reign in the Year of the *Hejra* LXXXVI, and of *Christ* DCCV, did very much enlarge the Extent of the *Mohammedan* Empire. *Katiba*, one of his Generals, conquered the *Mawaralnahra* or *Transoxane*, took *Bokara*, and *Samarcand* the Capital of the *Sogd*, or *Sogdiana* of the Ancients, together with *Farganah*, and many other Cities farther remote, beyond which the

the *Mohammedans* marched not, till a long time afterwards. It is true, the *Oriental* Histories tell us, that in the Days of *Malec-shah* the third of the *Seljukids*, their Empire reached to *Cashgar*, but this Kingdom was not subdued under the Kalifs, but by Kings, who not only disowned the Kalif's Yoke, but *Mohammedism* also; for Historians observe, that *Michael* the Son of *Seljuk*, was the first *Turk* that turned *Mohammedan*.

Elmac. Leb. Tarik. Emir. Cond. Abulfeda.

When our Authors wrote, the Mohammedan *Empire extended to the Frontiers of* China.

We must conclude then, that in the third Century of *Mohammedism*, when our Authors lived, the *Mohammedans* might go to the uttermost Parts of the *Mawaralnahra*, without exceeding the Bounds of their Empire; and that thus they were at no great Distance from the Frontiers of *China*: But it is not likely they were at that Time settled at *Cashgar*. Under the Empire of the *Seljukids*, indeed, they were a considerable Body there, and according to *Abulfeda*, this City produced a great number of Persons famed for Learning.

The Way by Cashgar.

Cashgar, according to both ancient and modern Geographers, was usually crossed by those who went either into *Turkestan*, or *China*. Some place this City in *Turkestan*, but others, upon better Ground, write it the Capital of a Kingdom of the same Name, inhabited by *Mohammedans*. According to *Abulfeda*, it is in 96 or 95, that is, in 105 or 106 Deg. 30 Min. of Longitude, and in 44 Deg. of Latitude, and so must be much more Easterly than *Samar-*

cand, which, according to the ſame Author, is in 89 or 88 Degrees of Longitude, and in the 40th Degree of Latitude; that is, according to the uſual Computation, 98 or 99 Degrees of Longitude, by adding the ten Degree neceſſary to make *Abulfeda*'s Meridian coincide with the Meridian of the other Geographers. After this Rate the Way the *Arabs* muſt have held for *China*, was by going firſt into *Choraſſan*, from thence into the *Mawaralnahra*; to have gone ſtrait from *Samarcand*, or ſome other City of the Province, deſtroyed by the *Moguls*, into *Tibet*, or to have gone into the Kingdom of *Caſhgar*, there to join the
Abulfed. p. 523. *Caravans*. They ſometimes alſo went by the way of *Gaznah*, upon the Skirts of *Choraſſan*, which had great Dealings; or by *Cabul* a City to the Eaſtward of *Gaznah*, and which, in *Abulfeda*'s Time, was the laſt City inhabited by *Mohammedans*, on the Borders of *Tokareſtan*, or *Turkeſtan*, and the Place where the *Indous* and *Moſlem* Traders uſually met. When theſe Travellers had got into *Tibet*, they might have entered *China*, by the Province of *Chenſi*, after they had croſſed the Sandy Deſart.

Another Way by Samarcand. But it was ſtill more eaſy to reach *China* by Land, if the Kingdom of *Samahand* be the ſame with that of *Samarcand*, and extends to the Sandy Deſart, as Father *Martini* has it in his Chart. Not but that the Diſtance is much the ſame, for theſe laſt Maps ſtretching *Samahand* to the Deſart, only allow it a larger Scope than the *Arabian*

bian Geographers. *Samarcand* is the Capital of the *Sogd*, and must be farther from *Tibet* than some Travellers give out, and among the rest *Benjamin* the *Jew*, who places it but four Days distant from the Capital of that Kingdom, whereas the Eastern Geographers clap ten Degrees between them. But there is no concluding any Thing from what they say; for they knew but little of the Provinces beyond the *Mawaralnahra*, and the Countries of *Cashgar* and *Cotan*; for under the general Name of *Turan*, or *Turkestan*, *Yajuje* and *Majuje*, that is, *Gog* and *Magog*, they comprehended all the Provinces Northward and Eastward of *China*. And some have enlarged *Chorassan* to that Degree, as to make it take in the greatest Part of the *Mawaralnahra* and *Chowarazm*, and so have made it a nearer Neighbour to *China*, than is allowed by the proper Limits of this Province.

Itiner. Benjam. p. 97.

What our Authors say to this Matter.

Our Authors seem to have been of this Opinion, and the last of them, giving an Account of a Man who went from *Samarcand* to *China*, observes it to be a two Months Journey from the Skirts of *China* to the *Sogd* of *Samarcand*, which is nearly the Distance of the two Ends of the *Sogd*, extending it to *Sicu*, which must be *Socheu*, on the Borders of the Province of *Chensi*. According to the Eastern Geographers, these two Cities * are 28 Degrees

* *Our Author is somewhat obscure in the preceding Period; but by these two Cities he seems to understand* Samarcand *and* Sicu *or* Socheu.

distant from each other; and these Degrees are equal to four Hundred and eighty *French* Leagues, at twenty to a Degree, which divided by sixty, give 8 Leagues for each Day, which, by the *Arabian* Geographers, are equal to a Days Journey for a Man that walks.

This Way was impracticable. But this Way by Land, whether by *Samarcand*, by *Cabul*, by *Gaznah*, or by *Cashgar*, was very impracticable in the Days our *Arabs* wrote, exclusive of the natural Inconveniendies of the Roads they were to travel. All the Trade of the *East* was then in the Hands of the Merchants of *Persia*, *Bassora*, and of the Coast quite down to the *Red-Sea*, which was the Center of the *Egyptian* Trade, and partly of the *Mediterranean*. They traded to the *Indies* by Land, in many Places, and particularly at *Cabul*. The Product of *Arabia*, *Egypt*, *Persia*, and the adjacent Provinces they exchanged with the Merchants of *Turkestan* and the *Indies*, for Musk, precious Stones, Chrystals, Spices, and Drugs: But it was almost impossible for them to go farther, or to drive a Trade quite home to *China*, because of the Desart, a dangerous Track; and still more, because of the continual Wars between the *Arabs* and the Princes of *Turkestan*. And the civil Broils which during the first Centuries, and afterwards were fomented between the different *Mohammedan* Princes of *Chorassan*, and the Tyranny of the Governors of Provinces in Times of Peace,

Peace added ſtill to the difficulties of Trading extenſively by Land.

Nor does it appear that any of theſe Obſtacles were removed for a conſiderable time; for the *Mahammedans* did not penetrate into thoſe Provinces of *Turkeſtan*, conterminous with the *Mawaralnahra* and *Chorasſan*, 'till three hundred Years after the firſt Voyages by Sea we are here to ſpeak of.

The Turks *came late into* Mohammediſm.

The various and numerous Nations, the *Arabs* comprehended under the general Name of *Turks*; came very late into *Mohammediſm*; and the *Moguls*, when become Lords of the *Upper Aſia* under *Jenghiz Khan*, were for the moſt part without any Religion, or had one to themſelves; ſo that it was under ſome of this *Khan*'s Succeſſors that ſeveral of the *Moguls* turnded *Mohammedans*; but the People of *Kipjak*, adhered moſtly to the Religion of their Anceſtors, contained in the famous Laws called *Yaza Jenghiz Khan*, as did moſt of the Hoards of the Deſart, according to *Cond Emir*, and even the whole Province of *Sejeſtan*, according to *Abulfeda*. The *Arabs* then could not ſafely venture a-croſs theſe Provinces, inhabited as they were, either by Enemies or by People of different Perſuaſions, who had moſt of them been driven out of *Chorasſan* and the *Mawaralnahra* by the prevailing Arms of the Kalifs. The Baits of a gainful Commerce could ſcarce bewitch the *Arabs* to run ſuch Riſques, and eſpecially as the

Bulk of Trade was negociated, as it afterwards was, upon the Sea of *India*; and indeed by the Accounts of Goods we read in *Arabian* Authors, we sufficiantly understand they had no large Dealings with those remote Provinces; that the Drugs they had from thence were brought to the *Mohammedan* Cities, by the *Turkish* or *Indian* Traders; and that all their Furs, in which may have consisted the most advantageous Branch of their Traffic, they had from *Armenia* and *Belad al-Jebel*, or from the *Barbarian* Coast, whence they had the Tygers and Leopards Skins, they so much valued for Caparisons and Saddles.

The Mohammedans *not prompted to these long Traverses by Curiosity.*

Nor does Curiosity seem to have prompted the *Mohammedans* to undertake such long Traverses, tho' it must be owned they sometimes went farther to hear some of their famous Masters. These Peregrinations did, with them, answer the end of a Course of Theology, and in some sort raised them to the Degree of Doctor. They would formerly from *Spain* and *Afric* go first to *Mecca*, then to *Bagdad*, thence to *Balk*, to *Samarcand* and to *Nisapor* to hear the celebrated Professors of those Academies. *Ebn Shalikan*, in his Lives of Illustrious Men, has many Examples of such Traverses, which in those Days were performed with ease enough. For at every Town and every Mosch, the Pilgrims met with charitable Entertainment, and with Persons who accounted it an Ho-

Honour to entertain them in their Houses. The *Mollahs* and the Learned in particular paid them great respect; many Princes had bequeathed Foundations for their Support; and if with some Knowledge in the *Koran*, and a parcel of traditionary Stories about *Mohammed*, they had some smattering of the Law, and a bent for the *Arabesque* Poetry, they were sure of a kind Reception throughout the extent of the *Mohammedan* Empire, just as our *Trabadours* were antiently received at the Courts of the European Princes.

History of the Provenc Poets of Nostradamus. *Hist. Manuscr.*

The Arabs *scarce knew any but the Maritime Cities of* China.

All this might induce us to conclude, that the first *Arabs* that went to *China*, were Merchants. The way thither by Land was so little used during the three first Centuries of *Mohammedism*, and even for some Time afterwards, that History scarce Records one Example of any Attempt of the kind. Now it cannot be very easy to suppose, that this Road was beaten by the Caravans, and the Geographers know nothing of the Matter; and yet *Abulfeda* and the other best Geographers seem to have known none but the chief Maritime Cities of *China*. They scarce ever speak of those towards *Chorassan*, and when they do, they have nothing but Fables to tell of them. These Countries of *Gog* and *Magog* are their Fairy-Land; it is here they suppose all the most wonderful Things to be, such as the Sping of Life *Alexander* sought for, and many other incredible

Particulars, which they have borrowed from the *Pseudo-Callisthenes*, and some such like writers.

When they tell these Tales in their Poems and Romances, we may say the Authors thereby mean to please and amuse us only: But when we meet with them in the gravest Works, and find they are to pass for the Geographical Description and History of a Country, we may safely pronounce the Author profoundly ignorant of what he would instruct us in, and especially when the more Judicious, not daring to relate them, give you to understand they have not much Faith in them. The very same Judgment may be formed in consequence of this, That the best Authors treating of the extraordinary, but true, Things of these same Parts, which the late Discoveries have confirmed and ascertained, do it with very great Caution, and as if they were not above half inclined to believe them.

Their Ignorance proved by their Geographers.

This Ignorance of the true State of *China*, particularly on the side of the Desart, beyond *Cashgar* and the Western boundary of *Tibet* may be proved upon them by us as many Eastern Geographers as there are in Libraries. Nor did this Mist continue during the first Centuries of *Mohammedism* only, it lasted down to the fourteenth Century, down to *Abulfeda*; tho' he, not barely satisfied with what was to be found in the best

Au-

Authors, had recourse to Travellers and Merchants for farther Information. Now it should seem there could be no going into *China* by Land, without knowing something of the great Wall: If a Traveller or two had gone through they possibly might have known but little of the extent and vastness of that Work; but had it been a common Road, Travellers would have made some mention of it; and yet we have not one Eastern Geographer, above three hundred Years old, that has described it, or that even seems to have known any thing at all of it: And those who have written the History of *Jenghiz-Khan*, seem to have been to the full as ignorant in this particular. *Golius*, it is true, in his Additions to the *Chinese Atlas*, cites a Passage in *Abulfeda*, which seems as if that Prince knew something of the Wall, but it is a Passage not to be found in old Copies of him; and the same may be said of what *Kircher* cites from *Nassir Eddin*, which is enough to make us believe they may be the Additions of some modern Hand.

The Eastern Geographers know but little of the Upper Asia.

But Eastern Historians and Geographers are not only so ill acquainted with this Part of the *Upper Asia*, they speak so confusedly of the Countries farther Northward, that it is impossible to imagin they knew much of them. In Truth, they comprehend all the Tracts beyond *Chowarazm* and the *Mawaralnahra*, under the general Names of *Turan*, *Turkestan*, or

Coun-

County of the *Turks*, *Igur*, *Catai*, *Shacatai*, *Caracatai*, and ſome others, without aſſigning any determinate Bounds to theſe Provinces, or if they attempt it, they vary ſo infinitely from each other, that there is no reconciling them; and juſt the ſame Stand they are at when they offer to fix the Poſition of the Provinces of *Turan*, or the ancient *Moguliſtan*, the Scene of the mighty Deeds of *Jenghiz Khan*. It was anciently the Opinion that all this vaſt Extent was inhabited by none but Hoards or Tribes of *Nomad Tartars*, Wanderers, and deſtitute of Towns; but in the Hiſtory of *Jenghiz Khan* you have Accounts of Sieges which laſted many Months, and ſuch Slaughters of the Inhabitants of the conquered Places as abundantly evince them to have been very numerouſly populous. *Jenghiz Khan* was a Deſcendant of *Buzanjir Khan*, who had been a potent King among the *Tartars*. *Ung Khan*, whom many, both antient and modern, have taken for the *Preſter John*, ſo famous in the Hiſtory of latter Times, was Lord of a very great Kingdom; and yet no Mention at all is made of it by the *Arabian* Geographers who wrote before the *Tartars* made a Conqueſt of all the *Upper Aſia*: And their Authors, that have written ſince the *Tartars* were driven out of *Syria* and *Meſopotamia*, ſeem to have made no uſe of the Communication they had with them, for a hundred Years, to inform themſelves,

Barros *Decad.* 3. l. 4. c. 1.

ſelves concerning the Countries ſo utterly unknown to their ancient Geographers.

Mohammediſm *but little known among the* Tartars *before* Jenghiz Khan.

To all this we may add the little Knowledge the *Tartars* of *Moguliſtan*, a Part of *Cashgar*, and *Tibet* had of *Mohammediſm* before the Days of *Jenghiz Khan*. The beſt Hiſtorians, and particularly *Emir Cond*, *Cond Emir*, and many that have followed them, obſerve that before *Jenghiz Khan*, the *Tartars* had no other Religion than what was contained in the *Yaza* or ancient Cuſtoms of the Nation; and ſo indifferent were theſe *Tartars* afterwards upon the Choice of Religion, that ſeveral of the Deſcendants of *Jenghiz Khan* became Chriſtians, while ſome of them embraced *Mohammediſm*, and others adhered to the old Religion of the Country. From this Piece of Hiſtory we may, almoſt, by a natural Induction conclude, That the *Mohammedans* had hitherto but a very ſlender Commerce with theſe People of the *Upper Aſia*; for they have ever made a Number of Converts in the Places were they have ſettled, or where they have had Liberty of Trade. Hence is it that great Numbers of them have been found upon all the Coaſts of *India*; for a few Families of them ſettling in ſome of the chief Cities of the Coaſt, were ſufficient to give Riſe to ſome ſmall Colonies, which, in Proceſs of Time, became very potent. Thus was it, that under the great Empire of the *Seljukids*, when the *Mohammedans* had Intercourſe with the Kingdoms of of *Cashgar* and *Cotan*, that *Mohammedism* was by little and little introduced; which they easily compassed, supported as they were, by the Power of *Chorassan*, the *Mawaralnahra*, and the neighbouring States, in Subjection to the Soltans, who, some of them, as *Malec Shah*, *Mahmud*, his Son, and some others of the same Family resided in those very Parts.

A Trade was not open'd with those Parts till after the Days of Jenghiz Khan.

It is certain, that after the Division of the Empire of *Jenghiz Khan*, and in the Reign of *Timur Beg* or *Tamerlan*, there began to be some Communication between *Chorassan* and *China* by Land; and that it was opened with a View to trade principally, and that some now travelled to those Parts out of Curiosity. The Merchants of *Chorassan*, who traded upon the Frontiers, did sometimes venture to cross the Desart in Caravans; but some of these Attempts miscarrying, the *Usbek* Princes, and some of the *Myrza Tartars*, mostly descended of *Jenghiz Khan*, by *Tuli Khan*, his eldest Son, began to send Ambassadors to *China*, by them to protect the Trade, which turned chiefly to the Advantage of these Princes. *Skah Rok*, the Son of *Tamerlan*, did in like Manner send an Embassy to *China*, which was joined by the Ambassadors of several other Princes and many Merchants. The Account of this Embassy is in *Persian*, and the Translation of it has been published by *Thevenot*. Father *Martini* acquaints us that these Embassies come to *China* every three Years, or that

Tom. 4.

that otherwise the *Chinese* would not admit the Merchants into their Empire. The *Caravans* usually attend upon these Ambassadors, who, as *Trigaut* tells us, come also from some other Neighbouring Kingdoms, with Presents to the Emperor of *China*, by way of Tribute. Thus is it they insinuate themselves into a Trade, and the Presents they receive are often more considerable than what they bring; for the *Chinese* Ministers of State make a grand Affair of these pretended Embassies, as if they derived a very great Veneration upon their Emperor, and perfectly answered the Flight of his Ambition. But though we were assured that for four Hundred Years past the *Mohammedans* have made it a Practice to trade with *China* by Land, it would not follow that they did or could do the same during the three first Centuries of the Empire, or that they resorted thither in such Companies as may be supposed to have settled in any Number in the principal Cities the Land way. L. 5. p. 545.

It is most likely that the Arabs *went first to* China *by Sea.*

All that has hitherto been offered, and much more that might be added, seems evidently to prove that the *Mohammedans* first went to *China* by Sea: It remains therefore that we examin into the Course they steered, the Nature of their Navigation, the End of their Voyages, and what Advantages they made of them.

Some are of Opinion they had the Use of the Compass before us.

Some there are who fancy the *Arabs* steered by the Compass before we had any Knowledge of that faithful Guide; that for

for many Ages paſt they have known how to take an Obſervation, to divide Sea Charts, and perform the ſeveral Parts of our moſt able Navigators. Granting all this, it muſt of Courſe follow that they made nothing of the great *Indian* Ocean, and that they traverſed it, backwards and forwards, as we do at preſent. Thus is it that a modern Author concludes, forming his Judgment from a Suppoſition that the *Saracens* had the Uſe of the Aſtrolabe long before the *Portugueſe*. " The *Saracens*, ſays he, " had uſed it a long Time before " upon the great *Indian* Ocean, to take the " Altitude of the Sun and other Stars ".

P. Bergeron Trait. des *Navigations*, p. 173.

And in another Treatiſe he ſays to the ſame Purpoſe :

Traité des Saraſſins p. 119.

" It is alſo of them we learned the " Uſe of the Aſtrolabe, for which they " have ſo many Names in their Tongue, " and for the ſeveral Parts of this ſo " univerſal and uſeful Inſtrument in Aſtro- " nomy; which they ſo well applyed on " the Mediterranean and the great *Indian* " Ocean, to take the Heighth of the Sun " and other Stars, in the midſt of their " great Conqueſts, Navigations, and Diſ- " coveries, as we have elſewhere obſerv- " ed. And indeed how could their Em- " pire, their Religion, and their Tongue, " ſo long have prevailed, and ſo exten- " ſively, among the remoteſt Iſlands, and " the fartheſt Eaſtern Shores, without the " Help of Navigation, and ſome Uſe of " the Compaſs in ſuch vaſt and perilous " Seas " ?

" Seas"? This Writer, tho' a very judicious Man, and many others, since him, at once suppose the Thing to have been as they would have it, and demonstrate a very uncertain Matter, by another abundantly more so. For if the *Mohammedans* have peopled a Part of the Coasts of the East *Indies* and *Afric*, it need not follow that they went thither by Sea, and tho' they did for certain reach some Parts by Sea, it is not certain that they sailed by Observation, or that they were skilled in all the Parts of Navigation required for the Conduct of a Ship in a long run.

We find not the least Proof towards this in their Books.

But to the Point; we do not find the least Proof of this ancient Use of the Compass in any of the *Arabian* Books; for tho' the Number of their Writers be almost infinit, and tho' no Man can be sure he has seen them all, yet may we say it is impossible that so useful and so marvellous a Discovery should be concealed in some rare and uncommon Books, if for so many Ages it was in the Hands of their Sea Artists.

Now there is not one original Word either in *Arabic*, *Turkish*, or *Persian*, which can properly signify either the Astrolabe or the Compass. The *Arabs* and the *Turks* commonly call the Compass *Bossola*, the *Italian* Name, which shews that the Thing signified is foreign to them as well as the Word. *Kotubnema* is a Compound, and a Word of modern Use with the *Persians*. Their Naturalists, who have so amply

amply expatiated upon the Virtues of the Load-ſtone, and repeated all they found concerning it in the ancient *Greek* Authors, have never once hinted at the Property of the Magnatic Needle; nor do we meet with one ſingle Obſervation, made, of ancient Date, by the *Arabs*, on the Variation of the Needle, or any Inſtruction conſequent thereto for the Aſſiſtance of Navigators.

The *Arabian*, the *Turkiſh*, and the *Perſian* Pilots, prefer the Compaſſes made in Europe to thoſe they make themſelves, and are not yet perfect in the Method of touching their Needles. Indeed ſince they have been taught by our Seamen, they know the Uſe of the Compaſs very well, and venture upon long Runs in the *Indian* Ocean, by the Help thereof, and ſucceed very well: But by this we underſtand, That if in leſs than two Centuries they have learned enough of the Franks to become intelligent Navigators, they could not have had the ſame Knowledge ſeveral Ages before, and at the ſame Time be ignorant of all the Principles of Navigation, as they were at the Time of the firſt Diſcoveries. The moſt ancient Mathematical Inſtruments they have for Nautical Uſes, can never be ſtrong enough to combat this Conjecture. Some indeed they have which are well enough wrought, and particularly ſmall Aſtrolabes, which their moſt skilful Pilots carry in their Boſom; and it is certain, that they

they have a long time made use of this Instrument, whence *Bergeron* gathers That they sailed by Observation, and even used the Compass : But no one is so ignorant as not to know the wide difference there is between these two Instruments ; or that tho', by the help of an Astrolabe, an Observation of the Stars may be taken, it is of no use to the Seaman in steering his Course without the help of the Compass.

Whether they had the Compass from the Chinese.

It is in vain to suppose the *Arabs* had the Compass before us, because they have had intercourse with the *Chinese* eight hundred Years past, and because the *Chinese* had it many Ages before we had. We very well know that Fath. *Martini* relates of the Emperor *Ching*, who reigned MCXV Years before Christ, that he made a Present of a Compass to an Ambassador from *Cochinchina* : *Auditus benigne legatus, adornansq; jam reditum, donatus est a* Cheveungo, *Machina summo artificio facta, quæ sua sponte respiciens Austrum, irrequieta lege certum monstrabat iter sive terra illud, sive mari facientibus. Ea duabus syllabis* Chinan *appellabatur, iisdem omnino quibus nunc Sinæ Magnesiam acum significant. Argumento haud dubio ejus usum illo jam tempore apud Sinas inventum ad alias inde Nationes, mea quidem sententia, transivisse. Hanc igitur Machinam ducem secuti Cochinchinenses unius anni spatio domum rediere.* We need not inquire into the Authority of the Authors Fath. *Martini* has compiled his History from; we ought to rely on the sincerity of that learned Man, to whom Europe is indebted for her most perfect Documents concerning *China*. But it seems extraordinary that the *Chinese* should have made so poor a Use of their Compass as to proceed in their Voyages as if they had none. The length of the time the *Cochinchinese* were upon their return from *China*, might tempt one to think this *Machine* was not altogether what we call a Compass.

The Opinion of Sir John Chardin *concerning this.*

Sir *John Chardin*, a famous Traveller, being consulted upon this Subject, returned Answer to the following Effect. "I
" cannot tell whether or no the *Chinese*
" of themselves found out the Art of
" Navigation and the Compass, as they did
" the Art of Printing and Artillery; we
" should consult their Learned to be as-
" sured of it. But for the other Asiatics
" I boldly assert they are beholden to
" us for this wonderful Instrument, which
" they had from Europe by the Hands of
" the *Arabs*, a long time before the *Portu-*
" *guese* Conquests. For, *First*, Their Com-
" passes are exactly like ours; and they
" buy them up of the Europeans as much
" as they can, scarce daring to meddle
" with their Needles themselves. *Second-*
" *ly*, It is certain the old Navigators,
" only Coasted it along; which I impute
" to the want of this Instrument, to
" guide and instruct them in the mid
" Ocean. We cannot pretend to say they

were

" were afraid of venturing far from Home;
" for the *Arabs*, the first Navigators in
" the World, in my Opinion, at least
" for the Eastern Seas, have, time out of
" mind, been from the Bottom of the
" *Red-Sea* all along the Coast of *Afric*
" down to the Tropic of Capricorn,
" which is a Space of fifty Degrees; and
" the *Chinese* have always traded with the
" Islands of *Java* and *Sumatra*, which
" is also a very considerable Voyage.
" So many Islands uninhabited and at the
" same time productive, so many Lands
" unknown to the People I speak of,
" are a Proof That the old Navigators
" had not the Art of Sailing on the
" main Sea. I have nothing but Argu-
" ment and Conjecture to offer touching
" this Matter, having never met with any
" body in *Persia* or the *Indies* to inform
" me when the Compass was first known
" among them, tho' I made the Inquiry of
" the most learned Men in each Country.
" I have been from the *Indies* to *Persia*,
" in *Indian* Ships, when no European
" has been on Board but my self. The
" Pilots were all *Indians*, and they used
" the Fore-Staff and Quadrant for their
" Observations. These Instruments they
" have from us, and made by ours, they
" not in the least varying therefrom,
" except that the Characters are *Arabic*:
" And, by the way, I observe that the
" *Arabs* are the most skilful Navigators
" of all the *Asiatics* and *Africans*: But

" they nor the *Indians* make ufe of " Charts, and indeed they do not much " want them; fome they have, but they " are copied from ours, for they are " quite ignorant of Perfpective.

It feems moft likely then that the *Arabs*, in the firft Ages of *Mohammedifm*, had no knowledge of the Compafs, and that they never failed by Obfervation till they imbibed the Precepts of that Art from the Europeans : And certain it is, by the Teftimony of our two Authors, and by that of all the Eaftern Geographers, who often take notice of Courfes and Diftances, That they were formerly mere Coafters, or that when they did venture to leave the Land, it was for no great Run, and this is what made their Voyages fo long and dangerous. They failed from the *Perfian* Gulf, and thence ranged along Shore quite down to the Point of *Malabar*, and having doubled it, whether they ftood over for the Ifles of *Andaman*, or made for fome other Port in the Gulf of *Bengal*, they did not ftir far from Land, and particularly as they came in with the Coaft of *China*.

They were very follicitous about Iflands and Anchoring-grounds, which our People now avoid as much as pofible, that their Voyage may not be retarded, and themfelves expofed to fuch dangers as they are in no fear of at Sea. The Built of the *Siraf* Shipping, as defcribed by by our Author, may satisfy us they were not calculated for the high Sea; for their Planks sewn, as we may say, together with Coco-nut Yarn, and almost destitute of Iron, could never have held in the tumbling Weather our Ships frequently meet with in those Seas.

We must not wonder then if the Discoveries the *Arabs* made by Sea, in six or seven hundred Years time, are not comparable to those of the *Portuguese*, *Castilians*, *Italians*, and, in a Word of all the European Nations, whom the Orientals commonly surpass in Industry; for the want of the Compass is ever an Obstacle in the way of long Runs.

The Arabs *inaccurate in their Reckonings at Sea.*

From what has been said we may safely conclude That the *Arabs* did not venture far out to Sea; that they sailed by an inaccurate reckoning and the Observation of the Stars; that the little Knowledge they had of the Winds and Monsoons, made them often mistake in their Run and the Distance of Maritim Places, as sufficiently appears by their general Measure of a Day's Sail by Sea, which is so vague and uncertain that there is no reducing it to any fixed Standard: And that thus they only coasted it along, or at least that they seldom left the Shore out of Sight behind them; and that, consequently, they are not to be supposed the Original Discoverers of the true Course to be steered for the Great *Indies* and *China*.

Now if we examin into the Cauſes of this Imperfection in their Science of Navigation, there are two which principally occur to us. *Firſt*, The *Arabs* being no great Inventors, as appears by the little Progreſs they made in Learning, beyond what they had from the *Greek* Books tranſlated into their Tongue, found no Inſtruction in thoſe ſame Books to make then Navigators. For the *Greeks*, tho' they had potent Fleets, knew nothing of launching out into the Sea, and many of the Learned think they hardly ever ventured upon the *Ocean*, but confined themſelves to the *Mediterranean*. The *Carthaginians* alſo were no more than Coaſters, and tho' it were certain *Hanno* ran down to the Cape of *Good-Hope*, and that the *Table Hill* is the Θεῶν ὄχημα, or *Chariot of the Gods* he diſcovered; we cannot conceive this Voyage to have been otherwiſe performed than from Headland to Headland; as the *Portugueſe* firſt did it. The general Form and Conſtruction of the ancient Ships was not adapted to the Ocean; for they all went with Oars which are not only uſeleſs but dangerous in Voyages of Length. The Deſcription of the great Coaſt of the *Indies*, or of the *Erythæan* Sea, as *Arrian* has left it us; and what we read in *Pliny* concerning the Courſe ſteered by the Ships, that traded to the *Indies* from the *Red-Sea*, can only confirm us in our Opinion. For if we except the Voyage to

Hannon Peripl. Ramuſ. Præfat. in Peripl. Navig. Tom. 1.

to *Taprobana* or *Ceylon*, with the Wind called *Hippalus*, that is, by obſerving the Monſoon, it does not appear they knew how to keep a Reckoning. The *Arabs* therefore could pick nothing out of the *Greek* Books to inform them of this neceſſary Art, and their very little acquaintance with the Latin would not allow them to underſtand what *Pliny* and thoſe he quotes had written. For the Book they have under the Name of *Pliny*, is ſo very unlike the Original, that we can ſcarce believe it was ever in the Hands of the Perſon who pretended to give it in *Arabic*. The *Arabs* then only continued to go from the *Red-Sea* to *Malabar* and *Ceylon*, but in time venturing farther than the *Romans* had been, they, from Iſle to Iſle, at length diſcovered the Shores of *China*.

In the ſecond Place, nor the *Kalifs* nor the *Soltans* who ſucceeded them, ever aimed at any great matter of Power by Sea, ſo that the Navigation was wholly left to the Merchants.

Their Kalifs never undertook any great Matters by Sea.

Theſe Princes never endeavoured to have Potent Fleets, as having no call for them, and as ſitting poſſeſſed of ſo vaſt and ſo rich an Empire, that they could have no Temptation to make farther Diſcoveries or new Conqueſts beyond Sea, or to conſult the Intereſt of their trading Subjects by procuring them the Benefits their Protection might have derived on them in foreign Parts. Some time, indeed

deed, after the first Wars beyond Sea, the *Soltans* of *Egypt* and *Syria* began to have some Shipping and even obtained some signal Advantages over the Christians at Sea; but it is plain That a Sea Strength had been of but insignificant Use in the other principal Affairs, and Revolutions of this great Empire.

They had every thing in abundance and Indian *Commodities were brought to them.*

To all this it may be added, That the general abundance of Things necessary for Life, or to supply Luxury in the *Mohammedan* Provinces was such, that they had no Occasion to expose themselves to the Dangers of a long Voyage to go in quest of them to the Places whence they came. For the *Indians* brought by Land to *Cabul* and some other Places, and by Sea to *Bassora* and *Siraf*, all the Commodities of the *Indies* and *China*. Furs were brought into *Syria* by the Provinces of *Adarbejan*, by *Curdistan* and other Parts more Northerly. Great quantities of the same they also had from the *Barbarian* Coast, by the way of the *Red-Sea*, from whence a great Trade was carried on with them all over *Egypt*. From the same Places they had Gold Dust; Gold also they had from the Mines of *Sofala*, brought to them by the Negroes who traded with *Egypt* by the way of the Desart, or from Port to Port quite to the *Red-Sea*. From *Ceylon* and the *Indies* they, by their Trade with the *Chinese* and *Indian* Merchants, had Silk, rich

rich Stuffs, and many other Manufactures; Drugs and Spices. With this Stock of Goods they drove a very considerable Commerce, by the way of *Kahira* [*Cairo,*] with the *Venetians*, the *Genoese*, the *Catalans*, and the *Greeks*; and therefore they were under no necessity of going so far as *China*. Wherefore it is very probable That the first Adventurers that undertook this Voyage were urged thereto by the Calamities of the Civil Wars, which, having reduced many Families to Want, obliged them to seek some Livelihood by Trade, deprived as they were of all other means of Subsistance. And accordingly one of our Authors observes of the *Arab* who had the long Conference with the Emperor of *China*, That he set out upon his Voyage after the Destruction of *Bassora*. There is some reason also to believe that the *Syrian* Merchants who went to *China*, and whom we shall mention hereafter, came to the same Resolution upon the very same Account.

The Navigation of the Chinese.

It remains now that we examin whether or no the *Chinese* had a different way of Sailing, and how far they went. If we hearken to some Authors, they came as far as the Cape of *Good-Hope*, and formerly Peopled and conquered the great Island of St. *Lawrence*. It is pretended also That they had the use of the Compass a long time before us; and that so they were able to undertake long Voy-

Voyages, and the rather as the Built of their Ships speaks them to have been more Skilful in nautical Architecture than any of the other Orientals. We have given you the Testimony of Fath. *Martini* as to the very ancient Knowledge they boast to have had of the Magnetic Needle; and our Authors assure us, That in their time the *Chinese* came to the *Persian* Gulf. So they had failed along throughout the Islands; and even had Settlements upon some of them, remains of which are at this Day upon *Malacca* and in other Parts. We read also in some Authors, That they conquered *Cochinchina*, and the Neighbouring States quite to *Pegu*; and others assure us That those States formerly paid Tribute to *China*. Now tho' the best Authors acquaint us that they marched their Armies by Land, it is nevertheless certain that, long before the Discoveries of the last Ages, they had Fleets which made them Masters of all those Seas, and it is thought they once subdued the Empire of *Japan* by means of their Shipping. But as it is above twelve hundred Years ago since this People, not very Warlike by Nature, have given over all thoughts of enlarging their Empire, they, as considerable Navigators as they were, made no Conquests among the Islands upon the Coasts of the Eastern Ocean, and have been very unwilling to admit Strangers among them under the pretence of Trade.

It

It is commonly reported that this Prohibition is almost as old as the Empire, and yet by the great number of *Mohammedans*, *Jews*, *Indians*, and even *Syrian* Christians that settled among them, it appears that this same Prohibition was not very strictly minded, as may be clearly gathered by all the Circumstances in our two Authors.

Navarette thinks they sailed no farther than the Straits of *Sincapor*, or *Sunda*, because their Ships are not strong enough to live in the heavy Seas of the great *Indian* Ocean; and will have it that there is not the least room to imagin they ever reached *Ceylon*, and much less St. *Lawrence* or *Madagascar*, as several of the *Portuguese* Navigators at first gave out. He adds, that they had never undertaken such long Voyages to conquer far distant Countries, seeing they never were inclined to spread the Fame of their Arms; that the Trade of Metals, Silks and the principal Drugs, could not have been their Motive for such Undertakings, seeing they were in *China* itself abundantly supplyed with all these Things; and that in short it does not appear they had any Instruments proper to take Observations, or that they ever knew how to divide, or project Sea Charts.

But our first Author partly destroys the Conjectures of *Navarette* by assuring us That in his Time the *Chinese* Ships came to *Siraf*, tho' they dared not go farther, because

cause of the bad Weather, and great Seas they could not endure, and that thus they did not offer to go quite up to *Bassora*, or into the *Red-Sea*. As for the *Portuguese* Writers who would have it they sailed as far as the Cape of *Good Hope*, they built their Assertion upon the uncertain Foundation of some Manners and Customs among the *Cafres* and People of the East Coast of *Afric*, which, as they thought, had some Resemblance of what they had observed among the *Chinese*. This is a Matter of great Obscurity, and can never be cleared up till we are more exactly informed of the *Chinese* History than we are.

It is very extraordinary also that the *Arabs* should have been eight Hundred Years acquainted with all the Seas of *India*, and yet never leave a Sea-Chart behind them, to ascertain their Discoveries, and guide their Posterity: And yet it does not seem that they drew up any Charts in the first Times, and we have very great Reason to suppose they are indebted for this Piece of Art to the Occidentals, it being but seldom that we meet with their Charts above three Hundred Years old.

Of the Sea-Charts and Maps of the Orientals.

These Charts are uncommon enough, and the very best of them are so imperfect, that the worst we have in our old Manuscripts, are far more accurate than the nicest of the *Arabs* and *Persians*; for they afford neither Bearings, nor the Course of Rivers, nor Order, nor Method. The best

best of them are those which consist of Squares, produced by the mutual Intersection of Parallels and Meridians, in the Midst of which is the Name of each principal City. They themselves have been sensible of their Ignorance in this Particular, and no sooner did the *Europeans* print their Maps than the *Orientals* put a great Value upon them: They have even endeavoured to make them their own, by writing the Names of the Places in their own Characters and Tongue, by the common Names current with us.

In the Commentaries of *Alfonso d'Albuquerque*, we read of a *Moorish* Pilot, at *Calicut*, who had a very exact Draught of all the Coasts of the *Indies*; and it is credible, that the *Arabs*, who, by *Egypt* and *Syria*, had a continual Commerce with the *Europeans*, had by the *Venetians* and *Genoese*, in those Days the greatest Navigators in *Europe*, been taught some Parts of Navigation, which they may have applyed in their Voyages to *India* and *China*. But these are very extraordinary Instances; for they had so little improved upon what they borrowed from our Seamen, That ever since the Discovery of the *Indies*, they have thrown aside their own Charts to make use of ours, which they prefer to those they may have drawn up from their own Observations.

The Arabs *made no great Discoveries by Sea.*

We must judge of the maritim Skill of a Nation by the length of their Voyages, their Discoveries, and bold Attempts, like

like thoſe of the *Portugueſe*, the *Engliſh* and *Dutch*, which had ſeemed incredible to the Ancients: The *Arabs* have undertaken nothing of the kind ſince the Riſe of their Empire. They went into *Afric* under the Protection of the Governor of *Egypt*, who ſent a Guard with them through the Deſart. Their Paſſage over into *Spain* was ſo mere a Trifle that it is not worth the naming, and even for that, it ſeems, they made uſe of Chriſtian Ships. The Conqueſt of *Majorca*, *Minorca*, and *Yvica*, was compaſſed a long time after, when the *Arabs* had by their Slaves and 'Renegadoes been taught what to do with a Ship: But all theſe maritim Enterpriſes, conſiſted of no more than embarking a Parcel of Troops on board of Flat-bottomed Veſſels, they had ſcarce any other, and landing with Diſcretion. Their Voyages to *Sicily*, *Sardinia*, and *Calabria* were to the full as eaſy. Their Fleets did not then ſweep the Seas, there were then but few Corſairs, and when the Chriſtian Princes began to fit out any conſiderable Strength, the *Mohammedans* were unable to ſtand againſt them; but in a very ſhort Time were driven from their Conqueſts, a certain Sign of the weakneſs of their Navy.

Their moſt formidable Sea Armament.

The moſt formidable Power they ever had at Sea before the middle of the Sixteenth Century, when they began to be dreaded in the Mediterranean, was that fitted out by the *Grand Signior*, in the Year MD XXXVI, under the Command of *Soliman* Baſha,

Basha, to drive the *Portuguese* from their *Indian* Conquests. This Fleet sailed from *Suez*, and reached *Diu*, which *Soliman* besieged with the unfortunate Event related at large in the *Portuguese* Writings. But, besides that this Expedition was set on foot above forty Years after the Discovery of the *Indies*, there was so great a Number of Christian Seamen and Officers on board of this Fleet, that we may fairly ascribe to them all the Honour of this Voyage.

Their Colonies in Afric *and the* Indies.

The *Arabian* Colonies discovered on the Coasts of *India*, since the *Portuguese* sailed thither, have made some believe they went to those Parts by Sea, and that they made their Settlements much in the same Manner the *Portuguese* conquered and Peopled a vast Extent of Country from Cape *Bojador* quite to *China*; but it is certain, these Settlements were owing to a very different Origin. The *Arabs* were at *Sofala* and *Mosambique* before the Discovery of the Cape of *Good-Hope*; and it was no very difficult Matter for those who were in *Afric* and in *Egypt*, to go down to the East Coast, which for many Ages had been famed for Trade. Thus it was that they peopled the *Egyptian* Side of the *Red-Sea*; because the Caravans of that great Province came usually down thither to trade with the *Persian* Merchants, who brought them all Sorts of Commodities from the the *Indies* and China, which they exchanged with them for those of *Egypt* and *Christendom*. They were Masters of *Arabia*,

bia, *Persia*, and all the Provinces which extend quite to the *Indies*, and so it was easy for them to have travelled from Kingdom to Kingdom, till they got to *China*. Had they been possessed of great Fleets to make them Masters of the Sea, it is very likely they would have undertaken the Conquest of this Country, as they did by all those they could get at with their Arms; but we do not understand by their Histories, nor even by the *Portuguese* Accounts, that their most considerable Cities were owing to any Thing besides Trade and Religion. It was Trade that formed the *Arabian* Colonies of *Monbaza*, *Quiloa*, and *Mosambique*, and some other Places on the Way to the Great *Indies*, where the first Families increased to that Degree, That, in Process of Time, they made a good Part of the Inhabitants of the Places. Religion also gave Birth to some Settlements, when Idolatrous Princes were persuaded to *Mohammedism* by Fakirs, who, as we shall observe hereafter, often devoted themselves to such Missions. Under these two Pretences did the *Mohammedans* get footing in several considerable Ports of the *Indies*: But, tho' they were in great Favor with the Princes, were very rich, and partook largely in the Government, they were never considered as the predominant Part, as they had not obtruded themselves by Conquest.

Mohammedan *Settlements*.

It is somewhat hard to account for the several *Mohammedan* Settlements upon the Coast

Coast of *Afric*, between the Cape of *Good-Hope* and the *Red-Sea*. These are of very obscure Rise, and of a very different Nature from those which brought the greatest Part of *Asia* and *Afric* under their Yoke. They were neither erected nor aided by the Princes or Governors of Provinces, equal in Authority to Tributary Kings, wherefore History has no Mention of them: And so little do we know of the interior *Afric*, that we cannot well decide the Way the first *Mohammedans* may have taken to the East Coast; the little we know of the History of these petty Kingdoms, we have from the Industry of the famous Historian *John de Barros*, who met with some of their Chronicles. *Coast of* Afric.

The *Arabians* subdued *Egypt* in the very first Century of their *Hejra*; and some Years afterwards they made a Conquest of *Afric*, were Masters of *Arabia*, and of all the Ports of the *Red-Sea*. There is some room then to believe that this stirring, this indefatigable and avaricious People, trading at first upon the Coast with the Negroes, understood they had their Gold from the Mines of *Sofala* and *Monomatapa*, that Ivory abounded in the Country, and that great Wealth might be thence accumulated; this was surely the Rise of the first *Arabian* Colonies in those Parts, tho' just at what Time we cannot say. It was easy for them to settle upon this Coast; because the Negroes who lived in the Upland had no Towns, but dwelt in Hutts

Abulfed. *Geogr. Perſ.* Kaſwini.

like Nomads. It is thought indeed, that their firſt conſiderable Settlement was at *Magadoxo*, a City known, tho' very obſcurely, by the *Arabian* Geographers, which muſt have been firſt inhabited, becauſe of its advantageous Situation.

The Cities they built upon the Coaſt.

The *Bedouin* or *Bedwin Arabs* had wandered to the uttermoſt Parts of *Egypt*, of *Nubia*, and, perhaps, even of *Barbary*, and had ſettled towards the Eaſt Coaſt; where they lived, in their ancient Manner, under Tents, feeding of Flocks, which were their chief Support, while they cultivated ſome Trade with the *Cafres*; but the Barbarity of theſe *Cafres* made them edge by Degrees to the Coaſt, and there build a City whoſe beginnings are to us unknown. After this, theſe ſame *Arabs* ſtrengthned by others, built *Brava*, and *Monbaza*, and ſome other Cities of the Coaſt quite to *Quiloa*.

Theſe Colonies, according to one of the Hiſtories of the Country cited by *Barros*, had been ſettled about the Year CCCXX of the *Hejra*, or DCCCCXXXII of *Chriſt*. About the Year of the *Hejra* CCCC, of *Chriſt* MIX, a *Perſian* Prince, younger Brother to the Soltan of *Shiraz*, came to ſettle at *Quiloa*. *Barros* calls Soltan *Hoſen*, the Father of this Prince, King of *Shiraz*; but at the Time he ſpeaks of he could be only *Khan* or tributary Prince of *Shiraz*, ſubject to Soltan *Addulat*, of the Family of *Buiya*, who was Lord of all *Perſia*, and the principal *Mohammedan* Provinces

Decad. I. l. I.

Provinces of the *Upper Asia*, from the Year of the *Hejra* CCCCIV, or of *Christ* MXIII, to the Year CCCCXI, of *Christ* MXIX, and the same succeeded him to the Year of the *Hejra* CCCCLXXXVIII, of *Christ* MXCIV. It is also said, that these *Persians* called themselves *Amozaydi*, or Followers of *Zaid*, the chief of a Sect which clashed with the *Arabs* and the *Africans*; but it is likely we must read *Imamzada*, as if they were descended from *Ali*, by some one of the *Imams* or Pontifs of the *Persian* Sect; this Difference was the Cause that this new Colony of *Persians* went to the Place where they afterwards built *Quiloa*.

Those at *Magadoxo* were the first that discovered the Gold Trade at *Sofala*, one of their Ships being horsed thither by the Currents: but they did not make the Discovery professedly, or on set purpose, tho' they had some Knowledge of it; because they dared not go near Cape *Currents*, which being still a dangerous Navigation, was abundantly more so to those who made as little free with the Offing as possible. The Kings of *Quiloa* made Discovery of a good Part of the Coast, and became Masters of *Monbaza*, *Melinda*, and the Isles of *Pemba*, *Zanzibar*, *Monfra*, *Comro*, and some others; they even sent some Colonies over to the Island of St. *Lawrence*, and their chief Residence was at *Sofala*. These *Persian* Adventurers, or their Descendants, were in Possession, here, long

Barros. Decad. I. l. 8. c. 5.

long before the *Portuguese* found out the Way to the *Indies:* And other Colonies, at different Times, from *Persia* and *Arabia*, did also seat themselves on many Parts of this Coast, and most of the Cities were so many Republics or little Kingdoms, when discovered by *Vasco de Gama*. Some of them were *Sonnis* or of the *Arabian* Sect, others were *Imamis*, or of the *Persian*; and these religious Dissensions, as well as a Jealousy of each other in Trade, stirred them to great Wars, which it seems the other *Arabs* knew nothing of, or any way concerned themselves with.

They force the Cafres *into the Country.*

The *Mohammedans* being thus in Possession of the whole Coast down to Cape *Currents*, obliged the *Cafres* to retire into the Country. It was seldom these *Cafres* came down to the Sea-Side, except to look for Ambergreese, which the Sea threw up at certain Times: But they found it also more Southerly, and trucked it with the *Mohammedans*, to whom they also brought Ivory, Gold-Dust, and Tygers, Leopards, and Lions Skins, which they had from the Desart.

What we know of the Origin of the Mohammedan *Settlements upon the Coast of* India.

It seems as if, in the third Century of *Mohammedism*, the Towns we are speaking of were not yet built, and that the Trade was immediately negociated with the Negroes themselves by the *Egyptian* Merchants of the Red-Sea, and the Coast of *Arabia*. This Coast was as yet called no more than the Country of the *Zinges*; and the Name of *Zanguebar*, since imposed on it, it, ſeems to be given by the firſt Navigators who came thither from *Perſia*. *Bar* in the *Indian* Tongue ſignifies a Coaſt, as *Abulſeda* and the other Eaſtern Geographers have obſerved: And the *Perſians* who were acquainted with the *Malabar* and ſome other Coaſts ſo called by the *Indians*, called this Country of Negroes *Zingebar* or *Zinjebar*, if we pronounce it as the *Arabs* do, or *Zinguebar* as the *Perſians*. All the Shores Northward and then Eaſtward quite to the River *Indus*, were in Subjection to the *Mohammedans*: And from the *Indus* down to Cape *Comorin*, they met with *Moors* in many Places, but particularly at *Calicut*. *Barros* relates, that *Sarama Payrimal* being ſeduced to *Mohammediſm*, and being deſirous to dye at *Mecca*, divided *Malabar*, his Dominions, between his Children and Relations, and that he gave *Calicut* to one of his Nephews who was his chief Heir, together with the Title of *Samorin*, or Emperor of *Malabar*. D. 1. l. 9. c. 5.

Their firſt Settlements there owing to Trade.

The *Moors* coming to *Coulam* to trade, this King *Payrimal* gave them *Calicut* where they kept their grand Warehouſes, not only of the Pepper and Ginger the Country abundantly produces, but alſo of all the Drugs and Spices which were brought from the Iſlands, and the uttermoſt Parts of the Eaſt. This Settlement and the Veneration the *Samorins*, who ſucceeded *Sarama Payrimal*, had for the *Moors*, gave them a great Sway at *Calicut*, and upon all the Coast, where they made Allyances with the Principal *Indians*, who thought it an Honour to give them their Daughters in Marriage. They insinuated themselves also into a great Interest with the Princes of the different Parts of the Coast, as *Idalcan*, *Nizamaluco*, *Cotalmaluco*, *Madramaluco*, for being at perpetual War with each other, they made great account of the *Moors*, and endeavoured all they could to engage them in their Service, they being, in those Times, the best Soldiers in all the *Indies*. Most of the *Patans* or Kings of the *Indies* were Idolaters, nor had *Mohammedism* taken any deep Root in the Country, nor did it till King *Ekbar*, in the beginning of the Seventeenth Century, made a Conquest of most of these States.

From Cape *Comorin* Eastward, the *Portuguese* did not meet with such Swarms of *Moors*; nevertheless they were settled upon *Malacca*, upon several Parts of *Sumatra*, and among the *Molucca*'s; but there was scarce any of them in most of the other Kingdoms. They were already at *Canton*, and in the other chief Ports, when the *Portuguese* arrived, but according to the Testimony of our two Authors, they had been there ever since the CCXXX Year of the *Hejra*.

They had four Ways of settling themselves in the Indies.

From these Premises we deduce That the *Arabs* formed their Settlements four several Ways; by Conquest, by Discovery, by Trade, and by Mission. By the first Means

Means they possessed themselves of all the Provinces which made their vast Empire: By the second they got footing in *Afric* down to Cape *Currents*, among the poor unarmed Cafres who had it not in their Power to prevent them from seizing on what Parts they saw good: Their Colonies of *Magadoxo*, *Brava*, and *Quiloa* were somewhat in the Nature of ours in these latter Times; but not so difficult to maintain, because of the Proximity of the *Red-Sea*, whence the *Arabs* had all Sorts of Assistance. By the two other they seated themselves in all the other Parts, but more especially by Commerce. These Voyages were not in those Days so safe and so frequent; wherefore the Merchants were under a necessity of making a long Stay at the principal Scales, where they took to them Wives, their Religion allowing them a number; these new Families brought on others, and the Princes being sensible it was greatly for their Advantage to draw the Trade of *Persia*, *Arabia*, and at the same time of *Egypt*, and *Europe*, by the *Red-Sea*, into their own Ports, these Merchants met every where with the kindest Usage they could wish. These Idolatrous Princes, confirmed in their old Superstitions, were not at all scrupulous about differences in Religion, but admitted all indifferently. So they readily allowed their Subjects to embrace *Mohammedism*, which they preferred to the rest; because of the hopes these *Arabs* gave them of Protection from the Soltans, whose Power was known in the remotest East: Even Princes themselves made profession of *Mohammedism* in troublesom Times, that the *Moors* might join them; for in latter Days they were so multiplyed, that they alone peopled whole Cities, or a part of the most considerable. Thus this Religion, which has nothing very inconvenient in it, did by little and little obtain in many Parts; and at length received an access of Power, when some of its Professors being raised to the first Posts in the Courts of *Cambaya* and *Guzarat*, invited a greater number of those Asiatic *Turks* called *Rumis*, and even seized on some Posts, as did *Malic Az*, who raised a considerable Settlement at *Diu*, from whence he a long time infested the *Portuguese*.

Their Settlements that were owing to Trade and to Religion.

By Trade and Religion the *Arabs* got footing in some Parts of *Malabar*, as has already been noted, and by the same Means they came to be very considerable upon *Malacca*. They first went thither as Merchants, and some of them there fixing their Abode, gained many of the Idolaters over to *Mohammedism*. From *Malacca* they sailed round to the *Molucca's*, and having prevailed on the Kings of *Tidore* and *Ternate*, together with several others to join with them in Religion, they reaped great Benefits from these Princes, whom the concerns of Trade, and the Protection these *Moors* gave them room to hope, confirmed in *Mohammedism*. According to the

the *Portuguese* Writers they had not been long upon the *Molucca's* before our Discovery of the *Indies*.

Their Settlement in China *not raised by Religion.*

They had been in *China* above five Hundred Years before, and, according to our two Authors, they were there very numerous; but the Severity of the *Chinese* Laws prevented them from propagating their Faith with the same Freedom they had been allowed in the *Indies*: So that they did not convert the *Chinese*; they could obtain nothing farther there than the free Exercise of their Religion. The great number of them, before the Year CCC of the *Hejra*, sufficed to People a Part of the chief Cities of *China*, where the *Portuguese* found them.

In what Manner they extended their Religion.

Our Subject naturally leads us on to say something of the manner how the *Mohammedans* extended their Sect to the Extremities of *Asia* and *Afric*. Now the Manner of this was widely different from the Way taken to proclaim the Gospel to the Universe, particularly by the Apostles in the first Ages of the Church: The Disciples of *Christ* were harmless, humble, poor, patient, and foes to Riches; and so averse were they to every sort of Violence, That many of the primitive Christians, moved by the Spirit of Meekness and Forbearance, forsook the Profession of Arms, deeming it unlawful to fight even with the Enemies of the State. The Apostles and their Disciples confined themselves to the pure Doctrine they had received

ceived from *Jesus Christ*; they exposed themselves to numberless Torments in Defence of it; they prayed for their Enemies, nor ever returned Evil for Evil; they hoarded not Wealth, and whatever the Believers deposited in their Hands, was faithfully distributed to the Poor: Thus was it the Gospel was first recommended to the World.

The Rise of Mohammedism.

The first *Arabians* were of different Manners, and had a contrary way of thinking; but without entering into a Detail of the personal Qualities of *Mohammed* their Prophet, a turbulent ambitious Man; let it suffice that we draw you the exact Picture of their reputed Saints, and principal Friends to the *Koran*. Their whole Religion consisted in a scrupulous Observance of Times of Prayer, Ablutions; in bestowing of some Alms, and in fighting for the Establishment of their Empire. Their Sermons were very short, and when they came into a Country they declared themselves Companions of the Prophet, that they were come to exhort them to embrace the Religion he had taught, and to root them out if they refused. Thus was it the Conqueror of *Afric*, addressed himself to the *Africans*; and all the Propagators of this pernicious Sect have always talked after the very self same Rate. And thus was the *Koran* erected not only upon the Ruins of *Paganism* in *Arabia*; but also upon the Ruins of all States and Professions, and that, by Blood, by Plunder, and by all the Cruelties to be imagined. History

History does not inform us that the *Mohammedans* used any other Means to spread their Doctrin. It is true, indeed, that in some of their Books we read of Disputes they had with the Christians of the Seventh Century, in which they boast of confounding them. *Emir Cond*, in his History of *Ali*, tells us, this Kalif disputed with a Christian Monk, and so clearly, from the Gospel, convinced him That *Mohammed* was the *Paraclete* or Comforter promised by *Jesus Christ*, that the Monk embraced *Mohammedism:* But such Examples, as liable as they are to doubt, are so very uncommon, that nothing can thence be inferred to satisfy us they made as many Proselytes by the Strength of Argument and Conviction, as by Might and Victory. In the Writings of the *Eastern* Christians we have Examples, and even the Acts of many Disputes upon Religion, but ever to the Advantage of the Christians. Accordingly the *Mohammedans* but seldom recurred to this Way of drawing Men into their Belief; it could not answer their Purpose, and varyed from the Beginnings of their Religion.

They did not spread their Doctrin by Conviction and Instruction.

When they were unable to propagate their Faith by Arms, as they had done in a Part of *Asia* and *Afric*, it does not appear They had recourse to any Thing but Cunning, Treachery, and their own Interest; they did not venture to condemn the Religion by Law established in a Country where they were Strangers, on the contrary,

They were very quiet about their Religion where they were weakest.

contrary, they were very cautious how they offended those they dreaded. But they had nothing to fear in the Sea Ports of the *Indies*; for the native Idolaters are not apt to take Umbrage at religious Differences, and have never made it their Endeavour to draw Strangers into their several Sects. The *Fakirs* or *Mohammedan* Devotees were by no means prone to the rash Doings they sometimes ventured on for the Sake of Religion; and if we make a Scrutiny into the Number of their Martyrs, we shall find them but few in Number, if we except those who dyed Sword in hand, who are all honoured with that Dignity. It hapned also, but seldom in the Primitive Times, That Dervises or *Fakirs* undertook long Journeys in the Cause of *Mohammedism*: But when any Prince was disposed to embrace it, then they sent for some who made an End of instructing him; and, upon *Tidore*, the *Portuguese* found one of this Sort, who was come to wash away the Lees of the old Idolatry in that Kingdom. The *Moors* expected to get by it if they undertook to propagate their Religion; and made themselves Masters of the Trade, by promising to defend the Princes against their Enemies; and sending for further Supplies of their own People, they added to their Strength, and often reigned Chiefs of the Ports that had received them as Foreign Dealers. Sometimes, under the Mask of Devotion, they persuaded the Princes, and the

the most considerable Personages to go Pilgrims to *Mecca*, or to send rich Presents thither; by which means they had so advanced their Affairs in the principal Empories, that, when the *Portuguese* arrived, they transacted all the Trade of the East. In this flourishing State, they without difficulty drew over to them a great many Persons, and particularly Slaves and Mestices, who thereby became exempt from all Tribute, as they claimed the advantages at first granted to the *Mohammedans* to allure them into the Ports.

By these Means and Methods did the *Mohammedans* propogate the *Koran*, which has still more extensively prevailed since the time the *Mogul* Emperors became Masters of the Kingdoms of *Cambaya*, *Guzarat* and many others, where this Sect had not yet admission, and where it was mistrusted, feeble, and in no condition to make any Attempt.

Now the difference between these Missions and those of the primitive Christians is obvious, as much as some modern Authors have dared to make the Comparison; they are not even to compare to those of latter Times.

Fath. *Naverette* writes that in his time there were about five hundred thousand *Moors* in *China*; and believes they had not been in the Country above five hundred Years, and that they had considerably multiplyed by Marriages: He adds that many of them took Degrees in the Sect of *Literati*, but that the rest considered them as Apostates, whence it is plain they thought this Sect incompatible with their Religion.

By what has been hitherto offered, we may pretty clearly discern how the *Mohammedans* may have at first got into *China*; and it seems that they did not force an Admittance as elsewhere, but insinuated themselves under the pretences of Trade chiefly; and that the Trade driven by the *Upper Tartary* was the most usual and expeditious: But we cannot tell exactly what this Rout may have been, because not only our Authors of the middle Ages and the modern *Greeks*, but also the *Arabs* and the *Persians* have under the denomination of *Turks* and *Tartars* comprehended many Nations of discordant Manners, Tongues, and Religion, besides that the most able Geographers have never pricked down the Limits of the Extent they place them in.

Many Nations comprehended under the Name of Tartars.

They most of them say that the Country of *Shash* is the boundary of the Provinces subject to the *Moslems*, and confines upon *Turkestan*. Then when they speak of *Turkestan* or *Tokarestan*, which is the same * they agree in nothing about it, but

* *Our Author here seemingly contradicts what he asserts in a Passage before, but he here understands that tho' these two were distinct Provinces considered as such, yet as they*

but in saying It is a very vast Province beyond the *Oxus* and Country of *Balk*; and that it reaches to *Badakshan*, which is thirteen Days distant therefrom. In *Tokarestan* they place a great number of Nations, which they comprehend under the general Name of *Turks*; and the chief of them are these. The People of *Bujak*, free, very barbarous, and their Country twelve Days in Extent: The *Najabis*, or *Nogais*, who inhabit a very great Country, a Month in Dimension: Those of *Ferak*, in a Country of the same Extent; they have a King and are *Mohammedans* of the Sect of *Ali*, whose Descendants they pretend to be, and whom they take to be the God of the *Arabs*. Abulfeda Yacuti EbnHawkal, *and other* Arabian *Geographers.*

Then they come to the *Tartars*, properly so called, whom they write *Tatars*; cruel, inhuman, lawless and without Religion, except that most of them worship the Sun; in Language they differ from the rest: They speak also of those they cay *Tagazgaz*, a Name variously written, from the aptness of taking one Letter for another, in a Character wherein a Point or two differently placed quite alters the Pronunciation: Others they have, called *Hakak*; these are free, and worship the

were included in each other, they are to be considered but as one when either of the Names is usurped in a general Sense.

Stars

Stars as did the ancient *Arabs*, and ſome of them were Chriſtians: Others, called *Hettis*, who inhabit a Tract of twenty Days Extent, more polite and ingenious than the preceding: Thoſe of *Harkir* the ſame, they had a King greatly reſpected by them, in whoſe preſence no Man appeared till he had attained his fortieth Year: The *Larkanjes*, the *Catlajes*, and ſome others are as unkown: The *Caz*, who were Chriſtians, and a very potent People, formerly ſubject to the *Seljukian Soltans*; but who waged War with *Soltan Sinjar* the Son of *Malec-Shah*, defeated him and took him Captive, tho after a Years Confinement he made his Eſcape: The Geographers ſpeak alſo of the *Bakara* or *Yabara* who poſſeſſed a Country of forty Days Journey, among whom there were *Chriſtians*, *Jews*, *Mohammedans*, *Idolaters*, and *Magians* or *worſhippers of Fire*: Many more are named in Hiſtory, the *Moguls*, the *Hiathelites*, the *Kipjaks*, the *Alains*, the *Karis* and *Markis*; in fine many numerous Hoards who were ſubdued by *Jenghiz-Khan*, but who before obeyed *Ung Khan*, whom he overthrew in Battle.

This detail may evince it impoſſible to know what People our Authors and even the Orientals mean, when they they uſe the general Denomination of *Turks* and *Tartars*. And if in Europe we are at ſo great a loſs to trace out the ancient Cities, and the many Nations whoſe

Names

Names ſtand recorded in Hiſtory, we muſt be infinitely more to ſeek when we attempt to recover Cities and Countries ſo very imperfectly known to the Ancients, who have ſo often changed both Name and Maſter, and who have been ſo harraſſed and ravaged by continual Wars.

Now, as it may be obſerved, among the People and Nations, ſo comprehended under the general Denomination of *Tartars*, there was a great Number of Chriſtians, not only when *Jenghiz Khan* erected his Empire but long before this Epoch: For in the Hiſtory of the *Neſtorians* we read that *Timothy*, their *Catholic*, who ſucceeded *Hananjaſhua*, the ſame mentioned in the *Chineſe* and *Syriac* Inſcription, wrote to the *Khan* or Emperor of the *Tartars* and to ſome other Princes of *Turkeſtan*, exhorting them to embrace the Chriſtian Faith, which he did together with two hundred thouſand of his Subjects. We may be ſure theſe People were true *Tartars* or *Turks*, the ſame Catholic being conſulted by the Biſhop, he ſent into the Country, concerning the manner how he was to make them keep Lent, and celebrate the Service; they being accuſtomed to Milk and Fleſh, and unuſed to Corn and Wine. His anſwer was, that in Lent they ſhould abſtain from Fleſh; but that during the ſame they might have Milk as uſual; and that as to the celebration

they should absolutely provide themselves with Bread and Wine. From that time we, in the Ecclesiastic *Notitia* of the *Nestorian* Church, have a Metropolitan of *Turkestan*, one of *Tangut*, one of *Chanbalig* or *Cambalu*, and one of *Cashgar* and *Nowakat*; as they had Metropolitans they must needs have had Bishops under them; and accordingly we
Abulfar. p. 286. find one called *Mar Danha*, in the History of *Jenghiz Khan*; *Mar* is conferred on Saints and Bishops, and *Danha* is a proper Name, very common among the *Nestorians*, but not to signify a Town as
Hist. of Jenghiz Khan p. 186. Abulfed. p. 522. *Jenghiz Khan*'s Historian mistakes. The best *Arabian* Authors agree that *Cabul*, which they place in an extent of Country they call *Bamian*, whose Capital was half a Day from *Balk*, was the last City inhabited by *Moslems*, tho' pretty much blended with *Christians*, *Jews*, *Magians*, or *Worshippers of Fire*, and Idolatrous *Indians*. Now altho' the *Mohammedans* were very powerful in *Chorassan*, *Chowarazm*, the *Mawaralnahra* or *Transoxane*, and tho' among the *Turks* and *Tartars*, we just now mentioned, there were those who had received *Mohammedism*; their Number was but small, and unable to extend their Colonies into *China*, so that tho' in the Course of several Ages some of them may have gone thither by *Tartary* and have settled, it is more likely the body of them went through the *Indies*. We have taken notice of the Settlements

tlements they had upon the Coast of *Afric*, and a Trade had been opened between *Persia* and *China* before, by the Canal described by our Authors: But the way was still made clearer for them, by the *Indian* Conquests of the *Gaznavid Soltans*, so called because the Seat of their Empire, which lasted one hundred and fifty Years, was at *Gaznah*, a City which some Geographers make the Capital of a Province of the same Name, while others place it in the Country of *Bamian*, and others in *Zablestaân* or *Gour*: For we cannot too particularly inform our Readers who have not applyed to the Oriental Tongues, That the Eastern Geographers, even those who are cryed up for their Accuracy, are seldom of one Mind as to the Division of Provinces. Ths first of these *Soltans* was *Sabactakin* whose Son, *Yaminaddulet Abulkasem Mahmud*, began his Reign in the Year of the *Hejra* CCCLXXXVII and of Christ DCCCXVII. The *Arabian* Historians and the *Persian* write that he compelled a great many *Indians* into *Mohammedism*, and among other things it is observed that he took the City of *Sumnat*, upon the Sea Shore, where there was an Idol which he ordered into Pieces. It is plain also that during the ceaseless Wars between these *Soltans*, and some others with their Neighbours, several of them, after a Defeat, took Refuge in the *Indies*. Whence this Part swarmed with *Mohammedans*, and es-

Cond. Emir *Leb. Tarich*

Leb. Tarich. Condemir Kazwini Abulfe. Geo. Per. Abulfed. n. 531.

especially after some of the Kings of *Indostan* had embraced their Faith, as did others in *Malabar*, *Malacca*, the *Moluccas*, and most of the circumjacent Islands; which we learn from the *Portuguese* Authors only, the *Arabians* having no mention at all about it.

They went to China *both by Sea and Land.*

They went to *China* then partly by Land through *Turkestan*, and by Sea from *Siraf*, as we read in our Authors, to whom almost alone we are indebted for this Information. The System of *Bergeron*, and some Moderns that have followed him, is grounded upon a false Suposition That the *Arabs* knew and used the Compass a long time before us, a Notion countenanced by our latter Accounts of *China*, that tell us the *Chinese* had that piece of Knowledge, which is an empty Assertion. Our two Authors report that *Siraf* was the Boundary of the *Chinese* Navigation, and that they steered the same Course the *Arabs* did; creeping almost continually along Shore, and keeping the Land aboard as much as possible. So that the great number of *Mohammedans* at *Canfu*, when that City was sacked, had increased there by the means of Merchants from *Persia* and *Syria*, partly by Sea and partly by Land, who there enjoyed the free Exercise of their Religion, as well as the *Jews*, the *Christians* and *Indians*.

They did not spread their Doctrin in China.

It is observable That the *Mohammedans* never attempted to spread their Do-

Ctrin

ctrin in *China*, as they had done in other Parts; either restrained by the Laws which made it Penal, or unable to win over the *Chinese* who may have been more hard to convince than were afterwards the Kings and People of the Neighbouring Islands, who professed *Mohammedism* before the *Portuguese* found out the way to them. The *Mohammedan* Missionaries have never been numerous, and of the great number of Saints of their Sect, concerning whom they have long and tedious Stories, not one Soul ever exposed his Life in the Propagation of *Mohammedism*. This abominable Sect was established by Violence only, by Slaughter, and the Horrors of War, and thus was it that it diffused it self over all the Countries subdued by *Mohammed* and his Successors. Thus was it that *Yaminaddulet Mahmud* the Son of *Sabactakin* conveyed it into a part of the *Indies* he conquered, since when it has insensibly over-ran the Country, but especially since the *Mogul* Emperors, descended of *Tamerlan*, have made public profession of it: Notwithstanding which, there are still a great number of Idolaters in *Indostan*, and in our Days there are many *Raja's* or *Indian* Princes who adhere to their old System, as do also most of the *Patans* or Nobles, the *Banians* or Merchants, and the body of the common People.

By our last Accounts there is a great number of *Mohammedans* in *China*, and *Navarette* writes That in his time they were

The number of Mohammedans *in* China.

were computed at above five hundred thousand, which is sufficiently confirmed by our *French* Missionaries. These assure us the *Chinese Mohammedans* take no Degrees, as do the rest of the *Literati*, to qualify them for Posts; and that this they observe out of a Religious Principle, thinking it unlawful to perform the *Chinese* Ceremonies, so long the Subject-matter of Dispute, and which, after a Deliberation of almost seventy Years standing, have been at length condemned by the Holy See. By several Accounts we are also informed That the *Mohammedans* who do take the Degrees, are rejected by the rest as Apostates, so that they on their part quite renounce the *Mohammedan* Faith, retaining nothing thereof but the aversion they have contracted to Swines Flesh.

AN

AN INQUIRY CONCERNING The *JEWS* discovered in CHINA.

OUR Authors observe that in the general Devastation of *China*, and particularly when *Cansu* was taken, a great number of *Christians*, *Jews*, *Mohammedans*, and *Farsis* [*Parsees*] were put to the Sword. In the preceding Inquiries we have discussed the Origin of *Christianity* and *Mohammedism* in this Country; but it is impossible to speak so positively concerning the *Jews* there; for the History of the Country affords no Light to guide us in this Research, the *Chinese* for the most Part, as is said, omitting all foreign Matter, or what relates to Strangers; and, if we may rely on the Testimony of the most learned *Jesuits*, their History is quite silent as to the Subject we are now upon: And yet there is a great number of *Jews* in *China*, as may be gathered from our two Authors, and the rather as they are ſtill in ſeveral Provinces, but particularly in the Trading Cities.

Fath. *Matthew Ricci*, whoſe Work contains the firſt genuin Informations we had concerning *China*, left behind him in his Memoirs, from whence *Trigaut* compiled his Book, *De Christiana Expeditione apud Sinas*, a very remarkable Story to our Purpoſe. A *Jew* of the City of *Caifamfu*, the Capital of the Province of *Honan*, coming to *Pekin* to take his Degrees, and hearing that this Stranger and his Companions adored one only God, and abhorred the Superſtitions of the idolatrous Nations and the *Mohammedans*, had the Curioſity to pay him a Viſit. Fath. *Ricci* conducting him into the Chappel, he there ſaw a Picture of the bleſſed *Virgin* with the Infant *Jeſus* in her Arms, and a St. *John* near at Hand, and taking them for *Rebekah*, *Jacob*, and *Eſau*, thought he knew them: And after the ſame Manner he gueſſed at Sight of the four Evangeliſts. The Father put ſeveral Queſtions to him, and by his Anſwers underſtood he profeſſed the Old Law; and that he acknowledged himſelf an *Iſraelite*, and not a *Jew*: Whereupon Father *Ricci* concluded him a Deſcendant of the Ten Tribes carried away into Captivity, and diſperſed over the uttermoſt Parts of the *Eaſt*. He ſhewed him the Bible of *Philipp* II. printed by *Plantin*, and this *Jew* knew the *Hebrew* Characters but could not read them.

Trig *ubi ſupra.*

He

He related that in the City whence he came, there were ten or twelve Thousand *Jewish* Families, who had a good handsom Synagogue, which they had lately rebuilt at a considerable Expence: That for five or six Hundred Years they had there preserved the *Pentateuch* written upon Rolls, which they held in great Veneration: That at *Hamcheu* the Capital of the Province of *Chequiang*, there was still a greater Number of *Israelites* and a Synagogue; That some also there were in other Provinces, but, that being destitute of Synagogues, they were greatly decreased in Number. We are told, that this *Jew* in pronouncing some *Hebrew* Words differed from our Manner, as in *Hierosoloim* and *Moseia*: He informed them That some of his Countrymen understood *Hebrew*, and among the rest a Brother of his: That for his Part, having, from his Youth up, applyed himself to the *Chinese* Literature, he had neglected the other: He frankly confessed, that for this Reason he had been deemed unworthy to enter the Synagogue, by the Person who was Chief of it: But that he was not very solicitous about his Exclusion, provided he obtained his Doctors Degree.

It were to be wished Fath. *Ricci* or some other Missionary had been a little better acquainted with *Hebrew*; for by the reading of their Books, they might have known the Difference between these Copies which must have been ancient, and those at present

Voyages, Tom. II. p. 316. *the* Dutch *Edition.*

ſent in the Hands of the *Jews.* *Bernier* is of Opinion there may have been of them in the Kingdom of *Kaſhemir*; and cites ſome Letters which Father *Buſæus* the *Jeſuit,* who was at *Dehli,* received from a *German Jeſuit* at Pekin, *which informed him he had ſeen ſome who had preſerved* Judaiſm *and the* Old Teſtament; *who knew nothing of the Death of* Jeſus Chriſt, *and who would have made the* Jeſuit *their* Kakan, *if he would but have abſtained from Pork.* Now this *Jeſuit* was Father *Adam Schall,* who lived above fifty Years in *China* with great Repute, being a Mandarin of the firſt Order, and Preſident of the Tribunal of Mathematics. He during his long Abode in the Country, by his Intereſt and by his Underſtanding, as well as his Succeſſors in the ſame Employs, might have diſcovered ſomething more than we have concerning the *Jews* in *China*; but they have neglected the Thing. It only appears, by what Fath. *Trigaut* writes, That their Number was not very great, and that it rather diminiſhed than not, becauſe many, to qualify themſelves for Offices, conformed to the Religion of the Country: And it is remarkable that the *Jews* excluded thoſe who applyed themſelves to the *Chineſe* Studies, which were neceſſary to attain to their Degrees; by which it is plain they thought the Practices of the *Literati* not free from Idolatry; and the *Mohammedans,* who were more in Number, thought the ſame Way, and no one of them could take his Degrees

Degrees without renouncing *Mohammedism*.

Father *Ricci* who thought these *Israelites* of *Caifamfu* might be some Remains of the ten Tribes translated by *Shalmaneser*, does not seem to be much out of the Way. *Benjamin* the *Jew* relates that in the Country of *Nisapor* there were some who pretended to be of the Tribes of *Dan*, *Zebulun*, *Asher*, and *Naphtali*: But we want many particulars to enable us to judge what there may be in this Notion, or whether it is a mere Conjecture or no. We should have their Books, we should know which they admit and which they are not acquainted with: For the *Israelites* of the ten Tribes could neither have nor acknowledge the Books of the Prophets which so severely reproach the Kings and People of *Israel* with their Idolatry; no more than what was written during and after the Captivity. Wherefore what Father *Trigaut* relates of the *Jew*, That he rehearsed the Stories of *Esther* and *Judith*, gives us to understand that he knew those Books of Holy Writ, which had been impossible if he had not been acquainted with the other *Jews*.

In Itiner. p. 97.

But what *Ricci* says of the Story of *Judith* must not make us suspect his Veracity, because that Book is not in the *Hebrew* Canon; for the *Jews* had some Knowledge of it as appears by *de Voisin*'s learned Preface on the *Pugio Fidei*, and by the *Hebrew* Translations of it that have been

been printed;, and what is more, the *Jews* of *Persia* have a Version of it in the Language of that Country, whence it may have reached *China*.

Father *Ricci* afterwards sent a Brother *Jesuit*, a *Chinese* born, to the City of *Caifamfu*, to inquire into the Truth of what the *Jew* had reported, and he found things to be exactly as he had said. He procured a Copy of the Beginning and Ending of the Books these *Jews* had in their Synagogue; and upon collating these Copies with the *Hebrew Pentateuch*, there appeared an exact Conformity of Passages and Characters between them, excepting, says *Trigaut*, that, according to the ancient Custom, these *Jews* had no Points. The Conformity of Character is a most certain Proof that these Books were not of the first Antiquity; and the Observation added, That they were written without Points is no Proof at all; for at this Day the Pentateuchs written upon great Rolls of Parchment, as the *Jews* have them in their Synagogues, are destitute of Points. So that from such uncertain Documents it is impossible to say whether the *Jews* went to *China* soon after the Transmigration of the Ten Tribes, or whether they came afterwards, as did the *Christians* and *Mohammedans*, which is most likely to have been the Case. For without enlarging on this Subject, we on all Sides learn That since the Destruction of *Jerusalem*, there is hardly a Country where they have not been

in

in great Numbers, besides those who were in *Persia* and *Egypt* before that Time.

Before *Mohammedism* there were whole Nations of them in *Arabia*, as may be proved by many Passages of the *Koran*, where they are mentioned. We have the Contest of *Gregentius*, Bishop of the *Saracens*, with a *Jew* called *Herbanus*, and by the History of his Life in the *Greek Menologies* and other Authors, we understand that he was sent to *Elesbaan*, King of *Ethiopia*, who was then at War with the Jew *Dunaan*, King of the *Homerites*, a great Enemy to the *Christians*, by the *Arabs* called *Dunaas*: But it is impossible to gather any help from the *Mohammedan* Authors about these Affairs; for all their Histories of the Times before their Prophet, are a Heap of gross Fables without the least Authority. We must therefore confine ourselves to the Time thereabouts, and to their Historians who have written since the Rise of their Empire.

Pocock. *Specim. Hist. Arab.* p. 33.

The *Jews* were persecuted by the Christian Emperors, and especially by *Heraclius*; who put a very great Number of them to Death, because, say the *Arabs*, he was admonished to beware of a circumcised Nation, from whom he had every Thing to dread: This he construed of the *Jews*, not dreaming of the *Arabs*, who were many of them circumcised, as were afterwards those who followed *Mohammed*; for all the *Arabs* were not so. This drove a great Multitude of *Jews* into the Domi-

nions

nions of *Persia*, where some of them had been ever since the first Captivity; and History informs us that they often stirred up those infidel Princes against the Christians: But they afterwards enjoyed more Liberty under the *Mohammedans*, who never disturbed them in the Exercise of their Religion; which was the Reason they multiplyed greatly in all the Provinces of the *East*. And when the City of *Bagdad* was built by the Kalif *Almansur*, and became the Capital of the *Mohammedan* Empire, the *Jews* settled there, and became very wealthy, and very potent.

They thrived by various Means; many of them cultivated the Sciences, particularly Philosophy, Astronomy, and Physic; others concerned themselves with Trade, in which the Nation has ever been very industrious; and some got into the public Revenues and Customs, as Receivers and Inspectors. In a Word, they became so numerous and so potent, that as the Christians had obtained the Privilege to have their Patriarchs, they obtained almost the same for a Chief of their Nation they called *Rash Haggola*, or *Haggalut*, whence the *Arabs* have their *Ras al Jalut*, or *Prince of the Exiles*, who exercised the same Jurisdiction over the *Jews* the Patriarchs did over the *Christians*.

In Itinerar. p. 71. This is what Rabbi *Benjamin* is very diffuse on, but with too much exaggeration, after the Manner of the *Jews*, saying he had

had a plenary Authority and a kind of Prerogative over those of his Nation. Some *Jews* by this imaginary Prerogative of their Chiefs, have thought to elude the genuin Drift of *Jacob*'s Prophecy, *The Scepter shall not depart from* Judah: But *Constantin l'Empereur* in the Preface to his Translation of *Benjamin*'s Travels, takes Notice of some Passages of this kind, and refutes them very solidly; for not to mention that all their Authors agree They have had no Prince of the Line of *David* to govern them since the Destruction of the second Temple; the Testimony of Travellers, Ancient and Modern, confirm this Truth beyond all Contradiction: But the *Jews* for want of Proofs have embraced and ever made a great Stir about the first Reports which have from Time to Time prevailed of *Jewish* Princes that have been said to be discovered in far distant Parts.

One of the most remarkable Instances of this kind, was upon the first News that arrived in *Portugal* of the Discovery of the *Prester John* or King of *Ethiopia*. Those who had been sent out reported that this Prince was of the Race of *Solomon*, that all his Subjects were circumcised, that they kept the Sabbath, that they abstained from the Flesh of Swine, and that they observed many *Jewish* Customs: And as there were two *Jews* among those who went on this Discovery they failed not to magnify every Object to their own People, who wanted nothing more to satisfy them there was a *Jewish* King in *Afric*, whence they deduced every Consequence that could flatter them. Thus Rabbi *Isaac Abarbinel*, who was then at *Lisbon*, did in some Parts of his Commentary upon the Prophets, recur to the first Accounts the *Portuguese* gave of the great number of *Jews* they found in the *Indies*. The *Jews* of *Constantinople* there printed a *Spanish* Translation of a pretended Letter from *Prester John*, in *Hebrew* Characters, and dispersed it about every where in different Languages. But the *Jews* did not long enjoy their Dream; for the *Portuguese*, going into the Country, found that as much as the *Ethiopians* were wedded to certain *Judaical* Practices, in which some Writers have in vain endeavoured to justify them, they were nevertheless *Christians*.

But, to drop this delusory Prerogative, it is certain the *Jews* have for many Ages swarmed all the *East* over; *Persia* is full of them, and they had a Synagogue at *Modain*, the ancient *Seleucia* of the *Parthians*, out of whose Ruins *Bagdad* was partly built; and when the *Jews* removed to this new City, they became very powerful, and obtained of the Kalifs such Privileges as differed but little from those the Christians were allowed. And particularly they attained to the Honour of having a Chief, the same the *Arabs* call *Ras al Jalut*, so much talked of by *Benjamin* and *Abraham Zacut*, the Author of the *Jukhassin*. Some learned Men of our own

own Times have doubted of what the *Jews* relate of the Ceremony of Installing this their Magistrate, but it is very true; and ought not to be reckoned a slight ensign of Sovereignty. We read in the History of the *Eastern* Christians, that it was the usual Custom for the *Mohammedan* Princes to leave them the free Choice of their Patriarchs; but the Person elected could not be invested with this Dignity, till approved by the Sovereign. There were even Canons which made it unlawful for Bishops to inaugurate or inthrone a Patriarch till his Election had been confirmed in public Form, which these Christians wisely ordained to obviate such Inconveniences as have frequently taken Birth from the Ambition and Jealousy of some private Men. Wherefore, before they Consecrated or installed a new Patriarch, they, besides the *Conge d'Elire*, usually brought him into the *Soltan's* Presence, or to the Governor of the Country; and when the Election was confirmed, the new Patriarch was in great State conducted to the Church, or the Patriarchal Palace.

We find many Instances of this in the History of *Egypt*, and in that of the *Catholics* or *Nestorian* Patriarchs; while nothing of the like is recorded of the *Jewish* Chief. But as they were very rich, and oftentimes very powerful at the Courts of these *Mohammedan* Princes, where every Thing gave way to Gold, it is very likely they obtained much the same Honours

n con-

conferred on the *Christians*. Accordingly if we examin the Recital of *Abraham* of *Salamanca*, and some other *Jews*; as *Benjamin* and others since him, it will be perceived these Cases were almost the same. It is impossible to suppose their Writings are fabulous; they do not prove That the *Princes of the Exiles* held any Sovereignty over their own Nation, nay, their best Authors ingenuously confess there was no such Thing, if we except private Regulations and Orders among themselves. So that they were not much better than Chiefs of Synagogues, or of the *Sanhedrim* of latter Times, and considerably inferior in Authority to the Patriarchs, when it hapned that the Prince confirmed the Election.

The main Difference between the Christian Patriarchs and the *Jewish* Chiefs, was, The former were invested with a Power over all the Churches within the Limits of their See, and such a one the latter seem not to have enjoyed. For what *Abraham* of *Salamanca*, and *Benjamin* say, That at *Bagdad* he was ushered in by the Title of *Son of* David, when he made his Entry, so proclaimed by the exulting Voices of the Croud; is in the first Place not much to be relyed on from such Hands, and, in the next, is but a feeble Proof of any Sovereign Power resident in the House of *David*. And besides that the *Jews* themselves confess There is a very great Confusion in their Genealogies, there is is hardly a County where there have not been Families who boasted of a Descent by that Line. The famous *Isaac Abarbinel* was of this Number, who has been so kind as to let us know that a Branch of the House of *David* migrated into *Portugal*, and that it was his own; this reflected an Honour on them from the *Jews*, but void of all good Authority.

It were needless then to recur to their Fables, now a-days sufficiently known, to inquire after their Origin in the East and at length in *China*. It is very likely some remains of the Ten Tribes existed in the *Upper Asia*. *Isaac Abarbinel* cites Letters from *Jews* in the *Indies* who laid claim to that Descent: But as they had Communication with the rest, they most certainly conformed with them; so that tho' we had any particular Tradition, or Account of a Custom, handed down to us by the former, this Medly would only puzzle us the more; and in Fact we find that almost all the Eastern *Jews*, mentioned in Histories, agreed with the rest in their Observance of the Law, and in the Reading of the sacred Books, excepting certain Things we shall mention in the Sequel.

We are assured by all Authors, that are come to our Knowledge, both *Christian* and *Mohammedan*; and by all Travellers, both ancient and modern, that the *Jews* have been found in *Persia*, in *Chorassan*

raſſan, in the *Mawaralnahra*, and in the Provinces fartheſt remote and neareſt bordering upon *China*, as well as in *Afric*, not to ſpeak of *Egypt*, where they have been always very numerous. *Antony Tenreyro*, a *Portugueſe* Gentleman, the firſt that travelled from the *Indies* to Europe by Land, whoſe Book was printed at *Coimbra* in the Year MDLX, found of them at *Lar*, and other Cities of *Perſia* in his way. *Abulfeda* often obſerves there were Multitudes of them in the *Indies*, eſpecially at *Calayata* and *Cingala*; as alſo at *Coulam*, according to *Marco Polo*. *Nuveiri* ſpeaks of them at *Modain* as being ſo powerful that in the Year of the *Hejra* DLXXIII, of *Jeſus Chriſt* MCLXXVII they had a warm conteſt with the *Mohammedans*. At *Cochin* there was a Jewry, where, according to *Diego de Couto*, they ſpoke the ancient Tongue: There were alſo great numbers of them all over *Malabar*, where they quite peopled ſome Places.

It is certain alſo that for many Ages paſt they have been very numerous in *Perſia*, and all the Provinces which formerly depended thereon, or that at preſent belong thereto; and in all the Parts where the *Perſian* Language is ſpoken, as it is in almoſt all the Dominions of the *Mogul*. This is confirmed by the Verſions of the Scripture the *Jews* have made into that Tongue, of which the Pentateuch only was printed, in *Hebrew* Characters,

at

at *Constantinople* in the Year MDLI. But there are almost all the Books of the Bible of this Version in Libraries, and particularly in Monf. *Colbert's*. The printed Version is by the *Jews* themselves supposed to be the work of one Rabbi *Jacob*, a native of *Tus*, a famous City in *Chorassan*. We have another to the full as good; and this as well as those of the other sacred Books is in *Hebrew* Characters, a Verse of the original preceding a Verse of the Version, just like the *Chaldee* Paraphrases in Manuscript. The Version of the Psalms, which *John Baptist Vecchieti*, a *Florentin* Gentleman, got copied at *Ormuz* in the Year MDCI, and which I have among my Books in *Persian* Characters, is from three very ancient Copies, in *Hebrew* Letters, whose various Readings are between the Lines of the Text. This is what *Vecchietti* has taken care to observe at the end of the Book, adding That this Version is the more to be esteemed as it has some old Words used by *Fardussi*, *Azraki* and other Poets, which being now obsolete prove its Antiquity.

And what still farther corroborates this; In these Copies, in *Hebrew* Characters, you have none of the Corrections and Variations the *Masorets* have introduced into the *Hebrew* Text, now in the Hands of the *Jews*, and much fewer of those various Readings called *Kari* or *Katib*, as I have paticularly remarked in the

Sapiential Books which I have in Manuscript, as well as in *Esther*.

Again, the same *Persian Jews* have Books in their Tongue which the others reject, as the Prophecy of *Baruch*, the History of *Tobit*, and the Additions to *Daniel*, which are not in the *Hebrew*. Many Conjectures might be raised upon this Foundation, but nothing certain can be thence deduced, no more than from what little we are told by the ancient Authors above cited. For the Antiquity of these *Persian* Translations tho' very great, is not sufficient to determin whether or no they precede the Revision of the sacred Books by the *Masorets*; and, indeed, that they did not precede them appears plain by the Version of the Psalms, which tho' in some Passages it varies from the *Masorets*, there are important Passages where it follows them: The first is in the 21 *Psalm* the 22 according to the *Jews*, and the 18th *Verse*, where the *Jews* instead of Reading כארו *foderunt*, as do the Septuagint and Vulgate, read כארי *sicut Leo*. The *Persian* reads the same. In the 144 or 145 *Psalm*, which is Abecedary, the 14 Verse is wanting in the *Hebrew*, tho' it stands in the Septuagint, the Vulgate and the *Syriac* Version which is very ancient, but is not in the *Persian*. As the *Syriac* is from the *Hebrew* Text, and as there is not the least Appearance that it was reformed by the *Greek*, it bids fair to have been once

once in the Original Text. For there is no Cauſe to be well aſſigned why in a Pſalm, whoſe Verſes are in Alphabetical Order, there ſhould be one Verſe wanting, and we not be able to gueſs at any Reaſon for it; and eſpecially as nothing of the like is to be obſerved in others of the ſame kind. As old then as the Books in the Hands of the *Jews* of *Perſia*, and the moſt remote Provinces of the *Upper Aſia*, where the *Perſian* Tongue was ſpoken, may have been, they cannot have been ſo old as the Tranſmigration of the ten Tribes, nor even as the laſt Diſperſion, when *Jeruſalem* was deſtroyed, ſeeing their Books conform in ſuch Eſſential Points, as theſe we have noted, with thoſe reviſed by the *Maſorets*.

It is moſt likely then that the *Jews* got into *China* as into all other Parts, and that they may the more eaſily have done it, if true it be, as *Benjamin* ſays, That there were about fifty thouſand of them at *Samarcand*, from whence they may have travelled into *China*.

A DISSERTATION ON THE *CHINESE* Learning.

What the Arabian *Author says of the* Chinese *Learning,*

WHAT our *Mohammedan* Traveller, in the first *Account*, tells us of the *Chinese*, That they have no Skill in the Sciences, must seem so extraordinary as to make us doubt every Thing else he says, after so many Elogies the Modern Travellers have lavished upon the Philosophers and Philosophy of *China*. We might at first imagin That illiterate Merchants could not perceive what has been since discovered, and that therefore we are not to mind them when they presume to go out of their Reach, but listen to the learned Men who know better. But it is not the Missionaries only that may be suspected of having talked a little too largely of the Wit and Learning of the *Chinese*, who have so done under a Notion of discovering such Truths in the Books of *Confucius*, as might dispose them to embrace the Christian Faith: For *Isaac Vossius*, a Man of great Erudition, has been more prodigal of his Commendations

very contradictory to Vossius.

dations than any Body else; * *If any Man*, says he, *should collect all that every Nation which is or has been, has invented, tho' they have all brought forth very great Things, the whole together would not be more excellent and various than those exhibited by the* Seres *alone, by the* Portuguese *improperly called* Chinese. This is the Opinion of a Man that was never in *China*; that was unacquainted both with their Tongue and their Books, but by Translations he could be no Judge of; and who, as some of his Friends say, was ready to believe every Thing, true or false, that could be told him concerning *China* and the *Chinese*. Now the *Arabian* Authors of these two *Accounts* had been in the Country it self, had probably some Knowledge of the Tongue, and consequently were better able to judge of the *Chinese* Learning than *Vossius* with his excessive and ill founded Prepossession. But let us see whether these *Arabs* knew enough of what Men call Learning, to qualify them to pronounce the *Chinese* Strangers thereto.

At the Time our Authors wrote, Philosophy was well cultivated among the Arabs.

Our first Voyage was made in the CC XXXVIII Year of the *Hejra*, which corresponds with the Year of *Christ* DCCCLI

* *Si quis omnium qui sunt vel olim fuere gentium, præclara simul conferat inventa, quantumvis ea multa & memoratu digna censeantur, tanta tamen & talia non erunt, quin longe inveniantur plura & meliora quæ a solis reperta fuere* Seribus, *quos* Lusitani *perperam* Sinas *appellaverunt.* Isa. Voss. de Magnit. Sin. Urb cap. 14.

and

and DCCCLII. Before that time of Day the *Arabs* had entered upon the Study of Philosophy, Astronomy, Geometry, Physic, and Natural History by the help of the *Greek* Books translated into *Arabic* in the Reign of the Kalif *Almamun*, the Seventh of the *Abbassids*, who dyed in the Year of the *Hejra* CCXVIII, of *Christ* DCCCXXXIII, having reigned Twenty Years and some Months; and there were some old Translations before his Time. The Sciences contained in these Books are those our *Arabs* mean, and when they assert them unknown to the *Chinese*, they advance no more than succeeding Ages have confirmed, as it were no difficult Matter to prove.

Elmac. p. 139. Ebn Shalik *Leb. Tarich*, *&c.*

The Chinese *Philosophy what.*

Philosophy, as defined by the greatest Names of Antiquity, *Is the Study and Knowledge of Things Divine and Human, their Causes and Effects.* We were formerly told Wonders of the *Chinese* Philosophy, contained in the Works of *Confucius* and *Mencius*; but the Translations we have of them, put it into our Power to judge for ourselves.

Their Metaphysics.

To begin with their Metaphysics, What can a People know of this kind, who have no Idea of the *Sovereign Being*, or any Name for him in their Tongue. Before the Disputes which so long perplexed the Court of *Rome*, nothing was more universally granted; Father *Martini* himself saying, *It is a wonderful Thing the* Chinese *should never talk of the* Prime *and* Supreme Author *of all Things; for in their Tongue, rich*

es

as it is, there is no Name for God. *Indeed they often use the Word* Xangti *to denote the great Ruler of Heaven and Earth.* * Again, we have a demonstrative Proof of this in the *Chinese* and *Syriac* Inscription discovered in the Year MDCXXV, and printed in the *China Illustrata:* For the *Syrians*, who erected it as a lasting Monument of their Mission, having been then one hundred and forty-six Years in the Country, could not be ignorant of the Tongue, and could they have found any Word in *Chinese* to express the *Sovereign Entity*, they would certainly have used it rather than their own *Aloho.* They did then as the *Spaniards* have since done in *America*, who were obliged to use the Word *Dios* when they instructed the *Indians*, who had no Idea of the *Supreme Being*, or Name to call him by. And all that has been since produced in the Progress of this long Contest, to make us believe there are some Words in the *Chinese* Books that may signify God, has been so solidly confuted, that it is not worth our Notice. All the figurative Expressions borrowed from the Heavens and the Sun, which some would have to be pregnant of a Mysterious Sense, and applicable to God, proves nothing in

* *De summo ac primo rerum authore mirum apud omnes silentium Quippe, in tam copiosa lingua, ne nomen quidem Deus habet. Sæpe tamen utuntur voce* Xangti, *qua summum Cæli Terræque gubernatorem indigitant.* Martin. Hist. Sin. l. 1.

favor

savor of the *Chinese*; for the same are common to the *Americans*, even to the most barbarous *Iroquois*, who certainly had no Notion of God. We might hearken to a well meaning Missionary, who, having never studied the Ancients, should be caught by such Ambiguities, and fancy the Ancients had never once thought of any Thing of the kind; but it is hard to conceive how a Man of such vast Reading as *Vossius*, should take it into his Head That the *Pythagoricians*, the *Platonicians*, *Aristotle*, and almost all the other *Greek* Philosophers, the *Epicureans* excepted, have not spoke of God more intelligibly and conformably to Truth than *Confucius* and all the *Chinese* together.

What they think of the Origin of the World.

As for the Origin of the World, Father *Martini* tells us they had various Opinions about it, all absurd, false, and common to other Nations; some believing it Eternal, others thinking it the fortuitous Work of Chance. Now can it be justly said That the ancient *Greeks* and *Romans*, informed only by the glimmering Light of Reason, did not treat more sagely upon this Subject? But it is observable that *Vossius* does not exclude the sacred Writers, not *Moses* himself, who in a few Words has taught us more Truths concerning the Origin of the World than all the Philosophers that ever wrote. We may judge what a Sort of Philosophy that must be, which is destitute of all Idea of a *Supreme Being*, and which knows no more of the

Creation

Creation of the World than is borrowed from the wild Extravagancies of Poets, and borders upon the Atomic Syſtem of *Democritus* and *Epicurus*.

The two Principles which Father *Martini* calls *Yn* and *Yang*, the one, as he continues, *Hidden and Imperfect*, the other, *Manifeſt and Perfect*, are the ſame the *Manichees* admitted, the one *Good* the other *Evil*; for this Doctrin has of old Time prevailed in the *Indies*, and over the *Eaſt*, whether it ſprung immediately from *Manes* himſelf, or whether it is of *Indian* Growth, and tranſplanted into *China* as ſome *Perſian* Hiſtorians relate.

Their two Principles. Hiſt Sinic. p. 14.

The Story of the Egg, whence *Puoncu*, their firſt Man, and all Things elſe were formed, was, as ſome take it, nothing unknown to the old *Greeks* and *Egyptians*; but if it was originally of *Chineſe* Extraction, it would not be much for the Honour of their Philoſophers: For the very ſame Thought came into the Head of the *Iroquois*, who, as ſome Perſons of great Sincerity report, believed That in former Times an Egg fell down from Heaven, near the *Huron* Lake, that falling it broke to Pieces, and that of the White were produced Men, and of the Yolk Caſtors. Their other Notions about the Birth of the World, according to ſeveral Authors, which the Moderns have endeavoured to embelliſh by allegorical Explications, are by no Means original, being known to the *Greeks* and *Egyptians*: But nor the one nor the

Fable of the Egg.

Spizel. *de Re Literaria* Sinarum. § 10.

the other of these Nations had them from the *Chinese*, with whom they never had any Intercourse; for not one of Philosophers who travelled to the remotest Parts of the Earth to seek Instruction, ever went to *China*; whereas many of them went to *Egypt*, to *Chaldea*, to *Persia*, and to the *Indies*, to consult the Sages of those Parts. It is very likely then that most of these Opinions which are ascribed to the old *Chinese* Philosophers, came to them from the *Indies* and *Persia*, as they had Commerce with those Countries; and that the superstitious Worship, so general in *China*, at least among the *Bonzes* and common People, they had from the *Indies*, as even those confess who speak of them in the most advantageous Strain.

Their Combination Tables. Their Table of the Combination of Lines, to the Number of Sixty-four, is a pretty useless Obscurity, whence you may deduce just what Sense you please; but besides that it teaches nothing, it were easy to perceive it is a confused Copy of some Fragments of the *Timæus*, and other Writings of the *Pythagoricians*: This is what Father *Martini* frankly confesses, when he speaks of the Book they call *Yexing*, "* which is, *says he*, wholly taken

* *Habent* Sinæ *librum* Yexing *dictum qui totus in illis figuris explicandis est, magni apud eos pretii ob res arcanas, quas in illis latere sibi persuadent. Mihi quædam* Philosophia Mystica *videtur esse, Pythagoricæq; persimilis; etsi multis sæculis prior; quippe quæ initium habuit à* Fohio. Martin. Hist. in p. 16.

" up

" up in explaining these Figures. They " value it at a high Rate imagining it re- " plete of many wonderful Secrets: But " to me it seems, *continues he*, a sort of " *Mystic Philosophy* somewhat like that of " the *Pythagorics*, tho' many Ages the " more ancient of the two, it being as " old as *Fohi*.

This Antiquity being vouched by the *Chinese* only, is not much to be relyed on; but tho' it were as far backward as these Moderns would have it, we must grant it can add no Sanction to so frivolous a System as this. But when we are afterwards told That the *Chinese* Philosophers pretend thence to derive not only the Principles of natural Philosophy, but the Rules also of Morality; it is almost impossible to think those who give out such Dreams, are in earnest with us. And what we elsewhere learn concerning the several Notions of the *Chinese* in the Philosophic way, is not a whit better, nor can we entertain any very great or very favorable Opinion of a People who talk of five such Elements as Metal, Wood, Water, Earth, and Fire.

It is Plain that the very best of the *Chinese* Metaphysics and Physics is by no Means comparable to what was taught by the ancient Philosophers, both *Greek* and *Barbarian*: That even their Fables cannot be said to be all their own, they being to be fonnd in other Hands and that this

this wonderful way of Teaching they had from the *Indians* and *Persians*.

This is self-evident from their Doctrin of a Metempsychosis which was very universal, as it still is with the *Chinese*. They have no rational Idea of the Immortality of the Soul, and a great Part of their funeral Ceremonies evince they have no System of Tenets upon so important an Article, the very Basis of all Religion.

Metempsychosis Mar. *Hist.* Trigaut Spizel.

The Guardian Angels they revere so superstitiously, are no other than *Genii*, Good and Evil, concerning which there are numberless Stories in the *Persian* and *Arabian* Writings. Fath. *Martini* says the *Chinese* call them *Tchin*, the very Name the *Arabs* give them; the *Genii* of the *Latins*, and the *Dæmons* or Spirits of several Classes or Orders, of whom *Jamblichus Porphyry*, *Plotinus*, *Eunapius* and others have written such and so many childish Things, as are a Scandal, to Philosophy, and quite foreign to true Religion.

Genii.

In short these great *Chinese* Philosophers were such Novices in Philosophy that they admired the Abridgments of the Schools, and among the rest That of the Professors of *Coimbra* which the Missionaries translated for them; but they were no ordinary Men that admired these Works, they were *Literati*, who, versed in the Books of *Mencius* and *Confucius*, acknowledged their Philosophy very imperfect

The Chinese *astonished at our Scholastic Abridgments.*

fect in comparison of that. What must they then have said if they had been informed of the great Truths to be found in the Writings of the old *Pythagoricians*, of *Plato*, and even of *Aristotle*, more happily and Usefully express than the small Number the *Chinese* have, which are not to be understood but by Paraphrases as obscure as the Text it self, and which it is oftentimes difficult to reconcile together. Father *Intorcetta*, *Martini*, *Rougemont*, *Couplet*, and others have given us Translations of some of *Confucius*'s Tracts, and their Classics, in which you must eternally help the Letter, and great Differences there are between these Fathers and what is cited by *Navarette* and other Missionaries.

Vossius does not much insist on their Philosophic Discoveries, but for Physic he cries them up to the Skies, and particularly for their Observations on the Pulse: he would have it that *Galen*, who treated the Subject very amply, was quite short of them: "The *Chinese*, says he, "not only feel the Pulse in one Part, "but in several, and that, for a considerable Time; which done, they are so "sure of the Disease that they tell all "the precedent Symptoms to a nicety." Fath. *Grueber* was a Witness to this, and told as much to the Sieurs *Lorenzo*, *Magalotti* and *Carlo Dati*; but added, that the Medicines prescribed to him thereupon, were so improper for his Disease that he

The Chinese Phisitians.

O soon

soon lost all esteem for the *Chinese* Practice. This Treatise on the Manner of Feeling the Pulse is turned into *Latin*; and *Vossius* Reading it, broke out into his Praises of this his favorite People: But very able Physicians have considered this Work and made no great Account of it, nor thought the Observations of any great Use. But were they as useful as is supposed, it must be granted That a Knowledge of the Pulse is but a middling Part of Medicine; and hitherto the *Chinese* have afforded us nothing to make us fancy they are as well acquainted with the Principles of this Art as *Hippocrates*, or that they have better explained them than *Galen*, and the other *Greek* and *Arabian* Physicians.

The Chinese *pretended to be skilled in Simples.*

They say the *Chinese* perform wonderful Cures with Simples; and so they may, tho' *Grueber* and the rest do not say much in behalf of their way of treating the Sick. But in this they do no more than the most barbarous Savages of *America*, who perform astonishing Cures as well in the Case of Wounds as of Diseases. Nor do we understand That the *Chinese* have been guilty of any great Improvements in Botany, and still less in Chymistry; but tho' their Books were richer this way than we imagin, we should, before we reason as *Vossius* does, inquire if these Books are old, or whether they may not have been touched up by the Mis-

Missionaries as well as their Astronomical Pieces, which is now time to speak of.

It is upon this Subject that our Moderns have expatiated the most, pretending That the *Chinese* Astronomical Tables, their Cycle of sixty Years, and the Celestial Observations in their History, are a standing Proof that they have surpassed all other Nations in Astronomy. This Notion gained considerable Ground, when Fath. *Couplet* brought Home these Astronomical Tables, which had never before been seen in Europe.

They were first examined by *Cassini* and *Picard*, who finding them to agree to a Minute, with the Tables of *Tycho Brahe*, began to mistrust them a little; and speaking of the Thing to Fath. *Couplet*, who was a very sincere Man, he ingenuously told them That the *Tychonic* Tables being by all Astronomers allowed to be the most exact, his Brethren had reformed the *Chinese* Tables by them; which I have since heard him say my self.

Their Chronology by Cycles of sixty Years.

In the Year MDCLXXXVII the same Father printed his Abridgment of the *Chinese* Chronology, together with the Cycles and some Astronomical Observations, particularly that of the Conjunction of the five Planets in the Constellation the *Chinese* call *Xe*: But *Cassini* undertaking to Calculate this Phænomenon, discovered an Error in it of five hundred Years; and the like in the Observation of a Winter Solstice, made, according to *Martini*, MMCCCXLII Years before the the Birth of Christ. This is to be seen at the end of *De la Loubiere's* Account of *Siam*, printed in MDCXCI, where also you have *Cassini's* Opinion of the *Chinese* Tables. "This Agreement between the *Chinese* "and *Tychonic* Tables, almost to a Mi-"nute, makes us believe they were cal-"culated by the *Jesuits* who have for "a Century past resorted to *China*, and "not by the *Chinese*. For if they were "not indebted to the *Tychonic* Tables, "how is it they so exactly tally with "each other? Our Astronomers of this "present Age, cannot well agree to a "Minute in the Places of the fixed Stars, "and we all know that between *Tycho's* "Catalogue and the *Landgrave* of *Hesse's*, "undertaken at the same Time by ex-"cellent Astronomers, there is a difference "of several Minutes. It is not likely "therefore That the *Chinese* Observations "should almost always agree with those "of *Tycho* to the same Minute. The Judgment of this great Man may teach us what to think of these Astronomical Tables which have tempted some People to prefer the *Chinese* to all the Ancients and Moderns.

The Ignorance of the Chinese *in settling their Calendar.*

To this Decision of one of the greatest Astronomers of this Age we may add a very natural way of arguing which every body may understand: *First*, The *Mandarin* Presidents of the Tribunal of Mathethematics, whose Business it was to fix their Calendar, succeeded so ill therein, that notwithstanding all their Interest and Intrigues, they were obliged to transfer the Task to the Missionaries, who were odious to them, both as Strangers and Preachers of a new Religion. The *Chinese* were first set right by Fath. *Matth. Ricci* ; but a few Years afterwards they were never the wiser ; so that Fath. *Adam Schall* was again obliged to reform their Calculations, and in spite of them became President of the Mathematic Tribunal, and *Mandarin* of the first Order, as were afterwards the Fathers *Verbiest* and *Grimaldi.* It is farther to be observed That these Missionaries and their Successors, were not profest Mathematicians, or known for such in Europe ; and yet they were able to discern and confound the Ignorance of these *Chinese* Astronomers on whom it was so incumbent to consult the Honour of their Nation, and keep themselves in Authority. The most rational of them were those, who, confessing their Ignorance, studied *Euclid*'s Elements, *Clavius*'s Sphere and some other Tracts, under the Direction of the Missionaries; and these they read with astonishment, which had never been the Case of those who had but the least smattering of the Mathematicks.

The Antiquity of the Chinese *Astronomy examined.*

We are now to discuss the Grand Point, and that is the Antiquity of the *Chinese* Astronomy, this is the most boasted by those

those who undertake to raise the *Chinese* above all the Nations that are or have been: Now for the famous Cycle of sixty Years, in which *Martini* and *Couplet* have ranged the principal Facts of the *Chinese* History, and the Succession of their Emperors. Father *Martini* led the way, and *Couplet* trod in his Footsteps. We are at a certainty about this Cycle from a Tract ordered by *Ulug Beig*, a *Tartar* Prince, deeply versed in Astronomy, who imployed very able Mathematicians to compile the Astronomic Tables we have in several Libraries. *John Greaves*, a learned *Englishman*, who was both a great Master of the Oriental Tongues and an excellent Mathematician, did in the Year MDCL print a Treatise, of this same Prince's, *Of the various Epochs and their Computations*. Therein the *Chinese* Epoch is called the *Cataian* or *Igurian*, which equally comprehends the *Chinese*, and the *Tartars* all over the vast Continent of the *Upper Asia*; and *Golius* in Conjunction with *Martini* have shewn That the *Cathayan* or *Catuian* Names therein, are *Chinese*. This same sexagenary Cycle is, by our late Informations, used in *Siam* and the adjacent Countries, who may have borrowed it from *China*.

Epoch Celebri. Johan. Gravii.

The *Greeks* had several Periods of Years; but as they doe not seem to have been known to the *Arabs*, the *Persians*, or the *Tartars*, who would have communicated them to the *Chinese*, it were a pre-

The Chronology according to their Cycles false.

presumption to deny them the Honour of having invented the Period before us; but we have two very weighty Remarks to make upon this Head.

The *First* is That after the Rate *Martini* and *Couplet* have marshalled the *Chinese* Chronology by these Cycles of sixty Years, either the *Chinese* or they must have been egregiously out, there being, as has already been observed, two Parachronisms of above five hundred Years apiece discovered therein; which makes us think it possible there may be more of them, if some skilful Man would but give himself the trouble of examining into all the Eclipses and Planetary Conjunctions they give us. But this done, there would be still another Obstacle in our way; for after the ingenuous Confession of those who give us these Tables, That they rectified them by those of *Tycho*, we should be at a loss to know whether they are the Observations of the *Chinese*, or of that great Astronomer.

The *Second* Remark is by no Means of less Moment: They exhibit this Series of Cycles as a plain Evidence of the Accuracy of the *Chinese* Science, and a Demonstration of the Truth of their History. But for this to be true, we should have some certain Epoch to count from, such as that of *Alexander*, of *Isdejerd*, of *Dioclesian*, of the *Hejra*, and of *Jelaloddin Ma-* *We cannot fix the Date of these Cycles.*

kee Shah; whereas they begin this Succession of Cycles from the Year MMDC XCVII before *Christ*. Now according to the *Hebrew* Copies and the *Vulgate*, there are but MMCCCXXIX Years between the Flood and the Birth of *Christ*; and to supply this Defect it is, that those who assert the Antiquity of the *Chinese* History, recur to the *Greek* of the *Septuagint*. They agree indeed that what is recorded in the *Chinese* Annals above *Fohi*, is fabulous, and no Soul doubts of it; so they dare not ascribe this Sexagenary Cycle to him, but bring it down to the Reign of *Hoamti*, who flourished the abovesaid Number of Years before *Christ*. But we shall not readily conceive how so very complex a Cycle as this should have been so soon discovered, or brought to Perfection as *Couplet* * advances; whereas *Martini* † tells us that Emperor himself invented it. This Disagreement between two Authors who had one and the same Drift, who wrought with the same Materials, and in Points of such Importance, makes us very much mistrust the History they so applaud. Turn this Fact which way you will, you must eternally be at a Stand.

It is difficult to reconcile the Chinese *Chronology with the* Hebrew *Text.*

The *first* and main Difficulty is how to reconcile it with Scripture, even with the

* *Usus opera Tanao Cyclum Sexagenarium perficit.*

† *Et ab hoc demum Imperatore tametsi bini illum antecesserunt, Sinæ Cyclum suum Sexaginta annis descriptum inchoant, quippe ab eo ipso inventum.* Martin. Hist. p. 25.

Septuagint

Septuagint itself; and this not only with Regard to Chronological Supputations, but in Things of greater Consequence; for if we admit the *Chinese* History, we must reject the Universality of the Deluge, not to say that it attributes many Inventions to the *Chinese* Emperors, which Scripture ascribes to others. This has been an Observation made by late Authors, and particularly by the *Protestants*, who adhere to the *Hebrew* Text, and therein agree with the *Catholics*, who acknowledge the Authority of no other than the *Vulgate*. Both the one and the other are most assuredly more ancient than the *Chinese* History as it stands with us; seeing they have none but printed Copies extant; and as old as the *Chinese* may boast their Invention of Printing, no Paper could last eleven or twelve Hundred Years. They have no Books so old, and when they have found an old Inscription they have not understood it, as is instanced by Father *Rougemont*.

These Cycles cannot be so old as pretended.

We shall always be at a Loss then to comprehend how the *Chinese* should have regulated this intricate Cycle two Thousand six Hundred and Ninety-seven Years before *Christ*; and much less how they should have contrived to teach it to others at a Time when they were very imperfect in Arithmetic, invented, as says *Martini*, under the same *Hoamti*, by Means of a Contrivance he represents. But after all, as exact and circumstantial as this Cycle appears to be, it was so defective, that

Hist. Sin. p. 21.

five

five Hundred Years after *Hoamti*, the *Chinese* Astronomers could not foretel an Eclipse which hapned under the Emperor *Choukang*, who for that Reason put them to Death. It is to our Purpose, that their Histories differ about the Time of this Eclipse; a plain Indication of the Insufficiency of their Calculations. Many Examples of the same kind might be produced, and the like have been very frequent in latter Times; for what reflected so much Respect on the Missionary *Jesuits*, was their Accuracy in these Predictions, while the *Chinese* themselves were out.

The point of Time they are deducedfrom, not the same we have been formerly told.

The *second* Remark we have to make upon this Cycle is, That those who brought it to *Europe* and made it the Standard of the *Chinese* Chronology, date it from the Reign of *Hoamti* MMDCXCVII Years before *Christ*, or twenty-eight Years afterwards, that is, MMDCLXX before *Christ*, when a great Mathematician called *Tanao*, rectified it. Now besides the Objections that have already been made to this early Epoch, so irreconcileable with Scripture, we have another; for Father *Martini* was the first that ever deduced these Sexagenary Periods from that Point of Time, which the *Chinese* themselves disown, and is merely of *European* Invention. For our first Travellers that went to *China* understood the *Chinese* to reckon after the Rate of eight Hundred and eighty Thousand sixty and three Years, from the Beginning of the World down

Scalig. *de Emendatione Temporum.*

to

to the Year of our Æra MDXCIV, and ſome of them made very great Additions to this enormous Number. And yet this is not to compare with what we read in *Ulug Beig*, who has treated more exactly of theſe *Chineſe* Cycles, than any Body elſe whatſoever: He tells us that in the Year of the *Hejra* DCCCXLVII, of *Chriſt* MCCCC XLIV, the *Cataians* or *Chineſe* computed Eighty-eight Millions, ſix Hundred thirty nine Thouſand, eight Hundred and ſixty Years from the Beginning of the World; which infinitely exceeds the immenſe Calculations of the old *Chaldees* and *Egyptians*, ſo juſtly rejected as fabulous by *Cicero* and other Authors, and which none have aſſerted but Libertins and the Author of the *Preadamitic Syſtem*.

Epoch. Celeb.

Thoſe who have favored us with Compendiums of the *Chineſe* Hiſtory, confeſs it fabulous till the Reign of *Hoamti*; but tell us that after his Days we are to deem it genuin, which they attempt to prove by a Series of theſe Cycles chiefly, according to which they compute the Years of the ſubſequent Emperors down to our own Times; but they cannot deny this Contrivance to be their own, not *Chineſe*. Its Outſet is fictitious, and no more to be relyed on than what we read, in *Greek* and *Latin* Authors, of the Aſtronomical Obſervations the *Babylonians* boaſted to have made for one Hundred and ſeventy Thouſand Years. Now many of their Eclipſes, as *Ptolomey* has them from *Calliſthenes*

Their Tables as they now ſtand with us, are rather an European *Work than a* Chineſe.

And yet they are faulty.

Simp. *in* l. 2. *de Cæl.* *Comm.* 46.

thenes who informed himself on the Spot, are right; but the chief of those in the *Chinese* Tables, tho' reformed by *Tycho*, are false. This is the Opinion of Mr. *Cassini*, the greatest Astronomer of our Time, whose Words it may not be amiss to produce:

Voyage de Siam. T. 2. "The *Chinese* Year, *says he*, has often "wanted Reformation to make it set out "from the same Term or Point, with Re- "spect to which our Modern Accounts "vary about ten Degrees; Father *Mar-* "*tini* fixing it in the fifteenth Degree of "*Aquarius*, and Father *Couplet* in the fifth "of the same Sign, as if it had retrogra- "ded ten Degrees since *Martini* wrote. "It is certain that a great many of the "Eclipses and other Conjunctions the "*Chinese* give as observed, cannot have "hapned at the Times they say, as their "Calendar stands at present; this we have "proved by the Calculation of a great "many of them, and may be discovered "by a bare Inspection into the Intervals "between them. For many of these In- "tervals are too long or too short to be "compleated by Eclipses, which never "happen but when the Sun is near one of "the Nodes of the Moon, whither he "could not have revolved at the Times "expressed, if the *Chinese* Year had been "the same formerly as at this Day". But

Hist. Lin. p. 33. Father *Martini* lays so great a Stress upon this first Observation that he breaks out into a kind of Oath, *Sancte assevero*, That he found it in the *Chinese* Books such as he gives

gives it; and so fully is he persuaded of the Thing, That he asks, What the *Europeans* have to say to it? Mr. *Cassini* has on the behalf of all *Europe* replyed, That this first Observation is false, and so all the Consequences thence deduced must fall to the Ground.

A Consequence thence deducible.

After this we may judge if *Vossius* could justly include the Astronomy of this People when he presumed to say of them, That they alone had invented more Things useful in Life, in the Arts, and the Sciences than all the Nations of the World put together. For we can know their Observations but by the Tables we have; and since those who turned them into *Latin* reformed them by *Tycho*; since the Conjunctions and Eclipses they contain prove false; and since by the Help of these Tables, rectified as they are, they have, for a Hundred and fifty Years past, never been able to settle a Calendar, or foretel an Eclipse; we must pronounce them far inferior not only to the great Astronomers that have graced our Days, but to the very meanest, such as were most of those who put them into some certain Method.

The Chinese *Astronomers not to compare with the* Greek *or* Arabian.

And far less are they to be compared with or preferred to the *Greeks*, whose Astronomical Observations are just and right; wherein no such Thing as an Anachronism of five Hundred Years is to be picked out, or any imaginary Eclipses, those in *Ptolomy* having been proved by the industry of our own Astronomers. Nor can the

Chinese

Almag. l. 4. *Chinese* be even compared with the *Arabs* or the *Persians*, who having imbibed the sound Principles of the Mathematics, in the *Greek* Writings, improved them so well, that when our Authors went to *China* they had able Geometricians and Astronomers, whose Tables and Observations served as a Rule to all *Europe* for many Ages together. For tho' there have at all Times been Men of some Skill in Astronomy, as were most of those who laid down Rules for the Church Calendar in the *West*, in *Asia*, and in *Egypt*; that was the sole Object of their Contemplations, they sought no further, nor had we any Astronomical Tables in *Europe*, before those which *Alfonso*, King of *Castile* and *Leon*, ordered to be drawn up in the Year MCCLXX: To do which he employed some learned *Jews*, as is observed by the Historians who speak of this Event: But they have not observed to us That these *Jews* were beholden to Tables which had a long Time before been prepared by *Arabian* Mathematicians, the most ancient of which were calculated at the Command of the Kalif *Almamun*, the seventh of the *Abbassids*, who got most of the *Greek* Books translated into *Arabic*.

Petav. *de Doctrina Temporum*

The Arabian *and* Persian *Astronomers.*

This general Translation is on all Hands applauded, and from that very Time the *Persians* and the *Arabs* began to have very good Mathematicians. By their diligent Observations they rectified the Tables of *Almamun*, in whose Days three famous Astronomers,

nomers, called *the Children of Musa*, made that famous Observation on the Measure of Earth, which they first did in the Plains of *Sinjar*, in Scripture *Shinar*, and which they afterwards repeated at *Kufah*. A little while after this, they had very learned Astronomers, among the rest *Abuabdallah Muhamed*, the Son of *Jaber*, who calculated Astronomical Tables very exactly, as did many others down to *Jelaloddin Malec Shah*, the third Soltan of the *Seljukid* Race, who had new Observations made to regulate the Epoch called *Malekean* or *Jelalean*. The *Jews* of *Spain*, who generally understood *Arabic*, it being common in the Country, while the *Moors* were Masters of *Corduba*, *Granada*, and many other considerable Cities; had translated the Astronomical Books and Tables of the *Arabian* Mathematicians into *Hebrew*, as well as most of those that treated of the Sciences in general, which gained them great Credit and Reputation. After this there was a great Number of very learned Astronomers among the *Mohammedans*, and *Ulug Beig*, a *Tartar* Prince, having caused very nice Observations to be made at *Sarmarkand*, ordered the Tables called *Ilakanian* to be formed, which have been admired even by the Astronomers of our Age. They did not, like the *Chinese*, mistake in their Calculations, they never obtruded false Eclipses, they never were at loss to fix the Beginning of their Years, tho', as they reckoned by Lunar Months, it is more

Ebn Kalikan.

Grav. Epoch Celeb. p. 38. *Praefat. in Tab. Geograph.* Ulug. Beig. Hyde. *Praefat. in Tab. Stel. Fix.*

more difficult to compute them than the *Chineſe* Cycles; and by what *Ulug Beig* ſays of the Matter, he ſeems to have known the Myſtery of theſe ſame Cycles better than the Mathematic *Mandarins* themſelves. We muſt not wonder then that *Mohammedan* Travellers from *Bagdad*, the Abode of the Kalifs, who were ſenſible how well theſe Sciences were cultivated in their own Country, ſhould, upon obſerving nothing like it in *China*, pronounce the *Chineſe* ignorant of the ſame.

The Arabs *were great Mathematicians.*

We might here exhibit a long Liſt of *Arabian* and *Perſian* Mathematicians from *Almamun* down to later Times; and their Works being extant and in our Hands, we find them to have been perfectly acquainted with all the Branches of the Mathematics. They had tranſlated *Euclid* from the Beginning, and their Comments upon him convince us they underſtood him thoroughly; ſo they tranſlated *Archimedes*, *Theodoſius*, *Apollonius Pergæus*, and almoſt all the other moſt difficult Authors; and by their Demonſtrations it appears, and by their Schemes That they were fully poſſeſſed of them, and that they made very intricate Calculations to the greateſt truth. We muſt confeſs then that in this Reſpect they were far beyond the *Chineſe* who have had ſuch Wonders told of them, Wonders not confirmed by a long Series of Time, or by Perſons not to be miſtruſted, but by a Handful of prejudiced *Europeans*, Tranſlators, and Reformers, as they themſelves

ſelves confeſs, of Books they could not underſtand. If the *Chineſe* had been but middling Geometricians, *Euclid's* Elements had not been ſo novel to them; if they had been grounded in the Principles of Arithmetic, they had long ago thrown away the Frame or Mechanical Contrivance they ſtill uſe; by whoſe Aſſiſtance it is hard to conceive how they ſhould have calculated their Cycles with as much Exactneſs as the *Perſians* did, who actually knew them, or as *Greaves* has done it for us in his *Epochæ Celebrires*.

The Chineſe *unacquainted with the Arts that depend on the Mathematics.*

Now if we take in Hand the Arts that depend on the Mathematics, we ſhall at the firſt Glance perceive the *Chineſe* are not only far inferior therein to the *Greeks*, and the Moderns; but alſo that they are quite ignorant in Optics, Proportions, Painting, Sculpture, Architecture, and in general every Thing that tends to the Improvement of the fine Arts. We cannot apprehend that any Body will compare the *Chineſe* Buildings, not even their Triumphal Arches, no nor the Porcelane Tower, with the noble Remains in *Greece* and *Italy*. If you will go ſtill farther back, there is *Shilminar*, which many take to be the old *Perſepolis*: The Ruins of this far exceed any Thing to be ſeen in all *China*. But if it is thought too much that we compare the *Chineſe* Architects with the *Greeks*, the *Romans*, and the ancient *Perſians*, compare them with the *Americans*, and they will ſtill be inferior: For what Authors of undoubted Credit report of the Edifices erected by the *Mexicans*, and *Inca's* of *Peru*, may convince us they far outdid the *Chinese* in Contrivance, it being very extraordinary they should have completed such vast Works as they did, without the Use of Iron. As these never had so great an Opinion of themselves as the *Chinese* have had, and were never shy of learning what they knew not, they in a very short Time attained to a Perfection in the Arts, as may be read at large in *Palafox*. This we cannot say of the *Chinese*, who in a Hundred and fifty Years Time, have not learned to make a Dial, or draw a Figure. But we shall resume their Arts hereafter; we are now going to touch on one of the principal Parts of their Philosophy, which is Morality.

Theve-not's *Col.* Vol. IV.

The Chinese *Morality*.

This is one of the Articles late Authors are prolix upon, particularly extolling the great moral Truths which so shine in the Works of *Confucius*, the most famous of all the *Chinese* Philosophers, honoured by the *Literati* as a Saint, and whom many compare with, nay prefer to the greatest Genius's of Antiquity. For a long Time we knew nothing of this Treasure but by loose Sentences, in *Martini* and others, till the Year MDCLXXXIII, when *Couplet* gave us a Translation of the Works of this Philosopher, or rather a Paraphrase upon it, without which it had been impossible to make Sense thereof. When we attentively consider these Works, we find it a difficult Matter to give a more natural Account of of this Philosophy than *Lorenzo Magalotti*, and *Carlo Dati*, Florentins, very ingenious and learned Men did upon the Conference they had about *China* with the *Jesuits Grueber* and *Orville*, who were just returned from thence, *E una specie di Filosophia morale, alterata pero con certi ingredienti di Theologia Scolastica.* They contain Truths as common to all Nations as to *China*; and when explained more amply by Interpreters and Commentators, they generally tend to trifling Ceremonies, and frivolous Superstitions. This it were easy to demonstrate, if we had leave to examin the chief of them, even the most marvellous; but as this would require a Volume by itself, let it suffice that we attempt a few important Observations upon this Chapter.

Moral Truths of Confucius *what we are to think of them.*

No Body can deny but that all the great Truths in *Confucius*, are more happily expressed, and more plainly taught in the Scripture: His Friends to be sure would never allow him to be beholden to the sacred Books, or that he thence exhausted his Lights, and indeed it seems he did not; for had he, in the least, known the Truths revealed to the Patriarchs and People of God, he had never contaminated those ascribed him, by such great Absurdities. And yet it is not impossible but some feeble Rays may have reached *China*, thro' other Nations; for the Antiquity of the Sacred Writings, is as certain as that of the *Chinese* is doubtful: But upon this Head we have wherewithal to suggest,

That moſt of theſe Truths ſo aſcribed to the *Chineſe* and to *Confucius*, are not of their own Growth, and that they had them from abroad.

Moſt of theſe Truths are in the old Gnomics.

There is hardly any Truth in Morals but is to be found in the old *Gnomics*, in the *Golden Verſes* of *Pythagoras*, in the *Sayings* of the *Seven Wiſe-Men*, and in the ſcattered Fragments of the *Pythagorics*. Now it is certain That the *Arabs* tranſlated moſt of theſe old Collections of Sentences, and that the ſame were afterwards rendered into *Perſian*; ſo it may have been That by this Means they made their Way into *China*; and that the exceſſive Vanity of the *Chineſe* may have prompted them to call that their own, they had only borrowed. For it does not appear by any Author, Ancient or Modern, That the *Arabs* or *Perſians* ever had any Thing from the *Chineſe*, not even Fables: In their fabulous Pieces mixed with Morality, as *Kalila-ve Damna*, and others ſuch, the grave Perſons introduced to pronounce Sentences are Bramins. They have many Romances, in Proſe and Verſe, which relate *Alexander*'s Travels to the *Spring of Life*, which, according to them, is in *China*, or ſomewhere in the circumjacent Provinces; and herein alſo they have Philoſophers but they are *Bramins*, not *Chineſe*. They have a Book in a more ſerious Strain, which they had from the *Greeks* of the Middle Age, and which they greatly eſteem; it is a kind of Dialogue between *Alexander* and ſome

ſome Philoſophers, each of whom delivers a Sentence, but they are ſtill *Indians.* In ſhort it is very poſſible that what the *Chineſe* have in common with all civilized Nations, may have been derived to them from the *Arabs* and *Perſians*; the Thing may have been, and that it was ſo, may appear by the Incoherence between theſe firſt and great Truths, ſuppoſed to be theirs, and the Conſequences they thence deduce for the Conduct of Life. This is what we muſt conſider at large.

" The *Chineſe*, ſays *Martini*, have ſtudyed " and ſtill carefully ſtudy to perfect them- " ſelves in the Knowledge of Heaven, of " Man, and of the Earth. Hence they are " very diffuſe on the Nature of Spirits, " Good and Evil, of the Principles of na- " tural Things, their Production their " Corruption, the Motion of the Stars, " the Variety of the Seaſons, and many o- " ther Things." If by their Study of Heaven we are to underſtand Aſtronomy, it has been ſufficiently ſhewn They have ſadly miſpent their Time: But this is not the true Senſe of the Words; nor by *Heaven* do they point at the true God, they being void of all Idea concerning him, and deſtitute of a Name to diſtinguiſh him. What they teach of the Nature of Good and Evil Spirits, is an inexhauſtible Source of the moſt ſtupid Superſtitions they obſerve at their Feaſts, and in their Sacrifices to *Genii* of the Mountains, Waters, Cities; as did formerly the ancient Heathens.

P. 148. *In what their Morality conſiſts.*

 The

The Writers who have given us Extracts from their most famous Authors, have been very brief upon this Head, seemingly aware That if it was explained we should therein discover something like the Doctrin of the old *Manichees*, or those the *Arabs* call *Tanwis*, because they admitted two equal Principles, the one Good the other Evil: But instead of this, some have thought them commendable for their Knowledge of, and Respect they pay to Guardian Angels.

" *The* Knowledge of Man, *according to* " *the same Author*, comprehends Morality, " Piety towards God, towards our Parents, " towards all Men, and towards ourselves. If we believe *Martini*, the *Chinese* by this Piety, recommended in the Books of *Confucius*, understand " The Love of God, of " our Relations, of our selves, and of all " Men." But how should the *Chinese* have prescribed Rules for the Love of God, and not at this Day have any Notion of him, no Name to signify this *Supreme Entity* we are bound to adore and to love as soon as we know him the Author of all Things, and of all Good. He endeavors indeed to make the Words *Thien* and *Xamti* expressive of our Idea of God; but this Point has been most minutely discussed in our Days, and given against *Martini*: And long before this Decision at *Rome*, *Navarette* and other Missionaries maintained, That the *Chinese* did not accept these Words in *Martini's* Sense, that they had no Idea of the true God, nor Name for him.

It

It follows then That *this Piety towards God* is not what *Martini* would have it, but what the *Chinese* practice. Now what they practice, are Sacrifices, in their Way, offered up to Heaven, to *Genii*, and their ancient Heroes; to *Confucius*, *Laossu*, and to *Foe* or *Fohi*, one of their first Emperors, whose Story is quite Fabulous. And herein consists the primary and principal Part of the *Chinese* Piety, void of any Vestige of true Worship, the Sum and Substance of Religion: But besides the undoubted Proofs we have of this, in the most sincere Travellers, we have speaking Proofs thereof in the Pictures we see in their Books; for above all the rest you have the Picture of *Fohi*, and very far beneath you have those of *Confucius* and *Laossu*. Now *Fohi*, according to the *Chinese*, was one of their old Emperors; according to the *Indians*, one of their Gods. The two others were their Saints, and great Philosophers; and before these Figures do the *Chinese* offer Flowers, Perfumes, living Creatures, and other Things; in this consists the Piety of the learned *Chinese*. If the Idolatry of the People be more simple and groveling, and if the Idolatry of these Grandees be more polite and refined; they are never the less equally Criminal, and equally Superstitious: In short, this first *Chinese* Precept is contained in the very foremost of the *Golden Verses*.

Chin. Illust.

Piety towards our Parents, in paying them the Respect due to them from Children, as long as they live, is by no Means

Piety towards Parents.

a Truth of *Chinese* Discovery, it being ordained and observed by the most barbarous Nations. What is peculiar to them, are the Funeral Honours they pay to their Memory, which they have carried to the highest pitch of Superstition; tho' the Laws of God, and those of the wisest human Institution have set Bounds thereto; no idolatrous Nation has pushed the Thing so far as the *Chinese*. For the Ceremonies called *Inferiæ*, Libations, and other the like Superstitions were not of that Import as the asking of such Favors from their Dead, the *Chinese* are guilty of. These Practices equally superstitious and frivolous, have ever been condemned by wise Legislators and Philosophers; and if they are called an Act of Religion, such a Religion cannot but be false, and all the Opinions conducive thereto, must be false likewise. They would be somewhat excusable in those who should believe the Immortality of the Soul, as did the old *Pagans*; but in the *Chinese* who, as we are told by the best Authors, have Faith in no such Thing, tho' they at the same Time unaccountably fancy the Soul of *Confucius* and the *Manes* of their Ancestors repose themselves upon Tablets they place upon their Altars, they are intolerably senseless. The *Iroquois* who believe there is a Country of Souls, where their Fore-fathers hunt the Souls of Castors, are scarce more absurd in their Notions than these wonderful *Chinese* Sages. To be brief, nothing can

can be more ridiculous than to suppose such mean Trash to be the Result of Philosophical Meditation, and, as it were, founded upon the original Principles of Wisdom.

The ancient *Greeks* and *Romans* were unhappily involved in the grossest Superstitions; but they were far from being approved by the Philosophers, tho' few of them ventured to attack them openly; they left the People to their Sacrifices, their Festivals, and all their religious Trumpery; the wisest Legislators gave Way to these popular Errors. But if they happened to ordain a Sacrifice or any religious Act, they did not derive it from Philosophic Reasoning; they had Recourse to Oracles, to Revelations, which the Philosophers always rejected, if we except the latter Times; when to maintain themselves in the Veneration of the People, and as much as possible to deter them from Christianity, they carryed the Error to its utmost Length. If then we are to say, as by all Accounts it seems we must, That *Confucius* and the other Sages of *China* taught the ridiculous Ceremonies in vogue with the *Chinese*, and considered the same as constituent Parts of Morality and Piety, it must be confessed They ill deserve the Name of Philosophers.

The Chinese *Ceremonies but ill became Philosophers.*

If it be asked what Order, what Geometrical Method there may be in the *Chinese* Philosophy? We shall be greatly at a Loss to find any. For *Martini* himself, who varnishes all they say and do, in the most

The Chinese *Philosophy destitute of Method.*

most beautiful Manner, having explained what they mean by Piety, proceeds to another Species of the same; "They acknowledge, *says he*, three Cardinal Virtues, Prudence, Piety, Fortitude or Magnanimity: That Prudence teaches the various Customs and Ceremonies; that Fortitude puts them in Practice; and that by Piety we are allyed and attached to the other Virtues." That is to say, a *Chinese* is prudent when he knows the Detail of their cumbersom Ceremonies; that he is magnanimous when he puts them in Practice; and that herein he displays his Piety.

Their civil Ceremonies a part of their Virtue.

We need only examin into the Nature of these Ceremonies, to be convinced That those who could imagin them in the least analogous with Virtue, had not the least Idea of Moral Virtues. The Chain of these Ceremonies is something so odd, that the like is not to be found in any of the Nations most civilized and most addicted to Form. They are so little of a piece with the Simplicity of the earlier Times, that we want no more to satisfy us They are not so ancient as the *Chinese* boast. The Manner of inviting to a Feast, of going thither, of receiving the Guests, of entertaining them; of going to a Funeral, of paying Visits, and of receiving them, which consist of an infinit Number of Circumstances, are the Science of a Gentleman-Usher, or some such Officer, not of a Philosopher.

But

Other Virtues according to the Chinese.

But it may not be amiss to observe what the *Chinese* understand by the other Virtues, which lead to this Piety of Ceremonies and Forms: *They are*, say they, *Justice, Fidelity to Friends, and the Virtue by which we measure the Sense of others.* We must not wonder That those who had learnt no better after so long a Study, should admire the Philosophy of *Coimbra*: Or that our *Arabs*, who had, perhaps in their own Tongue, read the Morals of *Aristotle*, should speak so contemptuously of the *Chinese* Learning. It were time lost to expatiate on such absurd Distinctions; nor can any Thing be more out of the way, than to make a Virtue of what they call *Measuring the Sense of others.* If these enigmatical Words are expressive of any Thing, they mean the Talent of diving into the Thoughts of others, of guessing at their good and evil Intentions, of getting at their Capacity, and of thence forming a prudential Judgment, according to which we are to behave. But this is not having the primary or simple Idea of Virtue, to apply it to such a Character; for a cunning, inquisitive, mistrustful, artful, designing Man, is for the generality better able to *Measure the Sense of others*, than an honest, plain, upright, and sincere Person.

A few fine Sentences no Proof of their Capacity.

But after all, say the Admirers of *Confucius* and the *Chinese* Philosophers, it cannot be denyed but in their Writings there are great Truths, among the rest this, *Quod tibi non vis fieri, alteri ne feceris*; We grant it; but

but we may, without any great Presumption, believe That this Maxim, and some others, came to them from abroad, in the manner above suggested. But it were straining the Point too much, not to suppose the *Chinese* may have known what Nature herself prompted to other Nations: Tho' the little Use they have made of it towards the Discovery of sublimer Matters, is a glaring Instance of the scantiness of their Genius, and a Proof of what our *Arabs* pronounce, when they report them unacquainted with the Sciences, and that all they know, they had from the *Indies*.

The Chinese *besotted with Chemistry.*

But if the *Chinese* have the finest System of Morality in the World, it does not appear That it has been of use to them in the Conduct of Life: The Cruelty of Fathers who sell or make away with their Children; the prodigious Number of Eunuchs, mutilated for the Use of the Court; the Pride and Cruelty of their Mandarins; their Dishonesty; the Fury wherewith they lay violent Hands on themselves; their Debauchery; their Luxury; and many other Enormities *Ricci* notes of them, are so many Proofs of their Deficiency in Morals. Add to this the Obstinacy wherewith some of their wealthy People seek after the *Philosopher's Stone*, and the *Grand Elixir*, which betokens a great Disturbance of Mind; which, as they say, has been upon them for above two thousand Years past: Tho', by the way, this their Attachment to Chemistry, makes their Antiquity look very

very doubtful. For notwithstanding the Fables the Chemists have forged among themselves, to prepossess us with a Fancy That their Art took Birth from the Patriarchs and Sages of the first Times, it was never heard of before the third Century of *Christ*. Most of the Learned have taken the Word Chemistry to be of *Greek* Etymology; but they are wrong, the Word being no where to be met with in ancient Authors, and being written with an H, whereas it should be spelt with a Υ to be *Greek*. It is on all Hands agreed that the first Books of this frivolous Art, that we know of, appeared first of all in *Egypt*, and that, as several relate, under the Empire of *Dioclesian*. Κημι is *Egypt* in the Language of the Country, where it is pronounced *Kimi*; whence the *Arabs*, who are as much infatuated with this Spell as any of the Orientals, have formed the Word *Chimia*. It is very likely then That by their Means it was the *Chinese* became acquainted therewith, there being, as shall be observed hereafter, no stress to be laid upon their Histories. The modern *Greeks* have many Treatises of this kind, which they set off with pompous Titles, to persuade us they are very Ancient: These the *Arabs* and the *Persians* have translated, and ascribed to *Hermes*, to *Pythagoras*, to *Aristotle*, and to other great Personages of Antiquity; but we have no *Arabian* Writer (and they are no very scrupulous Critics) that does the *Chinese*

the

the Honour of having been, in any degree, the Inventors, or Improvers of the Art they fo much boaft.

After Morality come Politics, as one of its moft noble Parts. Now we cannot fufficiently admire That Men verfed in Antiquity, as many were who have fo extolled the *Chinefe*, fhould fo emphatically infift on the Sentences of *Confucius* and *Mencius*, which are fo very trite, that the beft of them are not comparable to thofe which in a manner fill the *Greek* and *Latin* Writings, not to fpeak of Scripture which contains more political Truths than the whole Clafs of Profane Authors. But if the *Chinefe* Philofophers have uttered fome fine Sayings, It does not appear they have contributed much to the forming of great Princes, or able Minifters; to the Rife of wholfom Laws, or to make the People happy. For many Ages it has been a faying, *The People would be happy if Kings were Philofophers*, or if Philofophers reigned; and we may fafely fay That if Philofophers ever reigned in any Country, *China* has been the Place. For the *Mandarins*, who are all Men of Letters, and confequently Philofophers, Difciples, and Followers of *Confucius*; have for many Ages paft filled all the great Offices, both Civil and Military, have enjoyed all Governments, and prefided in all Tribunals. And yet if we fearch into the Hiftory of this Empire, embellifhed as much as poffible by fruitful Pens, we we ſhall not find Theſe Sages have been of any great Uſe in the extraordinary Revolutions that have hapned in their Country, or that they have exhibited ſuch Examples of Fidelity and Courage as abound in the Hiſtory of every other Nation. This is particularly obſervable in the very laſt Revolution, when the *Tartars* made a Conqueſt of *China*, and placed the reigning Family on the Throne. In ſhort, all the Defects which have been deemed the Ruin of the great Empires of the Eaſt, deſpotic Rule, the Luxury of the Prince ſhut up in a Palace with Women and Eunuchs, the Neglect of State Affairs, the Contempt of Military Arts; all theſe infect the Government of *China*. The *Tartars* without one jot of Philoſophy over-ran this vaſt Empire almoſt as ſoon as they invaded it; but when they conformed to the *Chineſe* Ways, they ſtood expoſed to the ſame Misfortunes as their Predeceſſors.

They have no Principles of Morality.

In truth it is hard to conceive how any body ſhould applaud a Morality and Policy ſo deſtitute of Principles, and ſo purely made up of common Sayings and Examples borrowed from Hiſtory; ſo void of all ſcrutiny into the Actions of Men and their Paſſions, their Spring, Tendency, and End; it being certain The *Chineſe* have no ſettled Doctrin on the Immortality of the Soul, and that they all agree the Good are rewarded and the Wicked puniſhed in this Life, either in their

their own Persons, or their Posterity. We can no longer hearken to those who would make us believe, among other Obscurities, that by Heaven the *Chinese* intend the true God; for the Persons themselves who give us this favorable Interpretation, grant, with the same Breath, That they have no Idea of God. The same must we think of all their Superstitions in honour of *Genii*, which are nothing less than Guardian Angels: Nor is it less absurd to imagin *Confucius* to have been a Man inspired of God, and that he foresaw the Birth of *Christ*, because in his Days certain Hunters killed an uncommon Creature which looked somewhat like a Lamb. The Holy Patriarchs and the true Prophets foresaw and joyfully expected the Coming of *Christ*: *Your Father* Abraham *rejoiced to see my Day: and he saw it, and was glad*: And by the same Spirit was *Jacob* moved to say, *I have waited for thy Salvation, O LORD*: But *Confucius* no sooner heard this Creature was slain, than weeping bitterly he cryed out, His Doctrin drew towards an End; whence we may infer it to have been quite different from the Doctrin *Christ* was to preach. *Martini*, who has this Story and gives us the mystical Signification of this Creature, puts it into the Mouth of a *Chinese* Philosopher, a Proselyte to Christianity, prudently avoiding to vouch for it himself. But if he and others could think That such were the Means to lead the *Chinese* into the Way of Truth; others have

Martin. p. 149.

have thought, and will upon better Foundation think, That this Condeſcenſion is rather adapted to confirm them in their old Errors. It were very ſtrange that God, the Father and Inſpirer of all Truth, and of the Way he is to be truly worſhipped, ſhould reveal himſelf in the Old and New Teſtament to plain illiterate Men without the Intervention of Philoſophy, and that to this general Rule of Providence there ſhould be an Exception for *China*. And it is ſtill more unworthy of the Divine Majeſty to ſuppoſe any Inſpiration in Men who had no Knowledge of his Supremity, of the Soul, of the Origin of Things, and who for two thouſand Years paſt have perſiſted in vain and frivolous Tenets. The *Mohammedans* with the bare Knowledge of an Almighty God, the Creator of Heaven and Earth, the Author of all Good, the Judge of the Quick and the Dead, the Avenger of wicked, and the Rewarder of good Works, could not but expreſs themſelves of the *Chineſe* with the Contempt obſervable in our two Voyages, a Contempt of ancient Date with the *Arabs*; for in Hiſtory we read of a Saying which came from *Muſa*, who conquered *Spain*, to the following Effect: *When Wiſdom or Knowledge was ſent down to Men, ſhe was lodged in different Parts of the Body according to the Difference of Nations; She ſettled in the Head of the* Greeks, *in the Hands of the* Chineſe, *and in the Tongue of the* Arabs.

Of the Inventions said to be theirs.

In the Dialogue between the Emperor of *China* and the *Arab*, in the second *Account*, we find that this Opinion concerning the *Greeks* had reached his Ears, and that he in some sort acquiesced therein. The *Arabs* have at all Times had great Notions of the Beauty of their own Tongue and Eloquence; but they yeilded the *Greeks* the Honour of having surpassed them in Philosophy and the Sciences, tho' they would never allow the *Chinese* to have been any thing but ingenious Mechanics. *Vossius* and the Authors of later Times, have not been unmindful to extol them as such, and at the same time allow them to be the Inventors of many useful and curious Things, which is not so certain as to be beyond all Dispute. For it will never be readily granted That they found out the Compass, and the Art of Navigation. The Antiquity of Printing among them is asserted from the Testimony of their own Histories only, which are much to be doubted, as is also the Claim they lay to the Invention of Artillery and Gunpowder, the Construction of Celestial Spheres and Globes, together with other Items of a Mathematical Apparatus. The Arts have every where else been perfected by slow Degrees; and if their first Inventors be as old as is supposed, it were astonishing That if we except their Varnish and Porcelane, every thing else attributed to them should be in such a State of Imperfection. For the Missi-

Mart. p. 44

Missionaries inform us, they were obliged to get Mathematical Instruments made to observe with, because what the *Chinese* had of the Kind would not do. As much as they are pretended to have been skilled in casting of Cannon, Father *Adam Schall* and *Martini* were at the Head of all the Meltings in their Time; and notwithstanding what is commonly said That the severe Prohibition against Infringements on the ancient Usages, or receiving Instruction from Strangers, has prevented them from improving the Arts they invented; these Strangers have taught them an infinit number of Things, before unknown in the Country. We must then confine our Elogies on the *Chinese*, to what they have actually invented and cultivated, and not extend them to Inventions which are none of theirs; for it can only serve to confound History, make us doubt of the Authority of Holy Writ, and administer to the Pride of a Nation already so puffed up therewith.

The Chinese *Characters.*

The Invention of Letters has ever been esteemed the most marvellous and useful; insomuch that many of the Ancients would have derived it from Divine Inspiration, as seeming, in some degree, beyond the reach of human Comprehension. The *Hebrews*, and after them the *Greeks* and *Latins* expressed an infinit number of Words with twenty-two or thirty Figures: The *Chinese* on the Contrary have so multiplyed their Figures, That they are computed at

upwards of ſixty Thouſand, and ſcarce can the Life of Man attain them all, even tho' they want the Sound of ſome of our Letters as R, and ſome others. Thoſe who have impartially conſidered this Matter, have agreed it to be a very grievous Defect, and it is eaſily conceived: For one and the ſame Noun, and one and the ſame Verb, admitting a great variety of Moods, of Tenſes, of Numbers, may always be diſtinguiſhed with us, becauſe the Characters never vary. But this Multiplicity of Characters is what *Voſſius* would have us moſt admire, adding That hence their Tongue has ſuffered no Alteration for three or four thouſand Years paſt, and that thus they muſt have retained all the Diſcoveries their ancient Sages had made in the Sciences and fine Arts, as well as the Hiſtory of their Empire. Theſe great and ſounding Words ſtrike us at firſt, eſpecially when delivered with that Air of Authority *Voſſius* aſſumed, when ſpeaking of Things he knew the leaſt of; but if we examin them nicely, we ſhall find that what they ſignify is quite falſe. For *firſt* he takes it for granted that the *Chineſe* Characters have always been as they are at preſent; *ſecondly*, that they underſtand them as readily as a *Greek* would read an old Inſcription, or a *Jew* the *Hebrew* Bible, which is a Miſtake. He might have informed him-
P. 25. ſelf from *Martini*, That the ancient *Chineſe* Characters differed widely from the Modern, and that they were not very unlike

like the *Egyptian* Characters upon the Obelisks at *Rome*. He adds, That he once saw a Book written in six several Sorts of these old Symbols, which the *Chinese* valued and admired for its Antiquity: But he does not say they understood them, and there is great Reason to believe they knew no more of them than of the Inscription mentioned by *Rougemont*, who frankly confesses That no Body could explain it. These Characters were strange to them, and consequently the Tongue had undergone a Revolution; which overthrows *Vossius*'s Argument.

But when he takes the *Chinese* Books to be so very old, he advances a decisive Fact without affording us any one Proof of it. He himself could furnish us with none, for he was ignorant of the Language; nor could he pretend to say any Thing he had not from *Martini* and others. These have indeed affirmed the *Chinese* History to be very Ancient, and seem unwilling we should doubt it; but they have never said They had any Books so very Old; nay they even supply us with a considerable Argument against this boasted Antiquity, by telling us more than once That they have none but printed Books; and altho' they disagree about the Time when the Art of Printing was invented, no one has given it out to be as Old as the earliest Times of the Empire, but only some Ages before it was known in *Europe*. It is also on all Hands agreed, That the *Chinese* Paper, which is very thin, and can bear printing upon one Side only, cannot last as long as ours, or as Parchment, which the *Chinese* use not. History relates That somewhat better than two hundred Years before *Christ*, the Emperor *Ching* caused all the Books to be burnt, and that *Confucius* and *Mencius* were preserved by an old Woman, who had pasted them against a Wall, whence they were afterwards taken; and moreover that some Passages were defaced by the Wet. These Books were written upon Bark, the common Paper being then uninvented: But we cannot perceive That those who for above six score Years past have been so minute in their Accounts of *China*, and have ran over all its Provinces under the Wing of Authority, have ever met with any of these Books written upon Bark, tho' such there are in several of our Libraries; or any Inscriptions upon Metal, or Stone of undoubted Authority, like the ***Eugubin*** Tables, the many *Etruscan* Inscriptions and *Punic* Medals, not to speak of Obelisks covered with long Inscriptions, by far more intelligible than the *Chinese* Characters; and yet they would persuade us these same Characters are much more perfect, because truly they have been always understood, tho' at the same Time it is confessed That no one understands the old Writing, and that scarce any Specimen of it is left; that those in present Use are liable to eternal Ambiguity, and that

Mart. p. 239.

Idem. p. 334.

that it requires many Years to get only a Part of them.

The Chinese *way of Writing very defective.*

If we examin the *Chinese* Writing and Language by the general Rules of Speech, and of expressing ourselves by Signs, it must appear there never was any more defective. For if we find fault with the *Hebrew*, the *Arabian* and *Persian*, these two the same, excepting some Letters, because they omit most of the Vowels, which are expressed another Way; this is nothing in Comparison of the *Chinese* Writing, which cannot be mastered but by a long and tedious Study of many Years. We shall never find that the *Greeks* and *Latins* were obliged to use the Pen to be understood in immediate Conversation together, as the *Chinese* are forced to do with their Pencil: This is what *Trigaut* expresly observes from *Ricci*'s Memoirs: For having said that each Word has its Hieroglyphic, and that there are as many Letters as Words; that they are to the number of Seventy or Fourscore Thousand; and that the Person who understands ten Thousand has as many as are necessary to write, and that no Man in the Empire can know them all, he continues, * " The Sound of these Chara-

---

* *Horum etiam characterum, ut plurimum, idem est sonus, figura non eadem, imo etiam significatio non una: unde fit ut aliud nullum idioma æquivocum æque reperiatur, neq; a loquentis ore scriptio ulla excipi potest, ab audientibus exscribenda; nec liber unus ab audientibus cum prælegitur intelligi, nisi librum eundem præ oculis habeant,*

" ѕters is commonly the same, tho' they " vary in Figure, and the Signification be " different. Hence it is there is no Ton- " gue more subject to Equivoques, that " there is no writing what is dictated by " another, or understanding a Book ano- " ther reads, if the same Book does not " ly before you, to ascertain the ambigu- " ous Sounds the Ear cannot distinguish. " It sometimes happens, That you shall not " understand a Man tho' he speak with the " neatest Propriety and Elegance, so that " he shall be obliged not only to repeat " what he has said overagain, but even to " write it down.

The great Defect of this Tongue.

This Defect is so great and of so extensive a Nature, that it may be pronounced to include all the rest, and that the Writing of no civilized Nation has ever been so imperfect and wanting. It is commonly said That the *Chinese* Characters amount to Seventy or Fourscore Thousand; and, as has been already observed, *Vossius* will have this Multiplicity to be a Sign of the Copiousness of their Tongue, but it is quite the Reverse. For were we, for instance, to reckon up all the Words in the *Greek* Language, we should have above five hundred

ut æquivocos vocum sonos, quos aurium judicio minime distinguunt, oculorum fide figuras intuentium internoscant. Imo etiam inter loquendum non raro evenit, ut alter alterius conceptum, accurate alioqui proferentis & polite loquentis, minime assequatur, ipse non repetere solum cogatur, sed etiam scribere.

dred Thouſand, and perhaps, a ſtill greater number if we took in the Variations of the different Dialects, and if we thereto added the vulgar Tongue, as the *Chineſe* reckon the ancient and modern together. If to this we accumulated all the Inflections of Nouns and Verbs, which have each a Character apart in the *Chineſe* Writing, the Number would infinitely ſurpaſs that of the *Chineſe* Characters. The ſame might be alledged of the *Latin*, and ſtill more of the *Arabic*, the *Perſian*, the *Armenian* and moſt of the Oriental Tongues.

Accordingly, as the *Chineſe* have thought it beneath them to learn any Thing of Strangers, the few who were rational enough to ſubmit to the Inſtruction of the Miſſionaries, have been obliged to uſe, or to form an infinite number of new Words, and conſequently new Characters; or it is impoſſible to conceive how they ſhould underſtand the Philoſophy of *Coimbra*, the Epitome of *Clavius*, his Sphere, his Gnomonics, Military Architecture, the Manner of compoſing and touching the Harpſicord, and other Tracts enumerated by *Kircher*. This ſuppoſed, we muſt needs confeſs the *Chineſe* Tongue to be very imperfect,as well in the Pronunciation, as in the Writing; and that the ancient *Hebrews* and *Phœnicians*, the *Greeks* and *Latins*, who were indebted to the former for their Knowledge and Uſe of Letters, did from the Beginning extend this admirable Invention to a Degree of Perfection the *Chineſe*

are

are far wide of to this very Day. For other Nations with less than thirty Figures have expressed almost all the Modifications of Speech, nay many the *Chinese* never heard, whereas these with an infinit number of Characters have never been able to settle their Pronunciation, or the Sense of their Words.

The Changes of Pronunciation have not prevented other Tongues from being understood.

The Experience of many Ages assures us it is impossible to fix any Pronunciation, and that it is liable to imperceptible Alterations in the Course of Time. We find the *Greek* Tongue was otherwise pronounced by the Ancients than by the Moderns; tho' we can neither discover the Time, or the Cause of this Change. We cannot doubt but that the ancient *Greeks* pronounced the B like the *Latins*, and yet they for many Ages past have been obliged to use the Conjunctive μπ, to express the Power of that Letter, especially in exotic Names. A like Alteration has befallen the *Latin* Tongue, whose genuin Pronunciation we rather guess at than know; and by the various Ways the *Hebrew* Words and Names are written by the *Greek* Interpreters, and by the *Masorets*, we learn that the same has betided the *Hebrew* Tongue: But this great Variation has been no Hindrance to the reading of the old *Greek* and *Latin* Books and Inscriptions, or the sacred Books of the ancient *Jews*.

Several barbarous Nations, as the *Goths* and *Saxons*, who had no Characters of their own, adopted the *Greek* and the *Latin*,

tin, and therewith expressed many Sounds unknown to those two learned Idoms, which they could not have done with the *Chinese* Characters. This want of some Letters has been the Cause we have for a long time been ignorant That *Samaband*, which the *Chinese* mention as conterminous with their Country, is *Samarkand*: But if since that Time the Missionaries have contrived an Alphabet and Syllabary for them, in the Nature of ours, they are highly to be applauded for having thereby supplyed what the *Chinese* so wanted; tho' at the same Time they furnish us with an incontestable Truth of what we have been saying.

The Chinese *Poetry*.

We have nothing to remark on the *Chinese* Eloquence and Poetry; to be a Judge thereof, requires a perfect Familiarity with their Tongue: *Martini* and others commend it much, the former writing That the Emperor *Ys*, who according to him reigned DCCCCXXXIX Years before *Christ*, did by his ill Conduct exasperate the Poets against him, and thereupon adding; "* There are many Poems of their Composition extant; for the Art of Poetry is of ancient date in *China*, consisting of several sorts of Verses of different Measure, and a certain number of Letters, with five Words ranged in Order." It is

* *Multa existunt etiam num ex eorum Carminibus, nam & ars poetica est apud Sinas antiquissima, & varia vario metro Carmina complectitur. Ea omnia legitimo literarum numero constant, & quinque vocum ordine.*

no

no easy Matter to get at the Meaning of these last Words, and needless to attempt an Interpretation of them: But we are much at a Loss to conceive what Poetry can be formed out of Monosyllables, which for that Reason should have but little or no Harmony; perhaps it is kept up by the Richness and Pomp of Expression. In this we must submit to the Judgment of those who are Masters of the Tongue, and the rather as there has been no Nation so barbarous but has had its Poets, and preferred its Poetry before all others. The *Americans* have their Poetry as well as the *Barbarians* of *Afric*, the old *Gauls*, the *Saxons*, the *Goths*, and generally speaking every Nation we have ever heard of, tho' infinitly inferior to the *Chinese* in point of Civility. Nor must we wonder at this Prepossession in Favor of our own Country; for in our Days the Learned of the *North* have bestowed great Elogies on the *Runic* Poetry, the *Iselandish* and others such. *Ludolfus* out of his singular Esteem for the *Ethiopian* Tongue, admires the *Ethiopian* Verses, the *Amharic* and *Gafatic*, as our Ancestors did the Hobbling-rhymed Prose of their Romancers.

The Arabs *make no mention of the* Chinese *Poetry as being too fond of their own.*

We are not to wonder our *Arabs* make no mention of the *Chinese* Poetry, which they may have known nothing of; but if they had really understood it they would have been more backward in their Praises of that than of the *Chinese* Philosophy. For the *Arabs*, besides the Opinion they have of of their own Eloquence, in which they imagin they surpass all other Nations, have still a fonder Conceit of their Poetry; and indeed were we to judge of it by their number of Poems and Poets, no Nation may compare with them: Were we to collect all their Pieces of this kind, we actually know of, they would form a Library of several thousand Volumes. But they kindled not their Genius for Poetry from the *Greeks*, together with their Taste for Philosophy, Mathematics, Physic, and other Sciences; for they seem not to have known any of the old Poets, tho', according to some Authors, *Homer* was formerly translated into *Syriac*. But the *Arabs* knew so very little of him, that when they happen to mention him, which is very seldom, it is as an old Philosopher, not as a Poet. This Genius obtained in the Nation long before *Mohammedism*; they spoke in Verse at their public Meetings, in their formal Visits, and even in the Field of Battle. In the first Ages of their Empire they had an infinit number of Poems, made by the old *Arabs* of the Times of Ignorance, as they express themselves; besides many that were particularly esteemed and lodged in the Temple at *Mecca*. A few Examples from History will enable us to judge of this Matter; in the Year of the *Hejra* CLV, of *Christ* DCCLXXI, Historians take Notice of the Death of a famous Man, called *Abulhasan Ahmed*, surnamed *Rowaia*, who was honoured and magni-

Abulfarag. Emir. Cond.

Hist. Aegypt. Taqr. Ward. Ebn Kalikan.

magnificently rewarded by the Kalif *Hisham* the Son of *Abdalmalec*, *Yazid* and *Walid*, for he lived ninety-five Years; because of his great Skill in the *Arabesque*, and because he was particularly versed in the old Poets before *Mohammed*. Another could repeat eighty thousand Distichs of these same Poets by Heart; this was the Abulfed. *Hist.* Ægypt. *Emir Ajama*, who dyed in the Year DLXXXIV. But *Jafar*, the Son of *Abdallah*, who dyed in the Year CCCLXXXIV, outdid him, he could repeat one hundred thousand. Their most serious Histories are full of Verses, and yet the Rules they are made by are as hard as the *Greek* and *Latin*, which they seem to have known as little of, as of the *Chinese*. But tho' the *Chinese* were more barren of Expression and Thought than the *Arabian*, *Persian*, and *Turkish* Bards, who err from our Rules, they might not be the less valuable; all that we have said of their Learning is not to take away from the Esteem we ought to have for them, but to reduce their Merit to its natural Bounds.

The evil Consequences which may attend our high Notions of the Chinese *Antiquity.*

The Writers of the last Age have strayed too far out of the Way, in preferring a few faint Sparks of Reason, and certain Truths veiled over with Enigma, to what has been started by all other Nations, and in offering to excuse the essential Defects of their Philosophy. These excessive Commendations might be excusable were they not productive of dangerous Consequences; but chiefly as they tend to make us us doubt the Authority of the sacred Books, which, setting aside Religion, ought not to be compared with the *Chinese* History. Those indeed who are most tenacious for them, give them up in this respect; but by labouring all they can to prove and confirm the Antiquity of this same History, the Answers they make to Difficulties are much weaker than the Objections raised, and thus they put Weapons into the Hands of Libertins and Free-Thinkers. An Instance of this we have had in the Author of the *Preadamite System*, who tho' as is said by his Acquaintance, he was so ignorant that he scarce understood *Latin*, yet having formed a System by wresting some Passages of Scripture to his own Mind; and being informed, by some, who had more Learning than himself, of what was reported of the great Antiquity of the *Chinese*; and the same being confirmed by *Martini*'s History, which appeared just at the same Time; he laid hold on it not only as a very valid Proof of his own Whims, but also of the infinit number of Years the *Assyrians*, *Babylonians*, and *Egyptians* reckoned, which the very Heathens themselves rejected as fabulous. He met with People who furnished him with the Memoirs in his second Dissertation, where the Subject is more amply treated; and but too true it is that many have been insnared thereby; not to become *Preadimites* indeed, but to harbor other Notions equally subversive of Religion. For these pretended Antiquities of the

Chinese

Chinese insensibly wipe away the Contempt which not only Christians but the old Philosophers have had for the *Egyptian* and *Babylonian* Traditions. On the other Hand we are told the *Persians* have Histories which go much farther back than the sacred Books; and tho superficial People, Sciolists, and those who believe they know every Thing, because they read much, do not absolutely admit these Fables, they yet suppose they must be founded upon some sort of Truth. They dive after this Truth in their wandring Imagination, but find it not, it being repugnant and foreign to what we know of the Origin of Things, revealed to the People of God, and contained in holy Writ. Now every Thing contradictory thereto, ought not only to be shrewdly mistrusted, but to be absolutely rejected as False, as well on a rational as a religious Account; for it must be allowed There is no Book so old as the Books of *Moses*; not even the *Chinese*, it being by themselves recorded That they were all burnt about two hundred Years before Christ, and that but a very small Number of them was saved.

Our Condescension of no Use towards their Conversion.

The Advantage the Missionaries thought to have obtained by flattering the *Chinese*, and letting them believe the most sublime Truths were in the Writings of their own Philosophers, has not always answered Expectation; this Complaisance has been more apt to swell their monstrous

monstrous Pride than to dispose them to an humble Reception of the Gospel Simplicity. The *Athenians* had at least as much Sense as the *Chinese*; we fancy no Body can prefer the Books of *Confucius* to those of *Plato* and *Aristotle*; or the *Chinese* Treatises of Physic and natural Philosophy to *Hippocrates*, *Dioscorides*, *Theophrastus* and several others; and yet when St. *Paul* preached to them he did not offer to convince them they had any Knowledge of God, but declared to them That they were Strangers to him, that they were ignorant of him; tho' at the same time he might have proved to them that their old Poets, and greatest Philosophers had owned a *Supreme Being*, much clearer than those who have undertaken to demonstrate *Thien* and *Xanti* to mean the same *Sovereign Entity*. For the old Philosophers at least, and even the Body of the People had some confused Idea of God, which ever obtained, notwithstanding the Cloud of Fables that interposed: But nothing can be added to what has already been said upon this Subject. what the first Authors of Accounts and Histories of *China*, cited as from Books of that Country, was implicitly believed by many learned Men; for as they knew nothing of the Tongue and Books of the Country, they were of Course to rely on those who had made it their particular Study; and others who since that time have applyed to the same, have powerfully asserted what the first had advanced. The Point was of immediate relation to the Missionaries, as they had taken on them to propagate the Faith; but the Learned who were not so immediately concerned look'd upon the Thing as a Curiosity that might help them to some Knowledge of those remote Parts; whence *Golius* and *Vossius* who had frequent Discourse with *Martini*, while he staid in *Holland* to print his *Chinese Atlas*, without any Scruple received all he told them about *China*. As for *Golius*, he applyed what he heard to the Improvement of Geography and Explanation of the Cycles, *Greaves* had given us by Translating the Original of *Ulug Beig*; but *Vossius* who was quite fond of the Marvellous, did not confine himself to what he had from *Martini*; he went on farther, he laid it down as a certain Fact, that the *Chinese* History was much elder than the Books of *Moses*, which the Missionaries never advanced; on the contrary, it is what they have endeavored to refute; tho' by very weak Arguments, it must be owned, while they supposed the *Chinese* History to be as ancient as they gave out. *Vossius* did not trouble his Head about the Consequences that might attend his Assertion he did not perceive what a Handle it might be made by Free-Thinkers and Libertins, but at once declares for the Antiquity of the *Chinese* Books: But, contrary to the common Custom of the Learned,

Learned, he affected to quote but little, especially when he was upon ſome new Paradox, tho' upon ſuch Occaſions, it is more than ever incumbent on the Party to call up Witneſſes. It hapned indeed he had none to call but *Martini*, who in the Year MDCL publiſhed the firſt Decade of his *Hiſtory of China*. This Author himſelf confeſſes The *Chineſe* carry their Hiſtory much higher; and when he allows the reſt to be fabulous, he only ſpeaks for himſelf, not for the *Chineſe*, who admit the whole as equally authentic, except they have been undeceived by the Miſſionaries. Before *Martini*, we had ſome Summary of their Antiquities, extracted from Books that are cited, but whoſe Falſehood is perceived at firſt Sight: This ſufficed to raiſe an equal doubt as to the one and the other, and no Man will ever be able to decide the Matter without underſtanding the Tongue, and actually peruſing the Books, which was not *Voſſius*'s Caſe. He could then only form his judgment by what he was told by Fath. *Martini*, who never pretended That the *Chineſe* Books were older than *Moſes*. On the contrary, he has endeavored to evince That by recurring to the Chronology of the Septuagint we may reconcile the *Chineſe* Hiſtory with the Scripture, which was the leaſt of *Voſſius*'s Care. This his Inadvertency is of ſuch a Nature as to ſap the Foundations of Religion; which has induced us to be ſomewhat

 dif-

diffuse in our Remarks thereon, to the end that no one may be prepossessed by the Authority of a Learned Man who pronounced upon he knew not what, who in his very Outset is guilty of a gross Mistake upon the Word *Sinæ*, averring the *Portuguese* to be the first who so called the People he would have to be called *Seres*. Our two *Arabs* use the Word *Sin*; they were there in the ninth Century, and the *Portuguese* went not to *China* till the sixteenth. Now they called the People of this vast Empire by the Name of *Sin*; because the *Persians* and *Tartars* had so called them, Ages before the *Portuguese* conducted their Fleets to the *Indies*.

FINIS.

INDEX

THE

INDEX.

N. B. There being two Chains of Numbers in this Book, the Reader is deſired to take Notice That the Pages of the firſt are diſtinguiſhed by the letter (*a*) and of the ſecond by (*b*).

A

Of

could

Fish,

INDEX.

Incarn-

INDEX.

Let-

Noah,

INDEX.

Re-

INDEX.

INDEX.

F I N I S.